EVERY WOMAN'S GUIDE TO Financial Security

Stephen Rosenberg, CFP, & Ann Z. Peterson

Chelsea House Publishers
Philadelphia

First published in hardback edition in 1997 by Chelsea House Publishers.

Note: This book is neither an attempt to provide legal or financial advice nor a substitute for the same. It is intended to provide accurate and authoritative information in regard to the subject matter covered. It is provided with the understanding that the publisher is not engaged in rendering legal, accounting, or other professional service. If legal advice or other expert assistance is required, the services of a competent professional should be sought.

1 3 5 7 9 8 6 4 2

Library of Congress Cataloging-in-Publication Data

Rosenberg, Stephen M., 1944-
    Every woman's guide to financial security / Stephen M. Rosenberg and Ann Z. Peterson
        p. cm.
    Includes index.
    ISBN 0-7910-4449-1 (hardcover)
    1. Women—Finance, Personal. I. Peterson, Ann Z. II. Title.
HG179.R683 1997   96-34994
332.024'042—dc20   CIP

Dedication

This book is dedicated to my loving wife, Nancy, a former widow who supported herself and two young daughters through difficult times. Her ability to survive and grow through her crises demonstrates the inner-strength and courage of women everywhere. Like the butterfly, she emerged from her cocoon and flourished. I'm so proud of her.

Stephen M. Rosenberg

This book is dedicated to my children, Tricia and Sharon, who encouraged and supported me, Ryan, who took on many of the family responsibilities, usually with good humor, and Laura, for the hugs and giggles at the end of the day . . . and to my husband and friend, Ricky. Their love gave me strength to grow beyond "mommyhood." I hope my professional achievements will inspire them to realize their dreams.

Ann Z. Peterson

Acknowledgments

We wish to thank the following people (in alphabetical order) who gave of their time and energy to help us with this book: Kay Bené, Lola Brooks, Kathy Rissmann, Anne Rosenberg, Nancy Rosenberg, Phyllis Thiele, Bryan Ziegler, and Norda Ziegler. Special thanks to the women who wish to remain anonymous, but shared from the depths of their hearts their own stories and personal diaries.

Thanks also to Mary Ann Fortenberry and Traci Parma, members of our dedicated staff, who efficiently ran the office and cheerfully provided excellent support to clients, all the while repeatedly proofreading this book.

Stephen M. Rosenberg is president of Rosenberg Asset Management, a firm specializing in financial and estate planning. He holds a Masters Degree in Psychology as well as the designation of CFP (Certified Financial Planner). The author of *Keep Uncle Sam From Devouring Your Life Savings*, Steve is nationally recognized as a leading authority in the field of estate and financial planning. He has appeared on radio and television from coast to coast, including CNN, CNBC, ABC, CBS, and NBC affiliates, in addition to being featured in major newspapers and magazines. He can be reached by calling (800) 777-0867 (toll-free).

Ann Z. Peterson is president of The Women's Network for Financial Security and vice-president of Rosenberg Asset Management. She holds a degree in education, with postgraduate training in psychology and finance. Her experience in education, church ministries, and business ownership have furnished Ann with a unique empathy for women that is often missing in the financial field. Ann is a financial columnist and teaches investment courses for universities, corporations, and other organizations. She can be reached by calling (800) 777-0867 (toll-free).

Table Of Contents

PART IV - APPLICATION

PART V - UPHEAVAL

PART VI - SPECIAL CONCERNS OF DIVORCEES

PART VII - SPECIAL CONCERNS OF WIDOWS

PART VIII - SETTING GOALS AND FEELING GOOD

Introduction

Why Did We Write This Book?

After years in the financial field, and having counseled literally thousands of individuals, we have concluded that one huge segment of the population has been ignored financially - women. This inequality is not because women aren't as smart as men, nor is it because they don't want to learn.

The reason is that over the years, society has delegated financial responsibilities to men and emotional responsibilities to women. Men have been praised for the ability to make great financial decisions; women have been lauded for the ability to handle emotional issues.

Even in our "enlightened society" this continues. There are tens of millions of women who are facing financial decisions for which they are not equipped. More than ever, they are forced into making decisions so they can support themselves and their families. In most cases, they are in unfamiliar waters. Sadly, most are ill-prepared for the challenge.

Statistics show that women live an average of seven years longer than men. There are five times as many widows as widowers, with the average age of new widows being 52. As a result, more women are going to have to personally handle their financial affairs for a number of years.

Divorce is occurring at record levels, with half of all marriages now ending in divorce. To make matters worse, men are better able to maintain their lifestyles after divorce than their ex-wives. Additionally, more men remarry than women.

Simple mathematics indicates that there are more widows

than widowers; more divorced women than divorced men. In addition, there are more single women than single men. Put all this together and you can see that as a society, women have, or will have, more financial responsibilities than men.

Yet society, which is predominantly male influenced, has kept women on a financial roller coaster throughout history. You're along for the ride, but have little voice or control.

You've heard it all:

- Don't worry your pretty little head about it.
- Women can't handle money.
- You take care of the house, I'll handle the business.
- Now, Mrs. Smith, you <u>know</u> your husband would want you to continue things just as he arranged them.

Well, the roller coaster has just reached the end of the line. The ride is over. It's time to get off and stand up for your right to make your own decisions. It's time to control your own financial destiny and secure your financial future!

Whether you are single, married, widowed, or divorced, this book is for you. Our goal is to provide specific help for **all** women. Whether you are taking up the challenge of handling your own finances for the first time, or you want to feel more confident about what you have been doing, you will find this book invaluable. We will help you understand your financial personality, educate you about choices, and enable you to apply the information to your specific needs.

If you personalize this book by completing the recom-mended worksheets and inventories, you will finish it with a new self-awareness, self-confidence, and assurance that you can handle the future. You can then face life straightforward and unafraid.

A note to women who haven't experienced divorce or

widowhood: we urge you to read the entire book, even the special sections. Statistically, you will face divorce or bereavement at some point in your life. If you are fortunate enough to avoid this crisis personally, you will certainly have friends who are not so lucky. When crisis strikes, those sections can help. Don't have the attitude of a woman that coauthor Ann Peterson recently met:

> *I was shopping for something to wear during book promotions and got into a discussion with the shop owner. She was intrigued that I was writing a book. She began to ask questions as she helped me with my selections. When I told her that it was a book on finances for women, her reaction was swift.*
>
> *"Oh, that's a wonderful idea for some women, but my husband handles all of our finances. I'm no good with any of that. And if something happens to him, my father-in-law will take over everything. He's so smart about money."*

For crying out loud, the woman runs her own business! Yet, she is playing ostrich with her personal finances. What if her father-in-law and husband are both gone? If she divorces her husband, will she still be "married" to her father-in-law? Doubtful. It would be funny if it wasn't such a typical response among married women.

Let's get a few things straight right off the bat. First, neither brains nor financial acumen are genetic characteristics based on gender. They are developed over time through a learning process. Second, if you are sheltered now, that does not mean you will always have that luxury. The best time to learn is **before** the fact. You don't want to be learning CPR while the victim is slipping away. At some point in your life, the odds are that you will become either divorced or widowed. Look at the following frequently quoted statistics:

- One of every three adults is currently non-married.
- One of every six is now, or has been, divorced.
- Women outlive men an average of seven years.

- Over a million women become widows each year.
- **Eighty to ninety percent** of all women will have to take charge of their own finances at some point in their lives.

If you learn to take care of yourself financially, you can handle any crisis. You become a wiser, more equal marital partner. Your future security will be assured. A crisis won't defeat you - whether it is due to death, divorce, disability, or other unforeseen event.

Women have great inner strength and capability, which is often obscured by poor self-esteem and lack of knowledge. You can uncover your own amazing abilities by learning the information, completing the worksheets, and applying it to your own life. If you take this book and make it a part of you, nothing will prevent you from reaching your fullest potential.

A note about cases

During our research for this book, we had the opportunity to meet hundreds of women. These special people have been through at least one crisis and survived to tell about it. Some of these women shared their personal thoughts during interviews; others loaned us their personal diaries or journals.

In each case, they gave of themselves to make things easier for you. This was the ultimate unselfish act: sharing very personal information with complete strangers. For that, we are very grateful.

This book contains writings, statements, and stories from these women. You can easily recognize their contributions by the different print style. You will probably personally identify with many of these - perhaps thinking that you could have written them yourself. We hope this information makes the book even more meaningful for you. Remember, no matter how tough things seem, others have already survived. You're a survivor, too.

Part One

Discovery

Chapter 1

Why Do Women Fail To Achieve Financial Security?

In our research, we isolated 12 reasons why women fail to achieve financial security. Most of these revolve around their relationships with men, both financially and emotionally, as well as their upbringing. Any one, or more, of these can result in financial insecurity.

This is not a putdown. To the contrary, successful women deserve much credit for their achievements, despite the numerous obstacles they have had to overcome. But most women have succumbed to the myth that they are not financially capable or that they have to fit into predefined female roles. Thus, we need to take a hard look at some of the barriers that are still holding women back.

Unequal pay. It is no secret that women earn only 70 to 75% as much as men. Despite all the years that women have worked toward equal pay, they still haven't arrived. In fact, not only is "equal pay for equal work" a myth, there is also a "glass ceiling" that prevents women from advancing to the upper levels of management and income. Less income yields less security.

Husband's ego. Married women face the problem of bruising their husbands' egos if their income is greater than his. Therefore, they tend to take the path of least resistance, which means sticking with lower paying jobs.

Play money. Many women (and men) treat the woman's income as "play money," while viewing the husband's income as "real" money that provides for the family. Since they don't think of the woman's income as significant, women don't demand advancement for greater earnings. If the husband is transferred, the wife is expected to quit her job. She looks for a job she enjoys, and doesn't worry about money or advancement.

Consolation spending. Many women console themselves after crises with unnecessary spending. For example, the woman whose spending habits were tightly controlled by her ex-husband glories in her new independence and spends money too freely. Or another might use spending to "get even" with her husband after an argument.

Insecurity. Women don't feel secure with their income or their future earning capability. They are afraid to invest money for long-term needs for fear that they may need every penny for today.

Dependency. Many women have been dependent on men their entire lives. This works several ways. If they're married, they expect their husband to always be around to take care of them. If they are unmarried, many expect "Prince Charming" to come along eventually and provide for their future. (If they're newly divorced, they think men should go straight to Hell!)

Lack of knowledge. Women, as a rule, haven't been taught about finances to the extent men have. As a result, they are behind the learning curve. This book will help alleviate that.

Honesty. Men tend to bluff their way through financial matters. If they don't know what they're doing, they'll act as if they do. Therefore, men invest more aggressively and take charge. Women, on the other hand, admit when they don't understand something. That reinforces feelings of inadequacy, so they are afraid to make investment decisions or take chances.

Spend assets. Many women want financial security, but

view all of their assets as available for current needs. In other words, they tap retirement plans, home equity, etc., for living expenses, children's college, and other special needs.

Dressing for success. Society expects business and professional woman to "look good." This takes money. Clothes, accessories, makeup, hair, nails, etc., are all very expensive. Men, on the other hand, can wear virtually the same clothes day after day, and it doesn't bother them one bit, nor hurt their job advancement.

Fear of mistakes. Women are afraid of making wrong decisions. They stick to the safe road, and it costs them dearly in the long run. They think that making a mistake will make them feel even more inadequate, which they want to avoid at all costs. Men, on the other hand, are willing to take chances, and view mistakes as learning experiences.

Wrong attitude. Women don't regard money as a measure of success like men do. Rather, women look at it as a tool to provide for themselves and their families, instead of as a vehicle to secure their future.

Guidelines

✓ *Regard your income seriously and use a portion to prepare for your future.*

✓ *Consider careers that have more earnings and advancement potential.*

✓ *View mistakes as "education" not "disaster." There is no real way to achieve wealth without some risk.*

✓ *Make your money grow and work for you.*

Chapter 2

How Do I Really Feel About Money?

The primary factor that governs how you treat your money is the way you feel about it, not the amount you have. We constantly meet women who, by anyone else's standards, have plenty of money. Yet, they **feel** poor. They don't **feel** like they can afford anything.

Why does this happen? Because they have "rules" concerning money - rules they learned growing up and still follow to this day. We recently asked seminar participants to tell us some rules they learned as youngsters and still think about today. Typical responses were:

> *Money is the root of all evil.*
> *A penny saved is a penny earned.*
> *Waste not, want not.*
> *We can't afford it.*
> *Money doesn't grow on trees.*
> *You can't live on love.*
> *If I don't have money, I don't have to worry about it.*
> *Save for a rainy day.*

Do these rules sound familiar? Are they similar to the ones you heard growing up? Probably so. Unfortunately, they can be a hindrance to your financial security.

We are often taught to think like we're poor, whether or not we are. We are taught to hoard our money because it might run out. We have learned to use money as a measure of our self-worth. We make ourselves feel better by spending wastefully, yet we deny ourselves the things we really want because "we can't afford it."

6

Lotteries have become very popular across the country. Studies show that the people who buy the most lottery tickets are those who can least afford them. How do people who "can't afford" decent clothes or nourishing food for their children manage to find the money to buy lottery tickets?

Choice

The point is that they **can** afford to spend their money wisely, they just **choose not to.** They feel it is okay to waste money on lottery tickets (I deserve a little fun), yet their self-esteem and/or education is too low for them to believe they can use that same money to improve their family's lifestyle. Their upbringing may still be preventing them from even expecting to improve their lot in life.

What you learned about money when you were young became the rules that govern how you choose to spend your money as an adult. Take a few minutes and think back. What rules did you learn and how have they affected your life? Have they kept you from enjoying yourself? Have they enabled you to be more financially secure? Have they kept you from taking risks to increase your wealth? Have you rebelled against them and found yourself wasting money? What has been the result? Do you want to change some of your rules? If so, which ones?

Space is provided to answer these questions. Decide which rules you wish to keep, and those you choose to discard. To give you guidance, we've included some client responses.

RULE: Money is the root of all evil.

RESULT: It made me think that I shouldn't have a lot of money, and I don't. As a result, I can't live the way I want. I have to worry about every cent, and I hate the pressure.

          Has that rule _____ helped or __X__ hindered you?
          Are you going to _____ keep it or __X__ discard it?

RULE: A penny saved is a penny earned.

RESULT: It kept me pinching pennies and made me so conserva-
          tive that I never accumulated any real money.

          Has that rule _____ helped or __X_ hindered you?
          Are you going to _____ keep it or __X_ discard it?

RULE: _____

RESULT: _____

          _____

          Has that rule _____ helped or _____ hindered you?

          Are you going to _____ keep it or _____ discard it?

RULE: _____

RESULT: _____

          _____

          Has that rule _____ helped or _____ hindered you?

          Are you going to _____ keep it or _____ discard it?

RULE: _____

RESULT: _____

          _____

          Has that rule _____ helped or _____ hindered you?

          Are you going to _____ keep it or _____ discard it?

Emotion

One thing we have learned in our many years in the financial business is that money is a very emotional issue. We have clients who are worth millions but who don't think they have a penny to their name. We also have clients who don't have a whole lot, but spend money as if they're loaded.

In fact, we found that the people who don't think they have enough, have the most. Those who like to think they have a lot, have the least. Yes, they have new cars, beautiful houses, and take great vacations, but they don't have much cash. Your feelings about money determine how you control it, or how you allow it to control you. That's why emotion plays such a large part in financial security.

Guidelines

✓ *If you follow the same rules you've always followed, you will continue to get the same results.*

✓ *You can choose your own rules.*

✓ *If you don't control your money, your money will control you.*

Chapter 3

How Have I Done So Far?

As Ralph Edwards used to say, "This is Your Life." Take time now to examine the money that has flowed through your fingers.

We don't know how old you are, but we'd guess you are probably between thirty and seventy. That means that during your lifetime you, and possibly your spouse, have earned a substantial amount of money. The question is, how much of it have you kept?

1. How many years have you (as a couple or individually) worked? _____

2. What were your average earnings? _____

3. Multiply the first two answers. _____

4. How much money do you currently have in savings and investments? _____

Compare the amount you've earned (number three) with the amount you've kept (number four). How much have you put away for yourself? Probably, not much.

Betsy is a 51-year old widow. Her late husband, James, worked for 35 years. His average salary was $25,000. Betsy has worked 20 years, with an average salary of $16,000. Naturally, both started out at lower wages and worked to higher levels.

James earned $875,000 ($25,000 times 35 years). Betsy earned $320,000 ($16,000 times 20 years). Together they earned $1,195,000!

Betsy figured the value of her assets minus her debts to be $90,000. That means that they spent over one million dollars!

The next questions are even more important:

- If you save the same amount over the next twenty years that you saved during the last twenty years, how well off will you be?

- Will you be satisfied with that?

- If not, are you willing to change?

You see, the problem is not that people don't *earn* enough money. The problem is that they consistently *spend* too much money. How often do we talk about the waste in our Federal government? It was Ronald Reagan who said the government doesn't tax too little, it spends too much. We, as individuals, are no different.

You're probably thinking: "I can't afford to save any more than I'm saving now. I have children to feed, bills to pay, and kids in college."

While that may be true, you're missing the real point. We're not saying you shouldn't spend money. We're not saying it's easy to raise a family. We're going through it ourselves and know what it's like. However, there are two things you can do to increase your financial strength. Coincidentally, these are the same things the government can do to solve it's financial problems.

- Stop spending (wasting) money needlessly.

- Begin saving money and investing it wisely.

We are not going to tell you how to live. You choose your own standard of living. And we're not going to tell you how to spend your money. We are, however, going to show you areas where you can **cut needless expenditures** and reveal places where you can put your money for **better returns**. There **are** ways to make your money work harder for you! Just by doing these two things, you will improve your financial picture tremendously.

Guidelines

✓ *Most people earn enough, but spend it all.*

✓ *Waste less, save more, and invest wisely.*

✓ *If you save and invest over the next ten years as you have over the past ten, you will still be where you are today.*

Chapter 4

Why Is It So Difficult To Make Decisions?

In our experience, women resist making the **necessary** financial decisions because they don't feel confident of their ability to make the **right** decision. "I just don't know a thing about money," is a common statement.

Ever since Bob left, I have found it nearly impossible to get anything done. I know I need to make some financial changes, I just don't feel I can handle it. I mope around the house all day, not knowing how to get started. But I can't leave things the way they are. I need more income from my savings, but I'm afraid to do anything.

Women avoid making decisions for a variety of reasons:

- They are **not convinced** they need to make decisions.

- They are **afraid** of making the wrong decision.

- They don't **know enough** to make a wise decision.

- Widows and divorcees are so **overcome** with grief that they can't even think about making decisions.

That is why we have included so many topics in this book. We want to show you which decisions you must make, even in crisis, and which decisions can wait. We want to help you work through your grief so you aren't totally immobilized. We want to convince you that your self-worth doesn't hinge on the success or failure of any one decision. Finally, we want to educate you so you can make good decisions.

Let's get to work on that. List some decisions that you

need to make. Beside each, list the reason you don't want to make it. Finally, list the worst thing that could happen if you made a poor decision.

Decision	Why not made	Worst result

Guidelines

✓ *List decisions that you should make, and prioritize them.*

✓ *Realize that a poor decision is rarely an irreversible catastrophe. It's a learning experience.*

✓ *You have not failed if you have learned from your mistakes.*

✓ *Reward yourself and be proud of each decision you accomplish. Build on your developing abilities.*

Chapter 5

How Can I Improve My Self-Esteem?

One of the most difficult aspects of our lives is dealing with the way we feel about ourselves. We call this self-esteem. Our self-esteem was developed by the way we were reared.

When we were born, we felt okay about ourselves. We had no biases. We were born with a clean slate. We had no chinks in our armor. However, as we grew older, those chinks started to appear. We were hit with negative statements that manifested into doubts about ourselves and our abilities:

How could you be so stupid?
Why can't you be like Marie?
Billie can do this. Why can't you?
You are such a klutz!
Boy, you sure are getting fat.
You can do better than that.
I'm so ashamed of you.

All our lives, people have bombarded us with hurtful comments. At first, we didn't believe them. But as more arrows were fired, they started to make little dents in our armor. The more they were fired, the more we believed them. One by one, they started piercing the armor.

Believing the put-downs

Every time another put-down pierced our emotional armor, we felt pain. It was small at first, but it began to grow and grow. When someone told us we were stupid, we believed them. And, to make matters worse, we started saying those things about ourselves:

I can't cook as well as Mom.
I can't believe how clumsy I am.
I just can't handle money.
I can't speak before a group.
I never could understand math.
I'll never get this right.
I am so uncoordinated.
I'm so stupid when it comes to money.

If you talk about your friends the way you talk about yourself, you won't have many friends. People are so tough on themselves, it's tragic. The more negative thoughts that enter your mind, the worse it becomes. In fact, those thoughts become self-fulfilling prophecies.

The way women were traditionally reared

Young women may have trouble identifying with this section if they have been reared with the newer, more liberated social consciousness. Perhaps that is why they can't relate to the low self-esteem and indecisiveness they see in their own mothers and aunts. Let's examine the upbringing of women, especially those over the age of forty.

Women as a group have been taught to subrogate their feelings to those of others. You have been taught that your role is to care for others. Caring. Nurturing. Loving. Yet, none of these things emphasize value on **you** as a person. Secure, independent women understand that a healthy self-esteem enables them to love and care for others. They enjoy nurturing, but not at the expense of their own self-esteem or self-worth.

However, insecure women experience the dark side of society's lessons. Continuous training to put others first teaches the negative connotation, "Other people are more important than you. Their needs count. Yours don't." Often that boils down to "putting myself first is selfish; being selfish is bad." Along with these feelings go excessive worry and guilt. Those feelings are all tied together by putting undue emphasis on others. This common misinterpretation has left an unfair burden on many middle-aged and older women.

> Betty and I were in a bookstore. I looked at a book I wanted, put it back on the shelf, and said to Betty, "It's not worth it." Betty turned to me and said, "Are you saying that the book's not worth it, or that you're not worth it?" That really hit me.

We can't negate all the propaganda you've been fed, any more than we can make the citizens of the former Soviet Union feel like free people overnight. It takes a lot of time to undo the wrong that's been done, but it's high time to begin.

You can do it

Our interviews with many, many women have proven that it is possible to overcome the myths and regain your self-esteem. Handling your life will become easier once you understand finances and feel more comfortable with them.

> As long as I can remember, I have felt inadequate. I was told growing up that I was not good enough. No matter how good my grades or accomplishments, I was told I could do better. No matter what I did, I couldn't please my mother. I couldn't wait to get married and get out of the house. But my husband was the same. He kept telling me I was lazy and stupid, the house was never clean enough, the meals were never good enough, and I was a "lousy" wife. Even after Chad and Brenda were born, it continued. Nothing I did was good enough for my husband.
>
> I devoted all my energies toward being the perfect wife, mother, and housekeeper, plus working at a full-time job for 20 years, and had nothing to show for it. I was sick and tired of the whole mess. My husband even turned Chad against me, although Brenda stuck up for me. Finally, I got up the courage to leave him. I decided that nothing could be worse than the situation I was in. He yelled and threatened. He told me I'd never make it on my own. My church friends told me I should try harder; it was my fault my marriage failed. They told me to remember my vows, "...for better or for worse." My mother told me I was selfish and

couldn't make it without him. But I could.

Glenda finally had the courage to do what **she** wanted. But it didn't stop there. She took some financial courses to understand how to handle her money. This helped her learn how to reduce some of her financial burdens. She also enrolled in psychology courses at the local community college. Feeling that she had a calling to help people, Glenda retired from her job, invested her retirement money, and went to college full-time. At the age of 48, she was the oldest freshman there. Nevertheless, Glenda proudly graduated with a degree in social work and a determination to help others.

Different paths

Life is not a dead end street. It has many paths, all leading in different directions. The path you choose has everything to do with the kind of life you live.

It all starts with feeling good about yourself. It's very difficult to make choices when you feel negative and powerless to make changes.

As you continue your journey, remember that everything you learn about financial matters will increase your self-esteem. This will lead to a better life for you and your family.

Guidelines

✓ *Although your attitudes and self-esteem are greatly determined by your upbringing, you have the power to change them.*

✓ *Educating yourself and taking steps toward change will increase your self-confidence.*

✓ *Pay attention to what you say about yourself and eliminate the negative thoughts.*

Chapter 6

How Can I Feel More
Financially Successful?

Janie spent considerable time talking with financial advisors. The following is an excerpt from a conversation with the last one with whom she met:

Q. Do you feel that you are financially successful?

A. No.

Q. Describe a person who is financially successful.

A. They would have lots of money, a good job, a big house and car, lots of investments, good retirement savings, and not have to worry about how they could afford anything.

Q. Can you define a financial failure?

A. I guess it's anyone who doesn't have all those things I just mentioned.

Q. Would that include you?

A. Yes.

Without continuing with the rest of the dialogue, we want you to see what has happened here. First, Janie doesn't feel very good about herself. She may have had some bad breaks in her life, however many people would trade places with her in a minute. Financially, Janie is securely middle-class.

Beyond that, take another look at her rules for success and failure. In order to feel successful, Janie must accomplish a whole list of things. If she doesn't accomplish **all** those things, she considers herself a failure.

That's a heavy burden to carry, wouldn't you agree? She established a definition of success that is virtually impossible to achieve. Does that sound familiar? Is your definition of success so difficult that you can't possibly achieve it? And is your definition of failure so simple that it's easy to achieve? Do you have one set of "success" standards for other people, but a tougher set for yourself?

Janie's problem is that she is living by other people's expectations. Society has expectations; friends and family have expectations. She can't possibly feel good about herself, because she can't live up to everyone's rules and expectations.

Setting your own rules

The way to feel financially successful is to tilt the rules in your favor. Make them easy, not difficult, to achieve.

Clarence is a pilot for Unlimited Airlines. He flies daily from St. Louis to Chicago, and back. Unfortunately, he is always late to work, constantly rushing to get on the plane. As a result, the plane is always late leaving the gate. By the time Clarence gets his clearance to land, the flight is thirty minutes late.

Is Clarence a successful pilot? You would probably say no, especially if your definition of a successful pilot is "one who gets his passengers to their destination, safely and on time." Obviously, the fact that Clarence's flight is always late violates your definition.

On the other hand, Clarence would say "Yes, I am a successful pilot." That's because his definition of a successful pilot is "one who lands the plane without killing anyone."

Each person establishes his or her own definition of success. Clarence considers himself successful because that's how he set the rules.

You need to do the same. Why go through life thinking of yourself as a failure, when it's just as easy to think of yourself as a success? Just set the rules to make success easy to achieve.

Your rules

You must set specific rules. Most people don't think they are a success unless they "feel" successful. That's not the answer. You must set definite guidelines. Take a few minutes to write your definition of success. Be easy on yourself. To give you some help, here are a variety of rules by people who have set themselves up for success.

I am a financial success if:

"I have developed some real goals and am working to achieve them."
"I am saving for my retirement."
"I am in control of my money."
"I use some of my money to help others."
"My financial situation improves each year."

State your new rules for success here. Make them easy to achieve.

_____

_____

_____

Failure

The same is true for failure. If you think of yourself as a financial failure, that's because you have made the rules too easy to achieve. So now, do the opposite of above. Make the rules for failure as tough as possible. For example:

I have failed if:

"I let money control me."
"I don't improve my financial condition each year."
"I use money to hurt others."
"I can't pay my bills and have no plan to improve."

State your new rules for failure here. Make them as tough as possible.

_____

_____

_____

Don't make winning so difficult. Don't make it impossible to feel good about yourself. Since you set the rules, set them in your favor. You'll see a world of difference in the way you feel about yourself.

Guidelines

✓ *I will believe in myself and have an "I can do it" attitude.*

✓ *I will educate myself about money, budgeting, and investments.*

✓ *I will learn about taxes and their effect on me.*

✓ *I will learn how inflation affects me.*

✓ *I will establish short-term and long-term goals.*

✓ *I will develop a plan for meeting my goals.*

✓ *I will start working today toward my goals.*

Chapter 7

Why Do I Feel I Must Live Up To Other's Expectations?

Women, more so than men, have been taught that they must act and feel certain ways. They've been taught to obey and please all the people all the time. Usually, that involves passive, caring behavior. There is nothing wrong with that, except when you compare it to the way men are reared.

From childhood, boys are taught to be tough and aggressive. "Don't take guff from anyone." When they get older, they tend to fight for what they want. They are assertive and seldom get pushed around.

Women, on the other hand, try to please. They don't want to rock the boat. They fall into their "place" in life. This is due to the way they were reared. Barbara's story is not unique.

As far back as I can remember, I had to be "Little Miss Perfect." I had to be concerned about everyone else's feelings. If I even looked cross-eyed at my mother, she would give me her "You're going to be dead soon if you don't straighten up" look. I knew she was serious. My brothers could get away with murder. They could yell, scream, and break things. I couldn't do any of that. I had to be "ladylike."

On top of that, nothing I ever did was good enough. If I got A's, my parents were upset that they weren't A+'s. "You can do better. Just work a little harder." When I played in the band, they were the first to tell me when I missed a note. Of course, no one else noticed that, except my parents. I had to be in every pageant and participate in every school activity. That meant spending time with many snobby, stuck-up girls. I had to be in the "right" sorority and wear the "right" clothes.

As I grew older, all that stuck in my mind. I continually asked myself, "Is this what Mother would want me to do?" I couldn't get her out of my mind. I always wanted to tell her, "I am my own person. Why can't I just do what I want for a change, instead of what everyone else wants me to do?" But I knew if I said that, I would get that "look."

My mother died recently, and I still resent her for what she did to me. Why couldn't she just let me enjoy life? Why did she have to put all those burdens on my shoulders? What difference did it make if I got high A's or low A's, or B's for that matter? It didn't make one bit of difference - except to make me miserable. Why was I always the one who had to consider other people's feelings? Why couldn't other people think of my feelings, just once? I got so frustrated!

The worst part is, I can see myself doing the same things to my children. I can see the tension in their faces when I disapprove of little things they do - the hurt in their eyes. It makes me want to cry, because I see myself as a little girl. I can feel the same look on my face now that my mother used to wear.

Luckily, I've started seeing a counselor who hopefully can help me get over this. I am paying more attention to how I treat my children. Maybe I'll even stop resenting my mother.

Expectations

It is very difficult to try to live up to other people's expectations, especially parents. Obviously, Barbara's mother didn't try to make her miserable, but she did. She put so much pressure on Barbara that, to this day, she hasn't recovered.

You can't feel good about yourself, or your accomplishments, when you feel like a failure. Financial independence requires positive self-esteem. It means feeling good about yourself and what you have accomplished from a financial standpoint. As long as you try to live up to the expectations of others, you cannot do this.

Whose expectations are you trying to live up to? Who

are you trying to please? Your mother? Your father? Your husband? Your children? Your church or synagogue? Your boss? Your friends? Your business associates?

How long are you going to let what these people think count more than what you think about yourself? When are you going to choose to take control of your own life? How much longer are you going to place more weight on the opinions of others than upon your own?

There's another point about expectations. Does everybody think the same way? Of course not. There are always going to be people who think you are doing the right thing, and those who think you are doing the wrong thing. How do you resolve this conflict? How do you choose whom to believe? How do you choose whom to please?

You can't. You'll drive yourself crazy. If you are a "pleaser," you know exactly what we're talking about. You spend all your energy trying to do what others want you to do, which is impossible. At some point, there will always be someone that you "disappoint."

If there are people in your life whom you are trying desperately to please, stop! Tell them that you choose not to live up to their expectations any longer. What **you** think is what counts. You are the only person you need to please.

Guidelines

✓ *Examine who you really are trying to please and evaluate why.*

✓ *Develop your own, personal expectations.*

✓ *Consciously take steps to make financial and non-financial decisions that satisfy your own expectations - not those of someone else.*

Chapter 8

How Can Assertiveness Be Financially Rewarding?

Women must be assertive to get ahead financially, as well as emotionally. Assertiveness means clearly, positively, and confidently getting your message across to others. It involves effective communication. Assertiveness is *not* being obnoxiously aggressive and demanding.

> Martha and Alice drove up to the bank simultaneously. Martha walked immediately to an officer and told her what she wanted. Alice stood around, waiting for someone to help her. Finally, a teller asked her if she could help. The teller had to strain to hear Alice say that she wanted to put some money into a CD. Alice was instructed to go see an officer. She meekly walked near the officer's desk and stood, with her eyes toward the ground, hardly noticed. Finally, the officer completed her other business and noticed Alice. Meanwhile, Martha had already transacted her business and left.

Learning to be assertive decreases your stress and improves your support system. It is good for everyone. You are acting, instead of reacting. You are in control, instead of being controlled.

When you need to make financial decisions, you can't do so while in a passive frame of mind. You must be confident, acting like you are certain of your decision. Then you can expect to be taken seriously.

When you first start being assertive, you'll probably feel some guilt. That is perfectly normal. And, in fact, you might not be taken seriously by family and friends. But that is no reason to stop. Just stick with it.

Like all new skills, it takes a while to become comfortable, but keep at it. Quit apologizing for your opinions and accepting the blame for everyone's problems. For the rest of your life, you will be thankful that you mastered this skill. Others will respect you more, and you will feel much better about yourself.

Take the analysis on the following page to see how you score on assertiveness. Record either an A or B to reflect the statement most correctly reflecting your behavior. The situations range from home, to finances, to the workplace.

If most of your responses are A's, then you are very assertive. Congratulations! You should go far. You can communicate clearly with others.

If most of your responses are B's, then you need to develop some assertiveness. Otherwise, you will find it difficult to accomplish your goals. Try practicing the examples in the chart, reworking them to fit your needs, until assertive responses are comfortable and automatic.

The choice is yours

Life is about making choices. Whether you are at work or in social settings . . . whether you are single, married, widowed, or divorced . . . whether you are young or old . . . **you** are solely responsible for making your own choices for today. Yesterday is finished. Today starts the first day of the rest of your life. What choices do you want to make for yourself? Who do you want to have control and power over your life, yourself or somebody else?

It's not enough to blame circumstances or other people for your situation. Sure, you may have been dealt a bad hand in the card game of life, but it's up to you to play that hand and come out a winner. Poker is a game well-known for people winning with terrible hands. They win because they use the

ASSERTIVENESS ANALYSIS

ASSERTIVE (A)	NONASSERTIVE (B)	A/B
I state my case without apology. "I'm looking for the loan officer. Is this the right desk?"	I apologize for myself when making requests. "I'm sorry to bother you, but I was wondering if this was the loan desk."	
I make suggestions confidently. "Try the growth fund. It will do better in the long run."	I ask permission to make suggestions. "Would it be okay if I change the television channel?"	
I try to handle confrontations in a positive way.	I try to avoid any confrontation.	
When making decisions, I state them firmly. "I'm changing my investments. I'm going to . . . "	I ask permission to state new decisions for which I am responsible. "Can I change my investments?"	
I stay calm and in control when others are upset.	I get upset easily and lose control during stressful confrontations.	
I try to pre-plan discussions that will be difficult, outlining my points mentally, and practicing ahead of time.	I try not to think about difficult discussions. I know I will forget what I wanted to say and mess up.	
I'm not afraid to praise my own efforts when deserved. "This cake looks great. I'm pleased with my effort."	I am afraid to praise my own efforts, even when deserved. "Do you think this cake looks OK?"	
I make sure people understand what I mean; I never just assume they do.	I assume people know what I mean. When they don't, I am frustrated.	
When my supervisor gives me a lot to do at once, I ask which things are most important. I let him know my limits or other conflicts.	When my supervisor dumps a lot of work on me, I stay until I get it all done or worry about what I couldn't finish.	
I check my time and job list before agreeing to any new responsibilities.	I say yes to anything I am asked to do. Saying no scares me.	
I know how to move up to the next job level in my organization.	I have no idea why other people are promoted instead of me.	
I make sure my supervisors and personnel counselors know that I am interested in a promotion.	I hope supervisors will notice how well I am doing and offer me a promotion.	
I regularly ask if any training, seminars, or new positions are available.	I would go for training or apply for positions if someone would tell me about them or invite me.	

proper strategy. They know the rules and how to make those rules work for them. They take control, instead of letting the cards they're dealt control them.

You, too, need to take control of your situation. This book contains the rules and strategies for making them work for you. Personal and financial concepts are covered, including taxes, credit, and investments. These subjects don't have to be foreign and frightening. You can use them all to your benefit. It's up to you to learn and apply these ideas and strategies to your life. Go for it!

One of the special challenges of being a woman is getting what you deserve. This is especially important if you are single, because everything is up to you. **You** have to make all the payments. **You** have to provide for your future. **You** have to make all the decisions, then live with the consequences. This is all made more difficult by people who treat women like second-class citizens.

Score yourself

Assertive people can accomplish much more than those who are non-assertive. On a scale of one to five, one being the least assertive and five being the most assertive, score yourself on the following:

_____ I communicate effectively with others by making statements that are concise, clear, and positive.

_____ I freely verbalize my experiences and accomplishments, without being boastful or apologetic.

_____ I stay calm under pressure and remain in control of my thoughts and emotions.

_____ I can make choices and stick by them, without buckling under to those who would sway me.

_____ I insist on fair treatment, and don't just assume that others will naturally treat me fairly.

_____ Without becoming hostile, I insist that others not make unrealistic demands of me. I set limits quietly, clearly, and confidently.

_____ I make other people believe that I am confident, even when I may not be.

_____ I am not defensive and don't feel I have to justify everything I say.

_____ I can take or share power in situations that affect me, even when I must insist on it.

_____ I know that I have the right to my own opinions and perspective, and am not threatened by the differing opinions of others. I do not feel the need to apologize constantly for my ideas.

Scoring results

40-50 You stand up for yourself without hesitation.

30-39 You have the general hang of things; you need to express yourself more.

20-29 You are easily manipulated. You need to work on your ability to communicate assertively.

10-19 You are extremely vulnerable to the desires and opinions of others. Take immediate steps to build your self-esteem and assertiveness.

It's up to you

In defense of others, no one can read your mind. You must state your demands clearly and concisely. Be brief and to the point.   Know the proper terms for whatever you are seeking. Do your research, then go to the proper person to transact your business.

At the same time, understand that people treat you the way you treat yourself, and they respond to the way in which you present yourself. If you think of yourself as "stupid," and act that way, that's how you will be treated. If you think of yourself as "smart," and appear to know what you want, then you will be treated with respect. If you act like you believe in yourself, then others will believe in you.

> *Ten years ago, Judith Resnick was divorced, broke, and alone with two teenaged daughters. She applied for jobs with major brokerage firms. Some refused to talk with her; one offered her a secretarial position. But that's not what she wanted. She kept looking until she found a company that would give her a chance to prove her capabilities. She found that company, and today is Chairperson and Chief Executive Officer of an investment banking firm that sold over $2.5 billion worth of bonds in 1992.*

When you speak up for yourself, you generally get what you are due. You cannot possibly get what you deserve if you don't speak up, demand your rights, and stand firm. If the person to whom you are speaking won't help, then go to his or her supervisor. Be as assertive and aggressive as necessary to get what's rightfully yours. That doesn't mean that you have to get ugly or obnoxious with people. Just be firm and don't back down.

Women should not be a silent majority. If all women would speak out, it would revolutionize the attitude of society.

> *I never wanted to speak out because I figured I'm only one person. One person can't make a difference. Then, after we had those bad floods last summer, I started thinking. Those floods were created one drop of rain at a time. While one drop of water alone might not make a big difference, when combined with all the other drops, that single drop can contribute to the devastation of cities. I'll never feel powerless again.*

There is power in numbers. Women need to speak out and network together. There are any number of groups that work toward that end. Join one or more with which you share a common purpose, and get involved in making change happen!

Guidelines

✓ *Learn to act assertively to get what you deserve.*

✓ *Speak up in situations that warrant it.*

✓ *Be decisive in your actions.*

✓ *If you want to be treated with respect, view yourself with respect.*

✓ *Learn the rules of life, and play to win.*

✓ *You are the only one who determines the respect you receive.*

Part Two

Financial Basics

Chapter 9

Why Do Most People Fail Financially?

It's sad but true: by the age of 65, most people are either dead or dead broke. In fact, government statistics show that out of 100 people reaching the age of 65, only two are financially independent. The rest must depend on relatives or the federal government, or must continue working in order to survive.

It's sad because proper planning can help you avoid the problems faced by most Americans. Notice, we said "proper planning." Anyone can plan; few plan properly. We're going to show you how. You can do it.

Of course, your biggest problem may be paying your current bills, not saving for retirement. However, they are interrelated. Problems during your working years, the only time you can save for retirement, result in problems during retirement. You cannot separate them.

There are any number of reasons why people have insufficient retirement income. Some of these reasons are unavoidable, such as an illness or tragedy that wipes out their life savings. Some are hard to overcome, such as loss of a job, divorce, or death of a husband. While these make it more difficult, they don't have to keep you from becoming financially secure. We have all read stories of people who have overcome terrible adversity to succeed emotionally and financially.

Most financial problems are not caused by laziness or stupidity. Rather, most people don't understand how money works or how proper planning and follow-through can overcome earlier adversities. As a result, they don't plan. Instead, they live for today, spending every penny on current "necessities," and saving nothing for future "necessities."

Education

There are several elements involved in financial management. The first is education. Few women have received the financial education and training that men have enjoyed. Thankfully, that is changing. But let's not fool ourselves. Many women were reared not to worry about money. As adults, they still don't want to worry about financial details. As a result, they live in a protective bubble, until it bursts. Their husbands are no longer around to handle things. Suddenly, they must make decisions for which they are not prepared. That's why the educational aspects of this book are so vital. You will learn how money works and how to make the most of it. Education, combined with assertiveness, makes you a strong force.

Discipline

Another element of financial success is discipline. Our parents and grandparents had discipline. They lived through the depression. They knew what it was like to go hungry and stand in line for food, and don't want to ever face it again. So they worked hard; they scrimped and saved. And no matter how much money they had, it was never enough. In the back of their minds was the concern that a depression might occur again, and they would be out in the street.

However, their descendants, the baby boomers and their children, haven't had this hanging over their heads. They've grown up in times of plenty. They see their parents and friends driving new cars and living in nice homes with pools. And they want this for themselves - now!

In fact, the most troubling aspect is that many don't want to work for a higher standard of living. They don't want to earn it. They want it today, whether or not they can afford it. They don't want to start at the bottom and work up . . . they want to start at the top and stay there.

Although this is not an indictment of all young people, it is a common thread throughout society. They want to travel, enjoy themselves, and live for today. Unfortunately, they will pay dearly for it when it comes time to retire and their income drops. Not only will they not be able to maintain their "exciting" lifestyle, they will have trouble simply getting by.

Most people lack discipline. They don't recognize that sacrificing today pays off in the future. They want to "enjoy my money now, while I'm young. After all, I may never live to age 65." Unfortunately, they probably will. We say "unfortunately" because by then, they will have spent all their savings and have nothing on which to live. They will become burdens on their children and society. All because they lacked the discipline to put money away - and keep it away!

Just a generation ago, fewer than one in 100 could expect to live past the age of 100. Now, one out of 85 live beyond the century mark. How will they afford it?

"Saving"

We see so many people who are "saving" money every month. But they are saving it like the Martins.

Jan and Larry Martin both work for major companies. They each participate in their company's retirement plan, to which they contribute 4% of their salaries. They'd like to put more away, but they have a new home and two new cars. The payments are quite steep, but they still save a few extra dollars each month in a savings account at the bank. Whenever they want to take a trip, they take the money from their savings. Whenever they want new furniture, they pay for it from their savings. They feel secure knowing that if they need money for college, or a major catastrophe, they can borrow from their retirement plans.

Jan and Larry are fooling themselves. They aren't saving anything! They are merely "parking" money in their savings account until they can find something on which to spend it. It's like the short-term parking lot at the airport. It becomes horribly expensive in the long run. In addition, they have a false sense of security regarding their retirement. Once the money is gone, it won't be available (or growing) for their retirement needs.

The Martins are no different from most people. They hate to see money in the bank when there are so many "better" uses for it. But when they get to retirement age, they will have to scrape by on what little is in their retirement plan. As you will see in Chapter 39, if they aren't saving a substantial portion of their income for retirement, they will face financial problems.

If this is starting to sound like a lecture, that's because it is. In our years of practice, we have seen problems faced by thousands of people who didn't plan properly. On the other hand, we've seen the abundant retirement benefits enjoyed by the relative minority that did. The difference is like night and day. It's payoff time when you retire with sufficient income. You finally get to enjoy the fruits of those years of sacrifice.

Again, we're not denying the special problems that you must face today, and we're not saying it is easy to save. In addition, we're not saying you have to put everything away for retirement. However, you probably need more long-term savings than you're putting aside today.

The reality is that the closer you are to retirement, the more concerned you become about having enough money. But no matter what your age, you must start planning today. As the old saying goes, "There's no time like the present."

Reasons for failure

Let's get back to the original question: "Why do people

fail financially?" There are many reasons.

- They don't know where they **stand** financially.
- They don't have financial **goals** for the future.
- They don't know about investment **alternatives.**
- They lack the **discipline** to make the tough decisions.
- They lack the **motivation** to make any decisions.
- They don't know how to apply the **tax laws** to their own advantage.
- They are afraid of making **mistakes.**
- They don't know where to **turn** for help.
- They don't know whom to **trust.**

For these reasons, and more, they don't make the moves that would help them financially. Instead, they wallow in instant gratification, inexperience, and indecision about planning for their future. Then they suffer for it in the end. Well, it doesn't have to happen to you. We're going to show you what you need to do to be financially successful.

Guidelines

✓ *To avoid financial failure, plan for your future.*

✓ *To have a comfortable retirement, you need to set aside and invest money regularly - starting today!*

✓ *Follow the guidelines set forth in Chapter 39 to determine how much you should set aside for retirement.*

✓ *Don't touch your retirement money until you retire!*

Chapter 10

Why Is It So Important
To Set Financial Goals?

There are many reasons why people run into financial difficulty. The primary reason, based on our experience, is they don't set goals. Goal setting involves defining exactly what you want, and then doing whatever is necessary to get there. You can't succeed without it.

> Judy takes her annual vacation the first two weeks of June. She always looks forward to this time of year, because it gives her a chance to get away from her job and unwind with her two children, Traci and Jake. Every day beginning in early March, the children ask her where they're going this year. She always responds, "I'm not sure yet. I don't have time to think about it. When the time comes, I'll decide." The days pass. The kids get excited. Judy keeps feeling more pressure because she knows she should make some plans. But, she thinks to herself, "It will be okay." Finally the big day arrives. They get up at 7:00, pile into the car, Judy backs out of the driveway, and stops. "Where are we going, Mommy?" asks Jake. "I don't know, honey," Judy replies. "I guess we'll just drive up I-45. It seems like a safe road."

Is this scene going to really happen? Of course not. Nobody would take a vacation without knowing exactly where they are going, where they plan to stay, how they are going to get there, what they are going to do when they get there, and when they're coming back. Yet that is how most people plan, or should we say "don't plan," their finances.

Most people have absolutely no idea of what they want financially. Oh, sure, they "want to be rich." They "want to retire comfortably." They want to send their children to the

40

"best schools." They want to have "no money worries." In most cases, that's just wishful thinking.

Importance of goals

If you ask successful people the secret to their success, they will tell you that they had specific goals. It didn't matter whether the goals were vocational or financial, recreational or educational. They didn't become successful by chance.

Trying to get by without goals is like trying to play golf without the hole - it's impossible. So, let's start at the beginning and learn how to set goals.

First, decide what is financially important to you. Next, break your goals into three time-frames: short-term, intermediate-term, and long-term. Let's look at each.

Short-term goals consist of what you would like to accomplish within a one to two year period. Some examples are:

- Paying off credit cards.
- Buying a new car.
- Changing jobs.
- Starting a college savings plan.
- Making a down payment on a new home.

Intermediate goals are those that you hope to achieve within a two to fifteen year period. For example:

- Funding a college education.
- Paying off your home mortgage.
- Buying a retirement home.
- Adding rooms to your home.
- Becoming completely debt free.

Long-term goals are those that you wish to accomplish

over a fifteen-year plus period. For example:

- Being able to retire.
- Starting another business.
- Paying cash for a retirement home.

These are just some general examples. Your particular goals depend on your own hopes and dreams. Obviously, age plays a part. For some, fifteen years is forever away. Others will be happy if they are still alive in fifteen years. No matter what your age and situation, however, it is vital that you have goals.

We will return to goal setting in Chapter 33. At that time, we will tell you, in more detail, exactly how to set your goals, and we'll walk you through the process.

Guidelines

✓ *You must have goals to succeed.*

✓ *Your goals should be established for various time-frames.*

✓ *Set short-term goals for 1-2 year time-frames.*

✓ *Set intermediate-term goals for 2-15 year time-frames.*

✓ *Set long-term goals for time-frames exceeding 15 years.*

Chapter 11

What Should I Expect From My Bank?

Most people have some money in a bank, savings bank or credit union. With only small differences among the three, they are the institutions where we deposit and borrow money.

Financial institutions are in business to make money. They do this by accepting deposits, investing them, and lending money to people in need, subject to their ability to repay the loans. They do not make money by letting the cash sit in their vaults. So, contrary to popular opinion, relatively little of your money remains with the institution as cash. Instead, it is invested to earn money for the bank.

Bank accounts

Banks offer several types of accounts.

- **Checking accounts** allow you to write checks against the money in your account.

- **Savings accounts** pay low rates of interest and hold money that you may need in an emergency.

- **Money market accounts** hold money that you may need within a fairly short period. They pay a rate of interest that is very low, since the money can be withdrawn anytime you want without penalty.

- **Certificates of deposit** hold money for longer periods of time. They range in duration from thirty days to five years. There is normally a penalty for early withdrawal.

Bank loans

Many people fail to realize that banks must lend money to stay in business; they can't make money by only taking in deposits. They lend money in a variety of ways.

- **Automobile loans** are discussed in Chapter 35.

- **Home mortgages** are discussed in Chapter 15.

- **Home equity loans** are discussed in Chapter 16.

- **Passbook loans** are loans against your own savings. This can be a good way to establish credit. On the other hand, paying interest to borrow your own money doesn't make much sense.

- **Credit Cards** are discussed in Chapter 14.

- **Personal loans** are based on your good name and credit worthiness.

FDIC Insurance

The main advantage of keeping your money in the bank is that accounts are insured up to $100,000. However, the FDIC (Federal Deposit Insurance Corporation) rules are confusing, not only to citizens, but to bankers as well. Here are a few important factors you must know.

- You are covered under FDIC insurance only up to $100,000 per institution, no matter how many different types of accounts you have in that bank. This also applies to branches of that bank. You gain nothing by spreading your money over different accounts or branches within the same institution.

- While you are covered for $100,000 for each "in trust

for" account, that only holds true when those accounts are for the benefit of your children, grandchildren, or spouse.

- When you hold joint accounts, the FDIC considers that you are the owner of **half** the account. You are still only covered up to $100,000 for the value of all your interests in all accounts in that particular bank.

Florence has three $50,000 joint accounts with her children in addition to a $70,000 account in her own name. According to the FDIC, she owns $25,000 of each joint account (total of $75,000) plus the $70,000 in her own name. Although her exposure is $145,000, she is covered only for $100,000.

- Under a law effective December 1993, the maximum insurance you can have for self-directed retirement accounts deposited in one bank is $100,000. Although you have different types of retirement accounts, the total coverage is still only $100,000.

What is the safest way to make sure you don't have any problems? Don't keep more than $100,000 in any one bank!

Choosing a bank

Bankers don't like to hear this, but in reality, all banks are pretty much the same. Their interest rates are similar; their checking accounts tend to be the same; their loan rates don't vary much. Location isn't even a factor anymore, since they seem to be on every corner.

The primary differences between banks are the people that work there and the services they provide. Basically, all banks do is take in deposits and make loans. How well they do this separates the leaders from the rest of the pack. That said, there are some subtle differences that can save you a lot of money, and those differences involve the costs.

Fees

One of the most aggravating aspects of dealing with banks is the fees they charge. You deposit your money in their bank, they make money while it's there, and they make money when they lend it out. Yet, they charge you fees along the way.

Use this form to compare your bank's fees against those of other banks to find the best banking deal. You'll be surprised how much money you can save.

Automatic Teller Machines	Your Bank	Bank #2	Bank #3
Charge for using your bank's ATM			
Charge for using any other ATM			
Checking Accounts			
Monthly fee			
Minimum balance to waive fee			
Number of free checks per month			
Charge per check above minimum			
Interest rate			
Interest paid on what balance			
Charge for stop payments			
Charge for bounced deposits			
Charge for bounced checks			
Charge for copies of checks			
Overdraft protection			

The key to choosing a bank is to do business with one that you like and that provides great service. Although banks gain or lose a few customers based on a half percent difference in interest rates, most customers deal with them because they like the employees.

It is a good idea to establish a banking relationship, then get to know the personnel. Find people who are pleasant to work with and appreciate your business. You don't want to be hassled every time you want to cash a check, are a few days past due on a payment, or unintentionally bounce a check. You want a bank that will work with you.

One mistake most people make is believing that the bank is doing them a favor by lending them money, or covering an overdraft. That's part of their business.

Don't walk into the bank hat in hand. It is a business relationship which is beneficial to both parties. Assert yourself and make sure that you get the service you deserve.

Guidelines

✔ *Compare rates of interest between various banks.*

✔ *Shop around for the lowest fees.*

✔ *Don't keep more than $100,000 in any one bank.*

Chapter 12

What Should I Know About Borrowing Money?

Establishing credit is a real Catch-22 situation. If you don't have credit, you need to establish it. But nobody will extend you credit if you don't have a credit history. Let's look at the different types of credit:

- **Secured** loans require you to pledge collateral. The two primary types are mortgages and automobile loans. In both cases, the bank or financial institution holds the title to your property until the loan is repaid. That allows them to repossess the asset securing the loan if you don't make your payments.

- **Unsecured** loans are based on your good credit alone. Primarily, we're talking about credit cards. The bank, retailer, or credit card company gambles that you will fulfill your obligations.

Qualifying for credit

No matter what type of loan you desire, you must be approved. In other words, you must qualify as to:

- **Credit worthiness.** You must have a good credit history.

- **Financial means.** You must have sufficient income to make the payments.

- **Debt structure.** You cannot be so overloaded with

debt that you will be unable to make the payments.

If you meet these qualifications, then you should be able to get credit. We say "should" because nothing is certain in the world of finance.

It has been especially difficult for women to get credit over the years. It is even harder for widows who have not established credit in their own names. That's why it is so important to get credit cards **in your own name** while you are still married, or never-married and employed.

If you are no longer married, however, it's not as easy. For divorcees, it can be especially difficult. Often, credit is destroyed during the final stages of a marriage, if not before. If the debt was in your name during your married years, that bad credit will follow you.

Establishing credit

The best way to establish credit is to pay your bills on time. For some, that's easier said than done. There are many factors that can negatively influence your ability to pay. Some you can't control; others you can.

The biggest factor you **can** control is the amount of money you borrow. One of the major problems today is the debt carried by the average family. The desire to "live for today" means that they want items they can't afford, so they put them on credit cards. That's where the trouble starts. Credit is a two-edged sword. While it helps people buy items they can't afford, it also makes it too easy to get into financial trouble. People are more concerned with the monthly payment than with total cost. That's how you get into trouble - fast!

The interest rate - APR

The interest rate is one of the two primary factors

affecting the total cost of your loan. There are many ways that rates are quoted, but the one you must concern yourself with is the **annual percentage rate (APR)**.

The government realized many years ago that Americans were being mislead as to the actual interest costs of loans. For example, one method of computing interest is known as "add-on." When this method is used, the 8% rate you are quoted is not a true 8% rate. The reason for this is that the interest you pay is computed as if the balance doesn't decrease as you make your monthly payments.

If you borrow $2,000 at 8% add-on, and make monthly payments for a year, you will pay $160 in interest. The only problem is, you are paying interest the entire year as if the balance remained at $2,000. This means that after six months, when the balance is down to $1,000, you continue to pay interest on the full $2,000.

The APR resolves the confusion. The annual percentage rate on this loan would be 14.14%, a far cry from the 8% you are quoted. The APR, which by law must be provided, is the **only** meaningful measure of your rate. Make sure you obtain it.

In addition, many mortgage lenders charge fees and "points," as explained in Chapter 15. The points are reflected in the APR. Again, the stated interest rate is meaningless.

Total payments

The other factor is the length of the loan. Together, the interest rate and number of payments form the total cost of the loan. Too often, people are concerned only with the monthly payment. A more meaningful figure, however, is the total of all the payments.

The following chart shows the total payments on a

$12,000 car loan at 9% APR for three, four, and five years.

	36 months	48 months	60 months
Monthly Payment	$381.60	$298.62	$249.10
Total Payments	$13,737.60	$14,333.76	$14,946.00

Your monthly payment depends on the interest rate and the number of years over which you repay the loan. Obviously, the longer you spread out your payments, the lower your monthly payment. Be wary of this trap. Though your monthly payments are lower, your **total payments** are greater. Therefore, it makes sense to finance for the shortest term possible.

Debt consolidation loans

Potentially the most expensive type of loan is a debt consolidation loan.

Beverly had $15,000 in credit card and automobile loans, with payments of $595 per month. Glancing through her newspaper one morning, she saw this headline for a debt consolidation loan: "Borrow $10,000 for only $78.67 per month. Home equity loans - rates start at 8.75%." The schedule of loans and payments in the ad showed that she could consolidate her debts into a single $15,000 loan with a monthly payment of only $118.01 for 360 months.

What a rotten deal! This chart shows the true results:

	Number of Payments	Total of Payments
Current Debt	30 months @ $595	$17,850
Consolidation	360 months @ $118.01	$42,483

She will have to pay $42,483 over a thirty-year period for her $15,000 debt. If she continues to pay $595 a month on her current loans, she'll be out of debt in 30 months. By consolidating, she won't be out of debt for 360 months. Even worse, since her car loan will be in her package, she'll be financing it for 30 years, long past it's useful life.

The advertisement is so enticing. Only 8.75% instead of the 15 to 18% she's currently paying. But you must look past the monthly payments and interest rate and consider the total payments. Unless you consolidate for a period no longer than the duration of your current loans, debt consolidation loans can only increase, not decrease, your total payments. Remember, **you cannot borrow your way out of debt!**

One final point. Many people who get debt consolidation loans to pay off credit cards invariably run them up again. They've not only failed to improve their financial position, they've made it worse! If you must get this type of loan, if that's the only alternative between you and bankruptcy, then destroy your credit cards and close those accounts. Keep only one credit card, and use it for **true** emergencies only.

Don't pay a fee to borrow money

Financially troubled people make their problems even worse by making foolish moves in desperation. One of these mistakes is paying someone to obtain a loan.

This can be done any number of ways. Some businesses and individuals advertise that they can "help" you get a loan. All you have to do is give them some money up-front. For that fee, they will either help find a lender, or send you information with a list of places to borrow.

There are others who advertise that they can get you a credit card, then tell you to call a "900" number. These "900" numbers are special phone numbers that charge from $1 to $5 per minute. To help run up the tab, they put you on hold for a few minutes.

Remember, nobody can perform miracles. These schemes only waste your money without providing any benefit. They make money for the other person, not you. All you will do is throw good money after bad.

Guidelines

- ✓ *If you don't control your debts, your debts will control you.*

- ✓ *Don't borrow money without considering the APR.*

- ✓ *Pay your loan in the fewest possible months.*

- ✓ *Avoid debt consolidation loans. They look good on the surface, but are very costly in the long run.*

- ✓ *Don't use long-term loans to pay short-term debts.*

- ✓ *Don't ever pay a "finder's fee" to get a loan.*

- ✓ *Don't ever call "900" numbers for financial help.*

- ✓ *It is important to maintain a good credit rating.*

- ✓ *You can't borrow your way out of debt.*

- ✓ *If it looks too good to be true, it probably is.*

Chapter 13

What If I Can't Pay My Bills?

Sometimes events occur which force our finances out of control. This is particularly true for recent divorcees and widows.

> Frankie had a difficult time during her divorce. She and her ex-husband owed money on two cars, their home, and several credit cards. She co-signed the mortgage and credit cards, and was sole debtor on her car. Upon their divorce, they sold their home and paid-off the mortgage, but realized no profit. They still had their credit card debts and car loans. The divorce decree stated that her ex-husband was responsible for 75% of the credit card debt, she for 25%. But her name was still on the line. A few months later, her ex-husband lost his job and couldn't make payments. She couldn't make them herself, since her salary was not sufficient to make the payments plus provide living expenses for herself and her children. Her total debt was $23,000, her income $21,000.
>
> This debt was a constant worry to Frankie, who finally reached the point where she could no longer stand the pressure and the calls from collection agencies. Enough was enough. She met with an attorney and filed bankruptcy.

Frankie's story is common. More and more people are finding themselves in the position of being unable to pay their bills. Once you get into that trap, the alternatives are not very pleasant.

Try to work with your creditors

The first step in resolving your situation is to stop charging and taking on new debt. Cut up your credit cards to limit the financial damage you are doing to yourself. Next, talk with your creditors and try to work out a payment schedule.

Let them know that you want to pay the debt and explain the reasons for your financial troubles. This may or may not work, but it's worth a try.

Don't bounce checks!

If you can't pay your bills, don't write bad checks. In many states, it's a worse crime to bounce a check than it is to fail to pay a debt. To make matters worse, your bank will charge you for bounced checks, and sometimes the party to whom you wrote it will get charged by their bank. It's a no-win situation. If you can't pay, level with your creditor. While it won't be easy, it will be better for you in the end.

Call Consumer Credit Counseling Service

If you are not able to accomplish anything with your creditors, call the Consumer Credit Counseling Service. This is a nonprofit organization that helps you analyze your current situation and set up a budget. In addition, if you are having trouble making your payments, they will present your repayment plan to your creditors. With the three of you working together - you, CCCS, and your creditors - you probably can resolve your financial problems.

To find the nearest office, look in your local white pages for a listing under Consumer Credit Counseling Service. If there is no listing, call toll-free 1-800-388-CCCS. You will be asked to enter your zip code, at which point they will give you the phone number of the nearest office. The service is free. However, if you do establish a debt repayment plan which is to be administered by CCCS, they may charge a small fee to help cover administrative costs.

Working your way out of debt is not easy, but it can be done in most situations. Just don't wait until it gets totally out of hand. Call CCCS now if you feel stressed by financial problems.

Last resort - bankruptcy

If all else fails, and if you just can't pay your bills, then the final step is filing personal bankruptcy. This can be done voluntarily, or you can be forced into bankruptcy by your creditors.

Although lenders hate bankruptcy, they also hate hanging onto a hopeless situation. They are more inclined to try to end it by writing-off the debt.

The two types of bankruptcy most often used for individuals are Chapter 7 and Chapter 13.

- **Chapter 7** is the most popular because it allows you to totally wipe out your debts. Of course, you also lose your assets, except for the small portion you may keep by law. Bankruptcy allows you to start fresh with no debts, but also with minimum assets. Nevertheless, there are some debts you cannot bankrupt against: child support, alimony, student loans guaranteed by the government, and income taxes for the three years prior to the bankruptcy.

- **Chapter 13** is known as the "wage-earners" bankruptcy. It is for people who have a regular income and want to establish a schedule to pay their debts. The court works with you in preparing a payment schedule. In return, the creditors agree not to take any further action, as long as you continue to make your payments. As long as you meet your obligations, you may keep your home and other assets. However, this is a form of bankruptcy, and your credit is still severely damaged.

The advantage of filing bankruptcy is that it ends attempts by your creditors to collect money and allows you to start all over. The disadvantages deal with moral and future credit issues. The cost of bankruptcy is born by everyone, because credit losses are factored into interest rates and prices. Additionally, it will be virtually impossible to obtain credit for many years, because bankruptcy remains on your credit record ten years for Chapter 7, and seven years for Chapter 13.

Repairing your credit

Credit repairing companies advertise that they can fix bad credit. That is totally untrue. It is not possible to legally erase bad, but accurate, credit data.

Your credit report contains your credit history as reported by banks, finance companies, and some credit card companies. It reflects your balances and your payment history. If you historically pay late, that is reflected. If you defaulted on your loans, that is reflected. If you filed bankruptcy, that is reflected. You can't change that. What is, is. Late payments remain on your record for seven years; bankruptcy information remains ten years for Chapter 7 and seven years for Chapter 13. No matter what people tell you, there is no way you can change it. That is why many states have outlawed credit repair services.

Don't make your financial situation worse by going to someone who says they can repair your credit. They just can't do it. The only thing that can repair your credit is time.

Correcting erroneous information

It is possible to have incorrect information on your credit history. It could have been entered or reported incorrectly. Your records might have gotten mixed with another person's having the same first and last name. Or, it could have been a spousal debt for which you had no liability. In fact, Consumers Union did a study of 171 credit reports and found errors in nearly half. That is why it is important to get a copy of your credit file.

You should write to each of the three primary reporting companies and ask for a copy of your credit report to make sure the information is accurate. Their addresses are:

TRW
P O Box 2350
Chatsworth, CA 91313
(800) 392-1122

TRW will send you a free copy of your report once per year.

Equifax
P O Box 740241
Atlanta GA 30374
(800) 685-1111

Equifax charges $8 for your credit report, but it is free if you've recently been denied credit.

Trans Union
Box 7000
North Olmstead OH 44070
(303) 689-3888

Trans Union also charges $8 per report, but it is free if you've recently been denied credit.

If you discover incorrect information, contact the creditor that reported it. If it is truly inaccurate, they should correct it. If the creditor disputes your argument, then you may write an explanation which will be attached to your credit report. If you don't get satisfactory results, contact:

The Federal Trade Commission
Division of Credit Practices
Sixth Street and Pennsylvania Avenue NW
Washington DC 20580

If your report is correct, but you have an unsatisfactory payment history, don't be surprised if you are denied credit. Lenders need to make loans to stay in business, but they also need to be repaid in a timely fashion. They don't want to extend credit to someone who has a bad payment history.

Reestablishing credit

One of life's most difficult challenges is reestablishing your credit after it has been ruined either by a history of late payments or bankruptcy. While it's very difficult to get credit with a bad record, it's virtually impossible after a bankruptcy. Though you may be a better *credit* risk because you don't have any debts, you are not a good *moral* risk, and that is just as important to a lender.

There are a few ways you can attempt to reestablish credit:

- **Secured credit card.** A variety of companies issue credit cards to individuals who deposit money equal to their line of credit. While this serves no logical purpose, it does at least provide a way to establish a payment record. If you cannot get a credit card through normal channels, a secured card is an alternative. The company has your money in case you don't make your payments, so they have no risk. In addition, they charge you interest, so they can't lose. Carefully read the next chapter on finding the cheapest credit cards. There is a big difference between the costs of secured credit cards issued by different companies.

- **Passbook loan.** Your bank should make a loan against your savings account or certificate of deposit at their bank. They hold it as collateral until the loan is repaid. Again, it can serve to reestablish your credit.

Even if you develop a good payment history with this new credit, it still takes a long, long time to overcome the damage that has been done. Since it was credit that got you

into trouble in the first place, that might not be so bad. You're
probably better off not having credit cards again, anyway.

Guidelines

✓ *Obtain a copy of your credit report to be sure there are
no errors.*

✓ *If there are errors, have them corrected yourself. Don't
pay someone else to do it for you.*

✓ *If you have a problem, discuss it with your creditors.*

✓ *Don't pay your bills with bad checks.*

✓ *Call Consumer Credit Counseling Service if your debt
becomes unmanageable.*

✓ *Don't pay someone to repair your credit.*

✓ *Use secured credit cards or passbook loans to reestablish your credit.*

✓ *File bankruptcy only as a last resort.*

Chapter 14

How Can I Use Credit Cards To My Advantage?

Credit cards have become part of our existence. You can't even cash a check without one for identification. Even Vice-President Gore, in his "Reinventing Government" program, recommended the option of paying income taxes with a credit card. With thinking like this, it is easy to see why so many Americans get into financial trouble. Some people will end up paying their taxes, plus monthly interest, to the credit company. Instead, by increasing their withholding they could do the same thing interest-free during the year (by paying the IRS directly). How interesting!

Like so many other financial products we've discussed, credit cards have their good points and bad points. Unfortunately, those bad points cause many people to get into trouble.

Allison was thrilled the day she received her credit card. Finally, she was a "real person" with "real credit." She had a $1,600 line of credit at a rate of 16%, and only had to pay $20 per year for the card. What a bargain! She couldn't wait for the weekend to arrive so she could go shopping. By late Saturday, she had charged over $900 worth of clothes. The next month, when she got her bill, she was pleasantly surprised that her minimum payment was only $25. "Wow," she thought to herself. "That's not so bad. I can afford that." A few weeks later, it was vacation time. Again, she pulled out her trusty credit card. In less than six weeks, she had reached her credit limit of $1,600. Her bill came the next month and her minimum payment was $35. She thought this was really great. "Thirty-five dollars a month is nothing." The next week she decided to apply for another credit card. By now, her credit was even better. So it went, until she was $18,000 in debt with a minimum monthly payment of $350.

Sound farfetched? Well, we're sorry to report, it's not. Stories like this occur daily. America has become a society of consumers. People want to enjoy themselves. They want all the comforts. And they pay for them by credit. Like Allison, many wind up in financial trouble.

Minimum payment

What really happens is that people get caught up in the "minimum payment" scam. Look at this example:

Credit Balance	$ 3,000
Finance Charge for the month at 16%	$ 40
Minimum Payment	$ 51

People don't realize that if they pay the $51 minimum, only $11 goes toward reducing their balance. Think how many months it will take to reduce a $3,000 balance at the rate of $11 per month. You may not live that long!

See why this is a scam? The credit card companies are collecting 15 to 21% on all those Americans who are only making minimum payments. No wonder they love the credit card business!

This is a national scandal, and one that must be stopped. Of course, the financial institutions aren't going to quit - they're making too much money from people willing to pay them 18% until the day they die. As long as people are willing to pay the interest, the financial institutions will be happy to collect it.

Is it any wonder that AT&T, General Motors, Ford, even Western Union have their own Visa and MasterCards? They're all making a fortune at our expense.

Charging to the max

Typical consumers, upon receiving credit cards, do what

Allison did - charge to the max. What they fail to realize is that once they have reached their limit, assuming they don't get any more credit cards, they have to pay cash for everything.   In addition, they have to make monthly payments on the "stuff" they bought months ago.

What have they gained? Very little. Most people can't even tell you where their money went. All they know is that they are now making monthly payments for something they bought a long time ago.

Why do people do this? Because they want things now. They want to "live for today." They want to "enjoy life." Well, that's fine if you can afford it. Unfortunately, most people can't really afford to do all the things they would like.

Reducing credit card costs

There are six ways you can reduce credit card expenses.

1. **Don't use them.** This is the best solution, but not realistic for all people.

2. **Pay your balance in full every month.** Again, this is not always possible.

3. **Shop for the best interest rate.** Rates vary greatly on credit cards. If you are not going to pay your balance in full every month, then this is very important. Why pay 19% when you can pay 8%? To find the best rate, contact either of the following companies for a list, including toll-free numbers.

   • Send $5 to RAM Research, P O Box 1700, Frederick MD 21702.

   • Send $4 to Bankcard Holders of America, 560 Herndon Pkwy, Suite 120, Herndon VA 22070.

4. **Shop for lowest annual fee.** If you are not going to carry a balance, then get a "no annual fee" card. If you pay your balance in full each month, then the interest rate doesn't matter.

5. **Get the longest grace period.** The grace period is the number of days between the day you make your purchase and the day the company begins charging you interest. This varies greatly between cards.

6. **Get the least costly calculation method.** There are several methods for calculating your interest. Bank-card Holders of America lists the most common, along with an example of the differences in cost.

   • **Average Daily Balance Excluding New Purchases.** This is the most favorable method because you aren't penalized for making additional purchases during the billing cycle.

   • **Average Daily Balance Including New Purchases.** This is the most commonly used method. The company takes your previous balance, adds new purchases, subtracts payments and credits to arrive at your daily balance. Then they compute your <u>average</u> daily balance. You are charged interest for new purchases if you have an outstanding balance, even if you pay your card in full.

   • **Two-Cycle Average Daily Balance Excluding New Purchases.** This is not very favorable if you sometimes pay your balance in full and sometimes make payments. The one saving grace is that it excludes new purchases.

   • **Two-Cycle Average Daily Balance Including New Purchases.** This is the worst method if you sometimes pay your balance in full and sometimes make payments. If you start with a zero balance one month, and don't pay in full, then you get penalized back to the previous cycle.

To reveal the impact of different calculation methods, Bankcard Holders of America did a study of charges if you began the month with a zero balance, charged $1,000, and made only the minimum payment. The following month, you charged another $1,000 and paid your balance in full. The card has a rate of 19.8%. Your finance charges would be:

- Average Daily Balance Excluding New Purchases $16.50
- Two-Cycle Excluding New Purchases $32.80
- Average Daily Balance Including New Purchases $33.00
- Two-Cycle Including New Purchases $49.05

The method used by the credit card company makes a big difference in your finance charges. However, if you always pay your balance in full, the finance charges don't matter.

If you don't pay in full, it is imperative that you understand the method being used by your credit card company. By law, they must make this information available to you. If you don't understand, then ask. Be sure to shop around and compare.

The key to successfully managing your finances is discipline and will power. If you don't have these, you'll end up with nothing. If you live only for short-term enjoyment, you'll have nothing left for your retirement. Remember, savings and investments buy security and peace of mind.

Cash advances

Besides charging purchases on your credit card, you can also get cash. This is called a "cash advance." Most credit card companies charge you a flat fee for a cash advance.

While on vacation, Judy needed $500. She went to the local bank and got a cash advance in that amount. When she received her bill, she noticed a $10 charge. She called her bank and learned they charge 2% on all cash advances, subject to a $2 minimum and $10 maximum. She paid the balance in full, plus the $10.

Judy ended up paying 2% on $500 for one month. That corresponded to an annual interest rate of almost 25%. In addition, if she had a previous balance, she would have been paying interest on her "average daily balance."

Payment holiday/prepaid payment

Many cards give you a "break." They let you skip a payment now and then. Some companies call this a payment holiday. Others just say your account is prepaid.

You might get a message on your statement like, "High Interest Card has received your recent payment which was more than the minimum payment. As a result, your due date was advanced to the date shown above and you may skip this month's payment. Congratulations on your good credit history."

Don't fall into this trap. It costs you more money and gives the credit card company full interest for an additional month. Remember, their goal is to keep you in debt as long as possible. Yours is to get out of debt as soon as possible. They are not your friends. Do the opposite of what they want. Aggravate them a little. Send in even more!

Total cost

I didn't pay much attention to the interest rate on my credit card. I just assumed they were all the same. It took me a while, but I finally realized there was a difference. When I calculated the cost, I was amazed how much I could save just by reducing the interest rate.

The following chart shows the impact of various interest

rates on a $2,000 loan balance.

	8.9% Rate	12.4% Rate	18.7% Rate
Annual Interest	$178	$248	$374
+ Annual Fee	$25	$25	$25
Total Cost	$203	$273	$399

The impact of lower interest rates is significant. If you make payments on your credit cards, as opposed to paying them in full, then the annual fee drives your costs up even higher. Contact the services on page 63 and apply for the lowest-cost cards.

American Express vs. Bankcards vs. Discover

The American Express Green and Gold cards differ from the others in that there is no limit to the amount you can charge, but also no extended payments. You must pay your balance in full when due. This is an advantage if you want to make sure you don't charge more than you can afford. However, there is a price. The Green card costs $55 a year; the gold card costs $75. It is better to get a no-fee bank card and pay the balance when due. In addition, bankcards (MasterCard and Visa) are accepted in three times as many locations as American Express.

The Discover Card contains a gimmick that pays you up to 1% of your purchases in cash at the end of each year. This is fine if (1) you charge a lot, and (2) you pay your balance in full each month. However, if you don't pay your balance in full each month, you are probably paying more in additional interest than you are receiving in rebates. That's because Discover uses the "two-cycle" method of computing interest. Change to a low-cost bankcard as described earlier.

The best investment you can make

Do you want a safe, high yield investment, with no risk of loss? Pay off your credit cards! If you have credit cards charging 18% and money in the bank earning 4%, why not take your money out of the bank and pay off your credit cards? That turns a 4% investment (before taxes) into an 18% investment (after taxes). What a deal!

If you can't pay off your credit cards totally, then at least pay more than the minimum. Anything above that will reduce your principal. As stated previously, just paying the minimum payment is a losing situation. How much of a losing situation?

According to Bankcard Holders of America, if you have a $2500 balance on an 18.5% credit card, and you pay only the minimum balance monthly, **it will take over thirty years to pay it off!** You will pay more than $6,600 in interest! Instead, make extra payments and get rid of that albatross.

If you can't pay off all your cards, then start making additional payments on the one with the highest interest. Once you have paid off that card, then make additional payments on the next highest one. You'll feel a real sense of accomplishment as you pay off each card.

Guidelines

✔ *Reduce your credit card costs by shopping for the best card for you.*

✔ *Don't get cash advances. The cost is too great.*

✔ *Don't take advantage of "payment holidays."*

✔ *Shop for the lowest "total cost" card.*

✔ *Make more than the minimum payment.*

Chapter 15

What Is The Best Type Of Mortgage For Me?

Very few people pay cash for their homes, instead choosing to finance them with a mortgage. Most mortgages are either fifteen or thirty years in length. Because most people want their monthly payment to be as low as possible, the 30-year mortgage is the more popular, but also the more costly.

Commercial banks, savings banks, and specialized lenders handle mortgages. Interest rates vary by institution and length of the loan.

There are two types of mortgages:

- **Fixed rate mortgages** provide a level interest rate throughout the term of the loan. This means that if interest rates go up, you get the benefit of your lower rate loan. On the other hand, if rates go down, you are stuck with that higher rate. Of course, you can always refinance to get a lower rate.

- **Adjustable rate mortgages,** also known as ARMs, provide a variable rate based on current interest rates. If rates go up, your rate goes up, and vice versa. These normally offer an unusually low rate the first year, and adjust upward from there. ARMs contain annual and lifetime caps. The annual cap limits the amount a rate can increase or decrease each year; the lifetime cap does the same over the life of the mortgage.

Adjustable rate vs. fixed rate

Choosing the right mortgage is extremely difficult because it depends on future interest rates. The low payments of ARMs make them attractive. However, there are some additional factors you must consider.

- If the only way you can afford the monthly payments is with an ARM, then that might be your only alternative. Remember, most first-year rates on ARMs are teasers - they are artificially low. They will invariably increase the maximum for the next year or two. This may mean that you won't be able to afford the monthly payments later on, so beware.

- There are limits to the increases in ARM rates. The loans contain annual and lifetime caps. These are the maximum rate increases for any year, as well as over the life of the loan.

- If rates go up, will you be able to afford it? Will it put you in a bind? Will you really be more able to afford the higher payment in two years than you are today? You must answer these questions honestly.

- Choosing the right loan was difficult in the past when rates were so high. However, it's easier now. With lower rates in recent years, fixed rate loans are the more attractive and prudent alternative.

In our opinion, fixed rate mortgages offer big advantages.

- You know what your monthly payment will be, and you can budget accordingly.

- You won't be shocked with increases in future years.

- If rates drop substantially, you can always refinance.

Before making any decision, you should first look at the length of your mortgage.

15-year vs. 30-year

If you want to make the most of your mortgage, get rid of it as soon as possible! In other words, pay it off. You will receive peace of mind, plus save thousands of dollars.

Mortgages differ from most other loans because your initial payments are almost pure interest. In the early years of a 7% mortgage, only 13% of the payment reduces your principal; the remaining 87% is interest. If the interest rate is higher than 7%, then even more of your payment is interest.

You must pay for many years before a reduction in your principal balance is evident. That is why we recommend a 15-year mortgage over a 30-year mortgage. Look at the difference in total interest on a $50,000 loan at 7% fixed.

Length of Mortgage	Monthly Payment	Total Interest Over Life
Thirty Years	$332.65	$69,754
Fifteen Years	$449.41	$30,894

By increasing your monthly payment only $117.24, you can reduce the total interest by almost $39,000! That's quite a difference.

Other costs

Mortgages are neither inexpensive nor simple. There are many additional expenses when getting a loan.

- **Points** are added fees that many lenders charge. Mortgages are quoted as the interest rate plus points. For example: "7% plus two points." Each point is

1%. On a $50,000 loan, two points equal 2%, or
$1,000. That fee is usually added to your loan.
When shopping for a loan, look for the **lowest
interest** rate and the **fewest points.**

- **Closing costs** are expenses that must be paid at
  closing. These include appraisals, inspections, credit
  checks, attorneys' fees, etc. While most of these are
  fixed, you can reduce attorneys' fees by shopping for
  an attorney who charges less. Closing costs vary city
  to city, state to state, and region to region. The
  national average is 3% of the loan amount.

- **Title insurance** is something else you want to have
  and your lender requires. It would be a disaster to
  purchase a house with a bad title. That could void
  the transaction, cause you to lose your entire investment, and still leave you liable for the loan.

- **Property insurance** is also required by your lender
  and necessary for you. As discussed in Chapter 21,
  this is a vital part of your asset protection plan.

You also have the expense of property taxes. These city
and/or county taxes are due annually. Most lenders require an
escrow account built into your monthly payment. It is a special
holding account for property taxes and insurance. When they
are due, the lender pays them. While this is not the most
economical way to pay, it does help you budget.

CHOOSING THE BEST MORTGAGE FOR YOU

*Elaine found a house she liked for $85,000. She got the Sunday
paper and looked at mortgage rates. How confusing! Not only
was there a big difference between the adjustable and fixed rate
loans, but there was a significant difference between financial
institutions. In addition, there were different rates for 30 and 15-
year loans. On top of that, some charged points and others*

didn't. She could put $15,000 down, but had a tough time deciding where to go for the loan.

Here are four of the twenty lenders listed in her paper.

Bank	30-Year Interest	Fixed Points	15-year Interest	Fixed Points	One Interest	Year Points	Adjust. Cap
A	7.38%	1.00	6.88%	1.00	4.00%	1.25	2/6
B	7.63%	1.50	7.00%	1.50	5.50%	1.50	1/4
C	7.25%	2.00	6.63%	2.25	4.50%	1.75	2/6
D	7.50%	1.00	7.00%	1.00	4.75%	1.00	2/6
Avg.	7.36%	1.70	0.85%	1.73	4.31%	1.71	2/6

Best rate

No two loans are the same, so making a decision is extremely difficult. Let's try to work through the numbers by choosing the best rate in each category.

Let's pick the best **30-year** loan. You can obtain the monthly payment by using a financial calculator or by calling a financial institution. Lender A has a lower rate and fewer points than Lender B, so B is out. Lender A has a lower rate with the same number of points as D, so D is out. Let's look only at A & C.

Lender	Monthly Payment	Points	Recovery Time
A	$483.71	$700	
C	$477.52	$1400	113 months

Lender C is lower by $6.19 per month but their points are $700 more than A. If you divide the $700 points by the payment difference of $6.19, you see it takes 113 months (over nine years) to make back the points you paid. This doesn't count the tax savings by deducting the higher interest, or the interest you could earn on your $700. Therefore, lender A is the winner for the 30-year mortgage.

Let's look at the **15-year** rates. Lenders B and D have the same rate, but D is charging fewer points, so B is out. A and D have identical points, but A's rate is lower, so D is out. Again, it's between A and C.

Lender	Monthly Payment	Points	Recovery Time
A	$624.49	$700	
C	$614.79	$1575	90 months

The monthly payment for C is $9.70 lower than A. Because C's points are $875 higher than A's, it takes 90 months at the lower rate to recover this expense. Again, we would choose A.

Now the **adjustable** rate. Lender B has a higher rate and more points than A, so B is out. C has a higher rate and more points than A, so C is out. That leaves A and D.

Lender	Monthly Payment	Points	Recovery Time
A	$334.19	$875	5.7 months
D	$365.15	$700	

A's monthly payment is $30.96 lower than D's but the points are $175 more. Dividing $175 by $30.96 reveals that it takes only 5.7 months to recover the points. In this case, the higher points are worth it.

There is one other factor that might give Lender B an edge - the cap. At the end of each year, when it is time to adjust the rate, B is more restricted than the others. They cannot raise (or lower) it by more than 1% in any year, or 4% over the life of the loan. That might be an advantage, but we don't know that now. It depends on what happens to mortgage rates. However, notice that their rate is 1.5% higher than A's. That means their maximum rate is 9.5%, while A's maximum rate is 10%. We would still choose Lender A.

Now we have narrowed it down to the best 15-year, 30-year, and adjustable rate loan. In all cases, Lender A has the best rate. Don't count on one lender having the best rates, though. This is an area where it really pays to do your homework.

15-year vs. 30-year

In Elaine's case, the total payments on a 30-year mortgage are $174,136. The total payments on a 15-year mortgage are $112,409. Elaine could **save over $60,000** by paying her mortgage over fifteen years, with additional monthly payments of only $140.78.

Fixed vs. adjustable

Choosing between the ARM and FRM is not as easy for Elaine, since she doesn't know whether mortgage rates will go up or down. Obviously, if rates stay the same, and the monthly payment stays the same, the adjustable rate is the best. However, rates always fluctuate, and the initial rate offered in an ARM is only a teaser rate. The actual rate is based on a formula: usually the 12-month treasury bill rate, plus 2.75%. On the date of her quotation, the formula revealed a rate of 6.25%, not the 4% offered by the lender. Therefore, even if rates stay the same, the interest rate on the mortgage will adjust upward at the first anniversary.

In Elaine's case, the 15-year mortgage is better than the 30-year rate. From a budgeting and practical standpoint, we would recommend the 15-year fixed even over the ARM, especially considering today's lower interest rates.

Additional payments

An alternative to a 15-year mortgage is to make additional payments on your 30-year mortgage. The following chart shows how additional monthly payments of $50 and $100 on a $70,000, 7% mortgage can reduce the number of payments and total interest expense.

Monthly Payment	No. of Payments To Pay Mortgage	Total Interest Paid
$499	360	$104,632
$549	275	$75,472
$599	226	$59,994

Guidelines

✔ *Choose a 15-year mortgage over a 30-year mortgage for lower total expenses.*

✔ *If you feel more secure with the lower payments of a 30-year mortgage, try to prepay the principal to reduce total costs whenever you are able.*

✔ *Compare lenders, considering rates and points.*

✔ *Shop for an attorney to reduce closing costs.*

✔ *Choose a fixed rate loan if you are concerned about interest rates going up.*

Chapter 16

What Are Home Equity Loans?

Over the years, homeowners with equity have used that asset to borrow money. "Equity" is the value of your home after deducting the mortgage balance. For example, if you have an $80,000 home and owe $30,000 on your mortgage, your equity is $50,000. When a home equity loan is made, the lender puts a lien on the home. Since the lien is second in line behind the first mortgage, it is called a "second mortgage."

Second mortgage vs. equity line of credit

A **second mortgage** is a fixed amount borrowed for a fixed period, usually at a fixed interest rate. For example, you may want to tap into your equity, so you borrow $10,000 for 15 years at 9% interest.

A **home equity** loan is a pre-approved amount (or line of credit) that can be borrowed as needed. You may get a $15,000 line and borrow only $5,000, leaving an available line of $10,000. It is a good way to borrow, since the interest rates are lower than credit cards and the interest payments may be tax-deductible.

Foreclosure

However, there is a risk when taking an equity loan, and that risk is the loss of your home.

Janet and Frank owned an $85,000 home. They owed $25,000 on their first mortgage and $40,000 on their second mortgage. Frank lost his job, and they were unable to get by on Janet's salary. As a result, while they could make the payments on the first mortgage, they were unable to do so on the second. The *second mortgage holder foreclosed. Janet and Frank lost their home and received none of the equity.*

Anyone who holds a lien on your home can foreclose if you violate the terms of the agreement. In Janet and Frank's case, that's exactly what happened. The home was repossessed by the second mortgage holder and sold for $70,000. Since they were second in line, the mortgage holder was only concerned about getting a sales price that would equal the total of the first and second mortgages, which it did. They didn't care about getting as much as possible for the house. That's why foreclosure sales often represent good buys. The balance was consumed in fees and expenses. Janet and Frank received nothing.

The second mortgage holder is in a riskier position than the first, so they will take action quickly to protect their position. In the above case, they started foreclosure proceedings after only two months of missed payments, before the situation could get worse.

The advantages of home equity loans include: the rate is lower than credit cards since the loan is secured; you can be approved for a line of credit and only draw on it as necessary; and the interest on the home equity loan is tax-deductible, as long as you itemize and the total of all mortgages is not more than the difference between the market value and your current mortgage balance. This is all subject to a loan limit of $50,000 if married filing separately, or $100,000 for everyone else.

> *Glenda bought her home in 1970 for $55,000. By 1990, the value had grown to $95,000, and her mortgage balance was down to $30,000. She may borrow up to $65,000 (the market value of $95,000 less the current loan of $30,000) and still deduct the interest.*

Danger ahead

We must insert a warning here. People see the words "tax deductible" and seem to think it means, "you must take advantage of this whether you need it or not." Don't fall into this trap.

Your home equity is your ace in the hole. It is available if all else fails. When you retire, things are much easier without a mortgage payment. Don't throw that away by needlessly borrowing against your equity. So many Americans are doing this that Congress is concerned about our tax policies encouraging people to borrow on their homes instead of reducing debt.

In addition, as with debt consolidation loans discussed earlier, many people borrow on their home equity to pay off other debts. Then they turn right around and use those credit cards again. This is a leap toward financial disaster. If you must use your home equity to pay other debts, then destroy those other credit cards and close the accounts. You don't want to risk losing your home.

Unless necessary, we recommend that you keep your equity and try to make it without borrowing. That's the safest thing to do. And remember our rule: **you can't borrow yourself out of debt.**

Guidelines

- ✓ *You can borrow money at lower rates by using home equity loans.*

- ✓ *The interest on these loans may be tax-deductible.*

- ✓ *You can't borrow your way out of debt! Use the money wisely.*

- ✓ *Shop for the lowest rate.*

- ✓ *Don't borrow unless really necessary.*

- ✓ *Plan to be debt-free by retirement.*

Chapter 17

Where Do I Go For Financial Advice?

There are many people who are available to help point you in the right direction. Let's look at a few.

- **Attorneys** handle legal matters, such as divorces, lawsuits, real estate closings, wills, trusts, etc. They either charge a fee for their work or receive a percentage of an award in the event of a lawsuit.

- **Accountants** specialize in tax matters, mainly preparing tax returns. There are public accountants and certified public accountants (CPA's). The latter undergo additional training and pass a rigorous exam. If you feel comfortable doing your own taxes, there are plenty of books and computer programs available. However, if you don't want to tackle them, then pay an accountant to do them for you.

- **Financial planners** are independent women and men who handle most types of financial products (stocks, bonds, insurance, mutual funds) in addition to preparing financial plans. Financial planners can earn the designation Certified Financial Planner (CFP) by undergoing additional training and passing a rigorous exam. Financial planners operate either on a fee basis or commission, or a combination of the two.

- **Insurance agents** sell the types of insurance discussed in Chapters 18-21. There are additional professional designations that insurance agents can obtain, such as Chartered Life Underwriter (CLU), Chartered Property and Casualty Underwriter (CPCU), and

Chartered Financial Consultant (ChFC). These designations show the agent has taken the time to study special material and pass the necessary tests. They earn commissions on the insurance they sell.

- **Stockbrokers** sell stocks, bonds, and mutual funds. Some of them also have earned the CFP designation. They work for national or regional firms and earn a commission on the products in which you invest.

The cost of advice

Many people hate to pay anyone for advice - they prefer to do things themselves. We can understand that, although it doesn't always make sense. Do you tune your own car? Diagnose and treat your own serious illnesses? Build or remodel your home? Most people prefer to have competent assistance and pay for that service. It is the same with financial planning. After all, how valuable is your financial security?

However, if you feel you have the expertise to handle your financial affairs by yourself, do so. If you need help, then be willing to pay for it.

Many people like to put their money in the bank because it doesn't "cost" them anything, whereas working with a brokerage firm or mutual fund does. Don't fool yourself. The bank makes loans and issues credit cards at interest rates up to 18%. They pay you 4%. Who says it doesn't cost you anything to deal with them? It costs you the difference between what you could make and what they pay you!

Of course, having a professional handle your personal affairs is no guarantee that everything will go smoothly. The sad truth is that professionals sometimes make mistakes, just like everyone else.

Beyond that, these people might not be trained in your

area of need. You must be certain that the person you are about to hire is competent to help you. It is also important to feel comfortable with him or her, and have a high level of trust.

WORKING WITH FINANCIAL PROFESSIONALS

Women have become a key target for the investment business because "they have all the money." Now that you've picked yourself up off the floor, we must tell you that, statistically, it's true. While you may not be in that elite group, many women are. Therefore, you are "fair game" for investment and insurance people.

Widows are hit the hardest. If you're in that position, you know what we're talking about. The average widow, unlike the average divorcee, ends up with money, primarily due to life insurance on the husband. This money attracts financial people like honey attracts bees. If you don't watch out, you'll be stung!

Selecting professionals with whom to work is an important task for women. There are so many from which to choose. How do you find the ones who are right for you?

Meet face to face

Make it a point **never** to deal with any person sight unseen, especially based on an unsolicited phone call. Many people try to drum up business using unscrupulous methods. Remember one thing: **if an offer sounds too good to be true, it probably is.** If someone contacts you with a hot new stock, an extremely high interest bond, prime lake property way below appraised value, a cellular phone deal . . . forget it. Scam artists successfully take advantage of thousands daily.

Ask friends

Ask your friends, co-workers, or respected acquaintances

for referrals. Ask why they like working with that person. While you may not enjoy working with the same personality type, at least you'll know what to expect.

Call around

Your yellow pages should list many firms, but don't judge the firm by the size of the ad. Call around to find out about their charges. Was your call handled professionally by someone who seemed an interested part of the team?

Ask for references

When you meet an advisor, ask for references. If they have written comments from clients and customers, great. If not, ask for names and make some calls. If they're not willing to give you names or show you comments, move on.

You're the boss

Never forget that you are hiring advisors to provide a service for you. **You** are the employer. **You** are in control. **You** are the one who must be satisfied.

Male or female?

Should you work with a male or female? Neither one is necessarily better. Individual personality, training, experience, and other factors are key. Some women, however, do feel more comfortable relating to females. Thankfully, these days well-qualified women are found in virtually every occupation.

Commission vs. fee-based planners

Financial planners earn money three ways: fees, commissions, or a combination of the two. There are two schools of thought on this. Some say you should only work with a fee-based planner, because he or she will be more objective and won't make money from the recommendations. Others say that if you have to pay somebody to carry out the plan, you're paying twice. You might as well use a commission-based planner.

This is just another area where the two sides will never agree. Remember there is nothing wrong with paying a fee or commission if you are receiving value from that person. If you need someone to help you with your affairs, then paying that person a commission is logical. After all, **you** get paid for doing your job.

The key is not whether you should pay a fee or a commission, it's whether that person is acting in your best interest. Obviously, nobody is going to be completely objective . . . everyone has biases. As long as you are aware of this, then you can be on the lookout and be cautious in your dealings.

Remember, it is **your** money. Nobody cares about it as much as you do. Nobody cares about your future the way you do. If you lose money, you will suffer, not your advisor.

This is the time and place to take control. Once you have completed this book, you will have the proper tools to know what to look for, and what to lookout for. Take control of your own financial destiny!

Unauthorized transactions

When Gloria retired, her retirement consisted of company stock. She met with a broker who recommended that she move the stock to his firm. He promised the stock would stay in an account until they agreed together what to do. However, he immediately sold it and put the money into mutual funds.

The broker obviously went against Gloria's wishes, as well as his word. To make matters worse, the stock went up immediately after he sold it, resulting in lost profits. After much discussion, and the intervention of a third party, the transactions were reversed and Gloria got her stock back.

Your broker is permitted to do only what you authorize. Do not put up with unauthorized transactions. Stand up for your legal rights.

Checklist

Use the guidelines below to hire professionals that best suit you. The way you relate to them is more important than any special degrees or letters tacked to the end of their names.

	Yes	No
Did they treat me with respect?	—	—
Did they ask about my concerns, then pay close attention to those needs?	—	—
Did they explain things simply, and to my satisfaction?	—	—
Did they talk to me as an equal, as opposed to talking down to me?	—	—
Was I encouraged to call with questions?	—	—
Was I allowed time to make a decision, as opposed to being pushed into one?	—	—
Will they let me retain control, as opposed to wanting me to sign it over?	—	—
Were they willing to give me references?	—	—

If you are unable to check **"yes"** to **every** question, then keep looking. You will eventually find the "right" person.

Warning

This is not an indictment of financial advisors, but do not write checks directly to them for investment or insurance products. There are many cases of trusted advisors absconding with the money. Once that happens, you have no recourse. If you don't want to lose your life savings, follow these rules.

- **Insurance.** Make all checks for all types of insurance directly to the company, not to the agent.

- **Stocks and bonds.** As a rule, you should make all checks for individual stocks and bonds directly to the brokerage firm, not to the individual broker.

- **Mutual funds.** As a rule, you should make all checks for mutual fund purchases directly to the mutual fund firm. Do not write checks to the individual broker or representative. The primary exception to this is when you pay the brokerage firm directly.

- **Taxes.** Make all checks for taxes directly to the IRS, not to the accountant or accounting firm.

For every investment you make, you receive a statement or confirmation. Make sure you get these statements and understand them. If you don't, call your broker. If your broker doesn't provide satisfactory answers, go to another broker with a different firm. That usually works!

You are ultimately responsible for your money. Make sure you know where every penny goes.

Guidelines

> ✓ *Do not invest any money with someone who is not known to you personally or hasn't been highly recommended by someone you respect.*

✓ *Educate yourself by using this book as a reference guide.*

✓ *Do <u>not</u> buy anything from somebody trying to sell you something over the phone.*

✓ *Make sure you meet with your advisors face to face.*

✓ *Do not invest in anything from anyone who tries to sell you something the first time they meet you.*

✓ *Ask for references. Then check them out.*

✓ *Make sure you feel comfortable with this person. If not, go on to someone else.*

✓ *If you don't feel comfortable with his or her recommendations, ask someone else for a second opinion.*

✓ *Do not give anyone authorization to make investments without your prior approval.*

✓ *Meet periodically with your financial professionals to review your goals and investments, to make sure you are still on track.*

✓ *Avoid anyone trying to sell you something without knowing your particular situation.*

✓ *Make sure your philosophies are similar. If you are conservative, work with someone who expresses a conservative attitude.*

✓ *Once you invest, make sure you review every statement you receive. Don't just throw them in a drawer.*

✓ *Don't make investment checks payable to individuals.*

Chapter 18

What Type Of Life Insurance Is Best For Me?

As you approach the subject of life insurance, remember this very important fact: the **primary** purpose of life insurance is to protect the family in case of the death of the breadwinner. It is **not** primarily a savings vehicle, although it can also be used for that.

You must have a sufficient death benefit before you begin using life insurance for savings. Too often we've heard of tragedies when that was not done.

> *Bob, age 30, was contacted by a life insurance agent. He had a wife and two children, but not much insurance. He could only afford to pay $50 a month. For that amount, he could have purchased $600,000 of 10-year renewable term, $51,000 of whole life, or $110,000 of universal life insurance. His agent recommended the whole life because it would also provide a "savings account" with lots of guarantees. When Bob died, his family only received $51,000, instead of the $600,000 they could have had.*

All too often, people purchase the wrong type of insurance. It's not because the coverage was necessarily bad. It's just that the type of insurance they purchased was not right for their particular situation.

Basically, there are four types of insurance products: whole, universal, variable, and term life. Let's look at each.

Whole life

Whole life is a traditional form of insurance with guaranteed premiums and guaranteed cash values. The policy is divided into two parts: death benefit and savings. Part of each premium payment goes toward each. In the early years, most of your premiums go toward death benefits. Over the years, however, cash values build up. As long as you continue to pay the premiums, the policy is guaranteed to remain in force, regardless of future interest rates.

The advantages of this type of insurance are: you know what the premiums will be; cash values grow tax-deferred; death-benefit is paid income tax-free; you can borrow your cash values tax-free; and your insurance remains in force as long as you continue to pay the premiums.

There are also a number of negatives: high premiums limit the amount of coverage the average person can buy; low interest rates make it unattractive from an investment stand-point; you have to pay interest to borrow your own cash values; and you lose your cash value when you die.

Losing cash value is probably one of the biggest disadvantages. You pay an additional premium to build cash value. Then you die and the insurance company keeps it.

Some of these negatives have been rectified with a new form of whole life called "interest sensitive whole life." These policies pay a more competitive rate of interest that results in lower premiums and higher cash values. In addition, you can choose a death benefit that will be increased by your cash values. This is called "Option B."

However, you are still paying a lot for the guarantees. Nevertheless, if these guarantees are important to you, then whole life is an alternative.

Universal life

Universal life is a relatively new type of insurance that is very sensitive to interest rates. It was designed to allow the policyholder to benefit from higher rates, but also accept some of the risk of lower rates. It provides coverage at a lower premium than whole life, but doesn't have the guarantees.

It has some advantages over whole life: you tend to get more coverage for your dollar; many contain a provision that you can "borrow" your cash values interest free; and you can increase and decrease both your premiums and your death benefit as you desire. Choose the "increasing death benefit" option (Option B) for the best long-term value.

However, it has some disadvantages relative to whole life. The primary one is that the values are not guaranteed. If interest rates drop, or the cost of insurance increases, you may have to pay more and/or longer than you originally thought.

Variable life

Variable life is a new type of insurance that combines death protection with an investment program with options for growth, similar to mutual funds. Whole and universal life invest in "fixed" accounts. In other words, their values don't rise and fall with stock and bond values. Variable policies perform only as well as their investment accounts.

This means you can have years with good performance, and you can have years in which you actually lose money due to a drop in the variable account. In addition, these policies are heavily loaded with fees. A few years of bad stock performance, coupled with the high fees, could totally wipe-out your account.

For these reasons, we are not fans of this type of insurance. While past performance has not been bad, we have had a good stock market for the past ten years, so almost anything looks good. Unfortunately, we're not going to have a good stock market forever. Remember, the purpose of life insurance is to provide money upon your death. If your account is wiped-out before that date, then you have defeated your purpose. Variable life is a disaster waiting to happen.

Term insurance

Term insurance provides death benefit only. As a result, it is the lowest cost insurance, at least over the short run.

Term provides temporary coverage. Generally, the premiums go up as you get older. Eventually, it becomes too expensive to own. Nevertheless, for young families who need large amounts of coverage on the breadwinner, term makes sense. There are several types of term.

- **Annual renewable term** has a level death benefit, but the premium increases each year. It eventually becomes too expensive to maintain.

- **Five, ten, fifteen, and twenty-year year** have premiums that are level for one of those periods. Five-year term starts out being less expensive than twenty-year term, but will probably cost you more over the twenty-year period.

- **Decreasing term** insurance provides a level premium while the face value decreases over a stated number of years. This is often used as mortgage insurance. Many people make the mistake of getting mortgage insurance from their lender. It is always better (unless you are uninsurable) to get it from an independent insurance agent.

Getting agreement on the "right" type of insurance is virtually impossible. On one side are the permanent (whole and universal life) advocates who think you should have protection plus tax-advantaged savings. On the other are those who think you should only have term. As usual, the truth is somewhere in between.

There is a place for each type of insurance. Term insurance provides temporary coverage at the lowest possible cost. Permanent insurance is used when you have sufficient income, but you want to accumulate money on a tax-advantaged basis.

Who needs insurance . . . and who doesn't?

Too many people buy inappropriate life insurance for the wrong reasons. Let's look at the need for life insurance in different situations.

- **Single with no dependents.** As a rule, you don't need insurance. Many singles buy insurance to cover their debts. But, legally, nobody is responsible for your debts, unless they are on the loan with you.

- **Single with children.** You do need insurance, but not your children. We'll show you how to calculate the amount in Chapter 38.

- **Married with no children.** You don't need insurance unless one spouse will suffer a drop in his or her standard of living (or lose the house and cars) upon the death of the other.

- **Married with children.** Sounds like a good name for a television show! You need insurance, but not your children. If both spouses work outside the home, you both need insurance. If one spouse works in the home, and you have young children, you both need insurance. We'll show you how much in Chapter 38.

- **Retired.** You probably don't need insurance unless the surviving spouse will suffer a significant decrease in income upon the death of the other. If all your income comes from your investment portfolio, then you probably won't suffer a drop. If, however, one spouse has a retirement plan from work, and income will decrease (or cease) upon the death of that person, then insurance is needed.

- **Estate planning situations.** Insurance can be used to pay estate taxes. This is covered in Chapter 25.

- **Divorced receiving child support or alimony.** If you have children, not only do you need insurance on yourself, you need coverage on your ex-husband.

Insurance on your ex-husband

If you have custody of your children, you are probably receiving child support and/or alimony. You have a vested interest in your ex-husband's ability to make the payments. If he should die, you and your children will suffer financially.

We recommend that your divorce decree contain a provision requiring your ex-husband to carry life insurance until his obligation to you and the children ends. You can compute how much he will pay in child support, and require insurance in that amount. The same goes for alimony.

You have to make sure he really carries the insurance. The best way is for you to be the **owner** of his policy, as well as the **beneficiary.** That way, if he stops making payments, the insurance company will inform you. That would also prevent him from changing the beneficiary, since only the owner can make that change. Another way to prevent a change in the beneficiary is to name an **irrevocable** beneficiary. That means that he can't change the beneficiary without that person's approval. But that wouldn't stop him from canceling the policy without notifying you.

Therefore, a good alternative is for the divorce decree to require him to pay the insurance premiums directly to you. You can then forward them to the insurance company, protecting yourself and your children.

Tax aspects

Life insurance death benefits are free from income taxes but subject to estate taxes if owned by the insured and/or his/her spouse. Estate taxes can be avoided by making the children or an irrevocable trust the owner.

Choosing the right company

You must choose a quality insurance company. Unless you are a financial analyst familiar with the insurance industry, you have to depend on rating services to do the work for you. Presently, there are three major services.

- **A. M. Best and Company** is the oldest insurance company rating service. They rate most insurance companies as follows: A++ and A+ (Superior); A and A- (Excellent); B+ (Very Good); B and B- (Good); C+ (Fairly Good); C and C- (Fair).

- **Standard and Poor's** rates the claims-paying ability for approximately 250 companies and provides solvency ratings for about 700 companies. In our opinion, the solvency ratings don't have much value. However, the claims-paying ability ratings are valid and important. Those ratings are: AAA (Superior), AA+, AA and AA- (Excellent), A+, A and A- (Good), BBB+, BBB and BBB- (Adequate) and on down as low as D.

- **Moody's Investor Service** rates approximately 90 companies for financial strength. The ratings are Aaa (Exceptional), Aa (Excellent), A (Good), Baa (Adequate), Ba (Questionable), and as low as C.

Our rule of thumb is simple: do not buy insurance from any company that is not rated at least A+ by A. M. Best & Company **and** at least AA by Standard & Poor's or Aa by

Moody's. While this won't guarantee against future problems, it will provide substantial protection. Ratings can be obtained from your local library or your agent. Don't be shy about asking. It's your money.

Guidelines

- ✓ *Don't buy credit life insurance. It's too expensive.*

- ✓ *Don't buy mortgage insurance from your lender. Purchase cheaper decreasing term insurance from a company or agent.*

- ✓ *Don't buy life insurance on your children. Spend the money insuring yourself. That is where the need is.*

- ✓ *Don't be too quick to drop your permanent coverage in favor of term insurance, and never drop old insurance before the new policy is in effect.*

- ✓ *Don't buy life insurance if you are single and have no dependents. Instead, invest the money for your retirement.*

- ✓ *Buy the lowest cost term insurance you can find. If a cheaper one comes along, switch.*

- ✓ *Make sure your insurance company is at least rated A+ by A. M. Best __and__ AA by Standard and Poor's or Aa by Moody's.*

- ✓ *Don't depend on accidental death as part of your coverage. You can't choose how you die.*

- ✓ *Don't buy extras, like "waiver of premium," on term insurance. It just increases the premium, with little chance of collecting benefits.*

Chapter 19

Do I Need Disability Insurance?

For a single, working mother, a disability that keeps her from earning a living is a financial disaster. Likewise, for a married couple, the disability of either working spouse can be catastrophic.

Disability insurance pays a monthly income if you cannot work as the result of either sickness or accident. A disability policy contains certain variables:

- The **waiting period** is the number of days you must be disabled before benefits begin.

- The **monthly benefit** is the dollar amount the company will pay each month you are disabled.

- The **benefit period** is the length of time benefits will be paid if you are disabled due to accident or sickness. Often, these are two different periods.

- The **definition** of disability determines when the company considers you eligible to collect benefits.

Short-term vs. long-term

There are two types of disability: short-term and long-term. **Short-term** is usually offered through a group policy at work to cover you for up to one year. The coverage usually begins when sick leave runs out.

Long-term disability pays for the rest of your life, or until age 65, depending upon the terms of your policy. If you have a technical job or profession, consider a policy with lifetime benefits. Otherwise, choose a benefit period of at least five years.

In addition, Social Security pays disability benefits, although they are difficult to collect. Some policies offset Social Security benefits. In other words, if Social Security pays, the company reduces your benefit by that amount.

How much to carry?

Disability insurance limits the amount you can carry based on your income and occupation. The insurance company doesn't want you to make more money from being disabled than from working. They want you to have incentive to go back to work.

As a result, you are usually limited to benefits of only 60 to 75% of your income. Your premium depends on the factors listed previously, in addition to your age and occupation. Obviously, the more dangerous your occupation, the higher your premium.

This is one of the most important coverages you can have, since your earning power is your greatest asset. Make sure you don't undercut yourself.

Guidelines

✓ *If your inability to work would result in financial chaos, you need disability insurance.*

✓ *If your employer offers disability insurance, take it.*

✓ *Make sure the insurance company is highly rated.*

Chapter 20

How Can I Cut The Cost
Of Automobile Insurance?

Automobile insurance pays if your vehicle is involved in an accident. The policy protects against a number of losses.

- **Liability** pays if you injure another party while driving your car. Your policy pays a maximum amount for each person injured and for each accident. With most companies, coverage consists of three parts, and pays:

    1. A stated amount for bodily injury to one person.

    2. A total amount of bodily injury for each accident.

    3. A maximum amount for property damage.

Coverage quoted as 15/30/10 means that each person is insured for $15,000 of bodily injury, but the total amount paid for any one accident is $30,000. In addition, you have coverage of $10,000 for property damage. As you can guess, minimum coverage won't help much in the event of a $100,000 lawsuit. Therefore we recommend higher limits provided by an umbrella policy, which is explained in the next chapter.

- **Medical payments** provide medical expense benefits if you are injured. Some say you don't need this coverage if you have health insurance. While that may be true, this coverage pays the deductibles and non-covered expenses. In addition, if you have a passenger in your car who lacks health insurance, this will go toward his or her expenses.

- **Uninsured motorists** coverage pays if you are in an accident with a person who doesn't have insurance. It pays bodily injury for each person, and per accident, besides paying for property damage. Again, there are some who say you don't need this coverage. Wrong! If the other party has no insurance, you may need money for medical bills or the replacement of your automobile. While your own health insurance may pay medical expenses, it also contains deductibles and limits on coverage. In addition, your health insurance won't cover a passenger if he or she is injured by an uninsured motorist.

- **Collision** pays for damage to your automobile if you are in an accident and it is your fault. This usually contains a deductible.

- **Comprehensive** (also called Other Than Collision Loss) pays if there is damage to your automobile by a cause other than an accident, such as theft, fire, vandalism, hail damage, etc. This also usually has a deductible.

Your greatest exposure is liability. While it would be tragic to lose your car, it would be a greater catastrophe to be sued for everything you own. Therefore, be sure you carry sufficient liability coverage.

Deductibles

We recommend that you have at least a $500 deductible for both collision and comprehensive. Face it, if you have a small claim, you probably won't submit it and jeopardize your coverage. So if you're not going to submit small claims, why pay for coverage on those claims? It makes good financial sense to have high deductibles, because that greatly reduces your insurance expense.

Eliminate collision and comprehensive

If your car isn't worth more than $2,000, don't bother carrying collision or comprehensive coverage. It is an added expense that, when added to the deductible, means that you're paying a lot for very little coverage.

For example, if collision and comprehensive cost you $400 with a $500 deductible, then you are really paying the first $900. If the car is worth $2,000, then you are paying $900 to possibly make $1100. That's too much. Just be careful and don't hit anyone!

Shop around

Finally, check with different insurance companies before choosing a policy. It is amazing how rates vary from company to company. Don't jump on the first one - shop around.

Guidelines

✓ *Use higher deductibles to reduce premiums.*

✓ *Buy medical and uninsured motorist coverage, even if it isn't required by your state.*

✓ *Don't buy collision coverage if your car isn't worth at least $2,000.*

✓ *Shop around for the best rates.*

Chapter 21

How Should I Insure My Home?

As a homeowner, you need to have proper insurance. Obviously, since your home is one of your largest assets, a loss could be devastating.

HOMEOWNER'S INSURANCE

Homeowner's insurance pays for damage to your home or liability for which you are responsible.

- **Dwelling** coverage pays a stated amount for damage to your home.

- **Personal property** coverage pays a stated amount in case of damage to your belongings. This is usually 50% of the home's insured value if insured for "actual cash value," and 70% if insured for "replacement cost."

- **Personal liability** pays a stated amount in the event that someone is hurt on your property, or if you cause damage to someone else or their property.

- **Personal article floater** pays for special items, such as jewelry, musical instruments, rare art, etc. Coverage for these items is usually limited under your homeowner's insurance. In addition, by submitting appraisals, you know you will get full value, regardless of the cause of the loss. For example, many floaters cover your jewelry even if you just lose it.

- **Temporary living expenses** covers food and lodging expenses while your home is being repaired.

Fire vs. all-risk

The old type of insurance (called "named perils") usually covered only fire, theft, etc. However, you can suffer losses not covered under that type of policy. Therefore, we recommend you purchase "all-risk" coverage, which covers everything except floods, wars, earthquakes, and a few other catastrophes. That does two things. First, you don't have to predict what type of loss you will suffer. Second, it takes the burden of proof off you to justify the loss as a result of specific causes. Instead, it puts the burden on the insurance company to prove it is not covered under your policy.

The floods of 1993 showed the need for flood insurance, which can be purchased for an additional premium in most parts of the country. If you live in an area that is susceptible to flooding, purchase this coverage. Likewise, if you live in an area that might suffer an earthquake, purchase that coverage as well.

Replacement cost vs. actual cash value

Insurance on your home and contents can be written on an "actual cash value" basis or on a "replacement cost" basis. The first is the cost of the property less depreciation; the latter is the cost to replace it today. Choose the latter (replacement cost coverage) for both your home and its contents. It doesn't cost that much more and it's well worth it.

Deductibles

Losses under homeowners insurance policies are relatively rare. Therefore, it makes sense to increase your deductibles and spend that premium savings to upgrade your coverage.

Amount of coverage

Many people like to save money by underinsuring their homes. However, that can be a big mistake. While some "experts" recommend that you insure your home for 80% of it's "replacement cost," excluding the land, we recommend 100%. Otherwise, the check from the insurance company might fall far short of the replacement cost.

Marie owned an older home that had appreciated, but she never increased her insurance coverage. Although the current value of her home was $80,000, she insured it only for $48,000. She suffered a small fire, which resulted in a $20,000 loss. She received only $12,000 from the insurance company.

Like most people, Marie assumed that her $48,000 policy would cover a loss up to that amount. As she found out, her thinking was flawed. Her coverage of $48,000 was only 60% of the value of her home. Therefore, her insurance company only paid 60% of her loss, subject to a $48,000 maximum.

Coinsurance

Most companies require insurance of at least 80% of the value to pay a full claim. For example, had Marie insured her home for $64,000, her entire $20,000 would have been paid. However, the maximum paid under any claim still would have been only $64,000.

The safest way to avoid any problems is to insure your home for 100% of its replacement cost. Although this may result in over insuring your home by a small amount, it guards against inflation and costs very little extra. You can buy inflation protection, but that doesn't help if your home value increases faster than inflation.

Obviously, you want to reduce your insurance costs. However, don't be penny wise and pound foolish. The purpose of insurance is to protect against catastrophic loss. Cutting

corners is a big mistake. Buy quality, and pay for it. A policy
that doesn't cover your loss is really more costly in the long run.

Discounts

Most insurance companies provide discounts for protection devices, such as smoke detectors and dead-bolt locks.
Discounts are also available if you carry all your coverage with
the same company.

RENTER'S INSURANCE

Renters usually ignore insurance, because they don't
think they have any exposure. This could be one of the greatest
mistakes you make. It is tragic when there is a fire in an
apartment complex, because most tenants aren't insured. Think
about what would happen if you lost everything in your apartment right now. Could you easily afford to replace it? Doubtful. Renter's insurance is not very expensive and pays for
damage to your property or liability losses.

- **Personal property** coverage pays a stated amount
  upon damage to your household goods. This can be
  written on a "replacement cost" basis or "actual cash
  value." Buy the former.

- **Personal liability** pays a stated amount in the event
  someone is injured on your property.

UMBRELLA POLICY

One of the best insurance buys is an umbrella policy. It
is so named because it provides liability coverage (usually
$1,000,000) above your homeowner's (or renter's) and automo-
bile liability policies. Since it only pays if a judgement against
you exceeds your liability coverage under your other policies,

the premiums are relatively low.

Some people say you only need an umbrella policy if your assets exceed your liability limits. We disagree. If you have $50,000 worth of assets and $100,000 liability coverage, but get a judgement of $300,000 against you, you still have major problems. Any income you receive, either as benefits or salary, can be garnished. We feel that you should carry a minimum of $1,000,000 umbrella coverage, whatever your assets, because your **exposure** is unlimited.

Guidelines

Homeowners:

✓ *Buy all-risk insurance.*

✓ *Buy replacement cost, not actual cash value coverage.*

✓ *Increase your coverage as your home increases in value.*

✓ *Do not underinsure your home to save money.*

✓ *Increase deductibles to save money.*

✓ *Buy an umbrella policy for additional liability coverage at a reasonable premium.*

Renters:

✓ *Insure your household goods for "replacement value."*

✓ *Carry personal liability coverage in case a visitor is injured in your home.*

✓ *Buy an umbrella policy for additional liability coverage at a reasonable premium.*

Chapter 22

What Insurance Is Unnecessary?

It is amazing how much money people waste not only on the **wrong type** of insurance, but on totally **unnecessary** insurance. Agents and companies make a fortune selling policies that consumers should avoid. Let's look at a few.

- **Supplemental** policies, such as intensive care insurance, hospital indemnity, cancer insurance, etc. Health insurance covers most of these, and the chances of collecting from supplemental policies are slim at best. While it would be great to have the coverage if needed, your chances of collecting, relative to the premiums you pay, are low. That is why these types of insurance are so profitable for insurance companies.

- **Extended warranties on new cars.** This is a special form of insurance that is very expensive and limited in scope. Manufacturers' warranties currently cover up to five or six years. Don't waste your money on extended warranties. All they do is give the dealer a bigger profit on your car.

- **Extended warranties on appliances.** Again, this is expensive coverage for products that don't break down very often. Manufacturers' warranties cover most problems, so this just needlessly increases the cost of the product. Why spend all that time shopping around for a great deal on a VCR and then get stuck with a needless additional warranty? Also, many credit cards now cover you for products purchased with their card.

106

- **More than one Medigap** policy. These policies pay for expenses that Medicare doesn't cover. Sales agents love to load older folks with these policies. You only need one, as explained in Chapter 23.

- **Credit life** insures you when you borrow money. Unless you are in bad health, you can get term insurance for a lot lower cost than credit life. If you are uninsurable and about to die, then load up on credit life! Otherwise, stay away.

- Ditto for **credit disability** insurance.

- **Service contracts** on appliances. Sears, among others, makes a fortune selling service contracts. Save your money.

- **Mortgage life insurance** covers you when you purchase a home. You can purchase decreasing term insurance from an agent for less than what your finance company charges for mortgage life.

- **Charge card insurance** covers your credit cards. You have no liability once you report your cards as lost or stolen, and until then your liability is only $50 per card.

- **Insurance by mail or television.** These policies tend to be very expensive. They seem attractive because they are packaged to appeal to your emotions and are so easy to obtain. Forget it. You can usually get it cheaper by working with a good agent or directly with a good company.

- **Accident insurance.** This is a big money maker for insurance companies because of the limited claims they have to pay. These policies are often marketed to parents to cover medical expenses in the event their child suffers an accident at school. As long as you are covered by medical insurance, you shouldn't need this coverage.

- **Accidental death and double indemnity.** These are usually add-ons to life insurance policies. In effect, you are gambling on how you are going to die . . . in this case, by accident. Don't do it! Spend these dollars on your primary insurance instead.

- **Flight insurance.** The chances of dying on a commercial airline flight are slim. In the few situations where a plane does go down, there are usually lawsuits against the carrier. Save your money.

- **Life insurance on children.** One of the biggest wastes of money is purchasing life insurance on children. It's an easy emotional sale by agents and companies who rake in big dollars doing this. While some policies give the child the right to buy insurance in the future, that doesn't justify the expense. And using it as burial insurance doesn't make a whole lot of sense, since the chances of death of a child are so small. Face it, no money you receive could ever replace the child. Instead, use that money to provide sufficient coverage on you.

- **Life insurance on singles with no dependents.** If you don't have anybody depending on you, then don't buy life insurance on yourself.

- **Waiver of premium.** Insurance companies like to add "waiver of premium" coverage on your policies. In theory, if you become disabled and can't pay your premiums, then the company will pay them for you. Don't fall for it. The coverage is expensive; the chances of collecting are small. If you have extra money to throw around on life insurance premiums, increase your primary coverage.

- **Rental car insurance.** Your personal automobile policy normally covers this. You will, however, be responsible for the deductible. Many credit card companies, such as MasterCard Gold, Visa Gold, and American Express, provide this coverage if you charge the rental on their card. Check with your insurance company and credit card company to determine what they provide.

One common factor among all these is that they are relatively inexpensive. You say to yourself, "Well, I might need the coverage, and it is pretty cheap, so I might as well get it." That thinking is costly. When dealing with insurance, look at the chances of collecting versus the premiums you will pay over the years. Remember, if the cost of insurance is low, so are the chances of a claim. As you know, insurance companies are not in business to lose money!

Guidelines

✓ *Spend your money for good, basic insurance, but avoid the highly advertised specialty policies.*

✓ *Don't buy insurance on any person, including yourself, who doesn't have others depending on them for support.*

✓ *Don't waste money on insurance on children.*

✓ *Don't nickel and dime yourself with worthless extra coverage . . . it adds up to wasted dollars!*

Chapter 23

What Can I Expect From Social Security?

Unfortunately, Social Security has turned into the **sole** retirement plan for millions of Americans. That is a far cry from its original purpose as a **supplemental** retirement program.

There are continuous discussions concerning the solvency of the program, and questions about whether it will be there when you retire. You can assume, if you are 40 or older, that Social Security will be there for you to some degree.

That said, Social Security should not, and cannot, be your only retirement plan. You must make provisions to save additional funds. Otherwise, you will live in poverty.

Who is covered?

Most working people are covered by Social Security. It is easier to identify those who are not covered: federal employees hired before January 1984; railroad employees covered under the Railroad Retirement System; state employees covered under their own retirement program; clergy who opt not to participate; employees of many school systems operating under older rules; and those who have not earned enough to qualify. If your payroll stub has no entry for "FICA Withholding," then you are not covered under Social Security.

How do you qualify?

You qualify for Social Security benefits by acquiring sufficient "quarters of coverage" to be considered **fully insured** or **currently insured.** In general, you receive "quarters of coverage" by having the required wages, or self-employment income, in any calendar quarter.

- Before 1978, you received one quarter of coverage for each quarter in which you earned at least $50. If your wages in any quarter didn't equal $50, but your total earnings for the year exceeded the maximum social security earnings base for that year, you received full credit.

- Starting in 1978, the earnings required for a quarter of coverage are as follows:

Year	Earnings	Year	Earnings	Year	Earnings	Year	Earnings
1978	$250	1979	$260	1980	$290	1981	$310
1982	$340	1983	$370	1984	$390	1985	$410
1986	$440	1987	$460	1988	$470	1989	$500
1990	$520	1991	$540	1992	$570	1993	$590

These are only general rules. Naturally, there are some exceptions that might affect your personal situation. Once you know this information, you can determine if you are "fully insured" or "currently insured." That is an important factor in your eligibility for benefits.

Fully insured

You are considered fully insured if you meet either of the following:

- Accumulate 40 quarters of coverage; or

- Accumulate six quarters of coverage and acquire at least as many quarters of coverage as there are years from your 21st birthday to either your 62nd birthday, disability, or death, whichever occurs first. The counting begins with the year 1936.

Currently insured

You are considered currently insured if you have acquired at least six quarters of coverage during the preceding 13 quarters in which you become eligible for **retirement** benefits, become eligible for **disability** benefits, or **die**.

YOUR BENEFITS

Social Security provides a number of benefits for qualified recipients. Those benefits are subject to rules and exceptions. Although you must check with your local Social Security office to find out what you are entitled to, here is a general review.

Retirement

You are entitled to retirement benefits if you are fully insured and have reached the age of 62. If you begin receiving Social Security at 62, you won't receive full benefits. For that to occur, you must refrain from taking benefits until the "normal retirement" age of 65. However, the "normal retirement" age will change in the years ahead.

- That age increases by two months per year if you reach age 62 in 2000-2005.

- It stays at age 66 if you reach age 62 in 2005-2016.

- It increases by two months a year if you reach age 62 in 2016-2022.

- It remains at age 67 if you reach age 62 after 2022.

Disability

You are entitled to disability benefits if you: are insured

for disability benefits; are under the age of 65; **and** have been or can expect to be disabled for 12 months, or have a disability which is expected to result in death. Social Security considers you disabled if you can't engage in any occupation.

Death

Upon your husband's death, assuming he was currently or fully insured, you are entitled to a one-time payment of $255 from Social Security. If you are divorced, you are not entitled to that money, but your ex-husband's children are.

Current wife

If your husband is retired or disabled, you may receive benefits when you reach the age of 62. However, if you are caring for your husband's child, and that child is under the age of 16 or disabled, you may receive benefits regardless of your age. To receive benefits, you must have been married to your husband for at least one year, and not be entitled to a retirement or disability benefit equal to or larger than one-half of your husband's primary insurance amount.

If you have earned income, you will lose some or all of your benefits if you or your husband are between the ages of 65 and 69 and earn over $11,160 (1994), or under the age of 65 and earn over $8,040 (1994). As a rule, you lose $1 for every $3 earned over $11,160 (between the ages of 65 and 69), and $1 for every $2 earned over $8,040 (below the age of 65).

Divorced wife with children

If your ex-husband dies, and he was fully or currently insured, then you are entitled to benefits if you are caring for his natural or adopted child who is under the age of 16, or disabled before the age of 22. Your benefits will be reduced if you earn more than $8,404 in 1994, or $11,160 if you are between ages 65 and 69. The child's benefits are not reduced by your income.

Divorced wife - retirement benefits

If your ex-husband is entitled to retirement or disability benefits, then you are also entitled to benefits when you reach the age of 62, as long as you have not remarried **and** had been married to him for 10 years before the divorce became final. However, you are not entitled to spousal benefits if your own benefits equal or exceed one-half of your ex-husband's benefit amount. If your ex-husband is under the age of 62, and you are over the age of 62, you must have been divorced for at least **two years** to qualify for this benefit.

Widow with children

If you are a widow with children, and your late husband was fully or currently insured, you are entitled to benefits as long as you are caring for a child who is under the age of 16, or who was disabled before the age of 22. Your benefits will be reduced if you earn over $8,040 in 1994 or $11,160 if you are between the ages of 65 and 69. Once your child reaches the age of 16, you lose your survivor benefits until you reach the age of 60 (50 if disabled). That period during which you receive no benefits is known as the "black-out" period. The child's benefits are unaffected by your income.

Widow - retirement benefits

If your late husband was fully insured, you are entitled to retirement benefits once you reach the age of 60 (or 50 if you are disabled) as long as you are not entitled to a retirement benefit equal to or larger than your late husband's primary insurance amount. You can lose part or all of your benefits if you are between the ages of 65 and 69 and earned over $11,160 (1994) or under the age of 65 and earned $8,040 (1994). If you remarry after the age of 60 (50 if disabled), you generally don't lose your benefits.

Child of retired or disabled parent

A child of a retired or disabled worker is entitled to the benefits of a retired or disabled parent if that parent is receiving benefits and the child is: under the age of 18; or between the ages of 18 and 19 and a full time high school student; or disabled prior to age 22; and is not married. In addition, the child must be dependent upon the parent.

The child's benefit will be reduced or ended if he/she earns over $8,040 in 1994. The benefits end when: the child dies; reaches age 18 and is no longer a full-time student; reaches age 19; marries; the parent is no longer eligible for benefits; or the child is no longer disabled.

Child of a deceased parent

If a child's parent is currently or fully insured and dies, then benefits are available to each child who is: under the age of 18; or is disabled from a disability that began prior to age 22; or is under 19 and still a full time high school student; and is not married.

By a rule change completed in 1985, students past the age of 18, attending post-secondary schools (college, vocational, etc.), are not entitled to benefits. Also, a child will lose part or all of his/her benefits if he/she earns over $8,040 in 1994.

Your future benefits

In our planning, we take potential Social Security benefits into consideration. However, trying to estimate retirement benefits can be a difficult task. The easiest way is to request your personal data from the Social Security Administration. Call your local office and ask for the **Request For Earnings and Benefit Estimate Statement** (Form SSA-7004-SM-OP2), or call (800) 772-1213. They will prepare an estimate of your future benefits for use in your planning. In addition, it will help you determine if any errors have been made. If there are errors, get them corrected.

Deciding when to retire

In the past, age 65 was the unofficial retirement age. That is no longer true for most Americans. More and more people are retiring, or hoping to retire, at younger ages.

Under current Social Security rules, age 65 is the "normal retirement" age - the age at which you receive full benefits. Retire earlier than that, your benefits are reduced. Retire later, your benefits are increased.

If you retire before you turn age 65, your monthly benefits are reduced by 5/9 of 1% for each month you retire before the age of 65. That works out to be approximately 6.7% per year.

> *The day Marilyn turned 62, she became eligible for Social Security benefits. However, she didn't know if she should wait until she reached 65 to begin her benefits. She talked with a Social Security official and was told that if she waited until age 65, she would receive $800 per month. If she began receiving benefits at 62, she would receive approximately $640 per month.*

What a difficult decision! There are a number of considerations:

- By beginning benefits at 62, Marilyn will receive $23,040 ($640 per month times 36 months) between ages 62 and 65.

- If she waits until age 65, all things being equal (which they never are), she will get $160 more per month. By dividing that into the $23,040 that she would receive by retiring at age 62, it will take her approximately 12 years to make it up. In other words, if she retires at age 65 and doesn't live 12 years, she would be better off retiring at 62. However, that doesn't take into consideration the economic benefit of having the money early.

- Since benefits are based on earnings, if she can earn substantially higher wages between the ages of 62 and 65, then it is worthwhile to postpone retirement and opt for higher Social Security benefits at age 65.

This is one of those decisions for which there is no exact answer. If you are not working and could use the money, then taking your Social Security at age 62 makes sense. You need the money earlier and you never know how long you will live.

Medicare

Medicare is a government program that provides health insurance for persons 65 and older. In addition, some younger individuals who are receiving benefits under Social Security may be eligible. Coverage is divided into two parts:

- **Part A** provides inpatient hospital care, inpatient skilled nursing facility care, home health care, and hospice care, subject to regulations.

- **Part B** is voluntary and pays for doctors bills and a number of services not covered under Part A.

MEDIGAP INSURANCE

Medicare provides health insurance to people over the age of 65 and a few others who may be receiving Social Security benefits. However, it doesn't pay everything. Therefore, Medigap insurance is available to fill in the gaps.

Coverage

Before looking at insurance, let's look at what is covered

by Medicare. You are responsible for what Medicare doesn't pay. These are the figures for 1993; they can change annually.

Part A - Hospital Services

SERVICE	BENEFIT PERIOD	PAID BY MEDICARE
Hospital Services, semi-private room & board, misc services	First 60 days 61-90 days 91-150 days 150 + days	All but $652 All but $163/day All but $326/day Nothing
Skilled Nursing Care Facility within 30 days of discharge from hospital	First 20 days 21-99 days 100+ days	100% of app'd am't All but $81.50/day Nothing
Home Health Care	Unlimited	100% of approved services
Hospice Care for terminally ill	One 90 day period and two 30 day periods. Can be extended beyond that	Reasonable cost of providing care

Part B - Medical Services

This coverage pays for inpatient and outpatient services by physicians and other approved practitioners.

Coverage: 80% of approved amount.
Deductible: $100.
Psychiatric: 50% for out-of-hospital.

There are many services Medicare does not cover. Therefore, Medigap insurance is available to cover the deductibles and many of the non-covered services. In the past, Medicare Supplement Insurance was the subject of much abuse by insurance companies and agents. It was complicated, unstructured, and difficult to compare. That is no longer so. Medigap insurance is offered in 10 varieties, A through J. The following chart shows the coverage for each classification. Since coverage is standardized, it is easy to compare.

COVERAGE	A	B	C	D	E	F	G	H	I	J
Basic Benefits	X	X	X	X	X	X	X	X	X	X
Skilled Nursing Coinsurance			X	X	X	X	X	X	X	X
Part A Deductible		X	X	X	X	X	X	X	X	X
Part B Deductible			X			X				X
Part B Excess - 100% (80% for G)						X	X		X	X
Foreign Travel Emergency			X	X	X	X	X	X	X	X
At-Home Recovery				X			X		X	X
Basic Drugs								X	X	X
Preventive Care					X					X

Every company must offer A; the others are optional. F is very popular since it pays 100% of excess doctor charges. However, C will become the coverage of the future as the government limits what doctors can charge Medicare patients. In 1993, that limit was 115% of what Medicare allows.

Guidelines

✓ *Get a "Request for Earnings and Benefit Estimate Statement" from Social Security.*

✓ *Call your local Social Security office to discuss your eligibility for benefits.*

✓ *Don't expect Social Security to provide sufficient income on which to live.*

✓ *Look at your Medicare card to check on your coverage. Add Part B if desired.*

✓ *Don't carry more than one Medigap policy.*

Chapter 24

How Can I Protect My Assets From Nursing Homes?

Statistically, women live longer than men. One out of four baby boomers is expected to require nursing home care. You are likely to end up in a nursing home . . . which could result in the potential loss of everything for which you have worked your entire life.

People are less afraid of **living** in a nursing home than they are of the **cost.** As usual, it is the middle class who is at risk.

Those who are "too poor to be rich" and "too rich to be poor" face the greatest jeopardy. The government cares for the poor. The rich have sufficient assets. It is the middle-class that suffers.

> *Sarah was concerned about entering a nursing home. Her health, while still fairly good, was starting to decline. Her assets totaled $105,000. She checked various nursing homes and learned it would cost her $2800 per month, which is about average. Her income from Social Security, along with her late husband's retirement, was $1350.*

She knew her income would not keep pace with the escalating cost of nursing care. What could she do? She could pay the shortfall between the cost of the nursing home and her income by liquidating assets; she could buy nursing home insurance; or she could qualify herself for government assistance.

Before reviewing the alternatives, understand that

Medicare, the health insurance program on which most senior citizens expect to rely, provides virtually no benefit for nursing home care. Most payments are made either by the patient or Medicaid. Let's look at Sarah's alternatives.

Pay in cash

For Sarah, the cost of paying the $1450 shortfall for a nursing home is not realistic. She just doesn't have the money. While she could pay for a few years, eventually she will have to tap into her $105,000.

Using her cash means that Sarah will probably deplete her life savings, leaving nothing for her children. That is not a pleasant thought. She and her late husband worked hard their entire lives, and were very frugal. Their intention was to enjoy their latter years and have something to leave their children upon their deaths. Now all that is in jeopardy.

Buy nursing home insurance

Another alternative is to buy long-term care insurance. This is not as easy as it seems. Over the years, nursing home insurance has been the subject of abuse by many insurance agents. Nevertheless, there are excellent policies offered by quality companies.

Nursing home insurance is not cheap if you wait until you are elderly to purchase it. The average person procrastinates, then is disqualified due to lack of money or poor health. If you decide to consider private nursing home insurance, here are some things that must be in your policy:

- **Guaranteed renewable.** The company should not have the right to cancel your coverage, no matter what.

- **Level premiums.** Your premiums should only increase if rates are changed statewide.

- **Waiver of premium.** Your premium payments should stop while you are a resident of the nursing home.

- **No pre-existing condition limitations.** The company must not be able to deny you benefits if you enter a nursing home due to a previous medical condition.

- **Alzheimer's disease** should not be excluded. This should also be true for other forms of senility or dementia. In fact, your policy must state specifically that these diseases <u>are</u> covered.

- **Underwriting after a claim** must not be permitted. Don't accept a policy that offers coverage but doesn't determine if you are qualified until you submit a claim. Why pay for something you'll never get?

- **No prior hospital stay required.** Most people go directly from their home into a nursing home. Don't accept a policy that requires you go to a nursing home directly from a hospital.

- **A+ rated.** At a minimum, you want the company rated A+ by A. M. Best & Company. Review Chapter 18 about the quality of insurance companies.

- **Review it.** Once you receive the policy, read it carefully to make sure everything you were told is actually in writing. Don't take the agent's word for it. If it is not in writing, send it back for a refund. You should have at least a "10-day free look" period.

Let the government pay

The answer for most people is Medicaid. Don't confuse Medicaid with Medicare. Medicare is health insurance for seniors 65 years and older. **Medicaid** is a welfare program designed to provide for people who are destitute. Like most government programs, Medicaid rules change constantly. The tax bill in 1993 made changes, with more to come.

Nevertheless, for most people, this is the only realistic alternative. Like Sarah, they don't have the money to pay for insurance or a stay in a nursing home. However, they don't want to lose everything, either. If you plan to give away assets to qualify for Medicaid, be sure to follow the current rules.

Many people have no choice but to depend on the government to pay their nursing home costs. Others, like Sarah, wouldn't qualify today . . . but after a short stay in the nursing home, they surely will!

New rules

The 1993 tax bill changed some Medicaid qualification rules. The effect was to make it more difficult for middle-class Americans to qualify for government assistance. Be sure you become familiar with those changes and how they relate to the laws of your particular state.

Guidelines

> ✓ *Prepare for nursing home costs years before you anticipate needing one . . . preferably by age 65.*

> ✓ *Compare the benefits and costs of several quality nursing home policies.*

> ✓ *Check the current cost of nursing homes in your area. Ask what their rates were five and ten years ago, and project those rates into the future.*

> ✓ *Find out the current Medicaid eligibility rules if you plan to give away assets to qualify.*

Chapter 25

What Should I Know About Estate Planning?

Estate planning is a highly complex subject, involving more than we can cover here. For a complete discussion of estate planning, we recommend the book *Keep Uncle Sam From Devouring Your Life Savings*, written by Stephen M. Rosenberg, coathor of this book. See the form on Page 355 for ordering information and other resource materials.

What is estate planning?

Mention "estate planning," and people say, "I don't have enough money to worry about that. It's only for the rich."

Nothing could be further from the truth. Estate planning is for anyone who cares about what happens to her family, and her assets, upon her death or mental disability. Wealth has nothing to do with it. The only determining factor is "do you care enough to plan?"

Why is it so important?

Most people leave everything to chance. They hope things will work out for the best. Unfortunately, things rarely do. There are many occurrences that can create untold problems for you and your family, including:

- Your husband's death or disability.
- Your death or disability.
- Leaving property to minor children or grandchildren.
- Entering a nursing home.

- Your will being contested.
- An ex-husband after your money.
- Property held jointly by parents and adult children.
- The wrong guardians for your children.
- Providing for disabled children.
- Estate taxes due within nine months.

This list can go on and on. The purpose of proper estate planning is to ensure that no matter what happens, your desires are known and followed. The horror stories are many; the people who plan are few. We want you to be one of the few.

YOUR SITUATION

The problems you face with estate planning depend upon your family situation. Let's review some typical situations to help you anticipate problems.

Unmarried without minor children

You must decide where your property will go upon your death. If you are young, then your parents or siblings are logical choices. Other alternatives are charitable and religious organizations. If you have no assets, or if your liabilities outweigh your assets, then you have no problems. If your estate is worth nothing, then don't bother planning. If, on the other hand, your estate has value, and you are concerned about what happens to it, then at least prepare a will.

Unmarried with minor children

This is the most difficult situation, because you have minor children. (This is not news, right?) Remember one thing: minor children cannot own property. You must resolve that problem through proper planning.

If you are divorced, there are special problems concerning your ex-husband that you must address. These revolve around guardianship of your children and their inheritance.

If you are a widow, you must make special provisions for guardianship of your children and their money upon your death.

Married with minor children

Although the chances of both of you dying together are remote, it does happen. You should plan to leave your property to each other, and then to your children. Minor children cannot own property. Therefore, you should set up a trust for them.

Currently, estates over $600,000 face federal estate taxes. Special planning can help you reduce those taxes.

Married with adult children

Plan ahead to ensure that your assets pass according to your wishes. The issues aren't as pressing since you don't have minor children, however they still need to be addressed. Currently, estates over $600,000 face federal estate taxes. Special planning can help you reduce those taxes.

PASSING YOUR PROPERTY

Upon your death, your assets pass in one of five ways. Let's look at each.

- **Joint tenancy.** Any property you own as "Joint Tenants With Rights of Survivorship" automatically passes to the surviving tenant(s) upon your death and avoids probate.

- **Beneficiary designation.** Life insurance and retirement plans paid to a named beneficiary (as opposed to your "estate") go to the named beneficiary(ies) upon your death. This automatically avoids probate.

- **Your will.** If you have a will, your assets pass according to the instructions in your will. Property that avoids probate (joint tenancy, life insurance and retirement benefits paid to a named beneficiary, and property titled in a trust) passes according to its own rules. Everything that passes via your will goes through probate.

- **Trust.** Any property titled in the name of a trust (whether revocable or irrevocable) passes according to the rules in that trust and avoids probate.

- **Intestate.** If you don't have a will, your assets pass according to the laws of your state. Property that avoids probate, however, passes according to its own rules, as explained previously.

CONCERNS WITH CHILDREN

Minor children (under 18 in most states, 21 in others) can't own property. That means if you leave assets (cash, property, life insurance, etc.) directly to your children, they cannot control that money until they reach majority. Until that time, that property is under the control of the probate court. Upon reaching the age of majority, they receive all the property.

Guardians (custodians) of the person

You probably want to name a guardian (custodian) for your children. That is the person who cares for them upon your death. You name the guardian in your will. However, that is just your preference. The court has the final say. If you don't have a will, the court names a guardian.

Making your wishes known is especially important if you want to name someone other than the natural parent as guardian. However, your wishes may not be followed, since the courts generally give preference to the natural parents.

Guardians (trustees) of the money

In addition, the court will name someone to handle the money you leave your children. This is usually the guardian of the children, although others can be named.

This is very important if you are divorced and concerned about your ex-husband getting his hands on the children's inheritance. There are only two reasons why a person would want to be the guardian of your children: they love them, or they want access to their money. This latter reason, while disgusting, happens more than you realize. Frequently it occurs with ex-husbands . . . they want to get to the money, and they do that through the children.

No matter what a creep your ex-husband may be, he can dress up, go to the courthouse, and impress the heck out of the judge. Therefore, if this is a concern, you must make special provisions.

The solution

The best way to protect your minor children's inheritance is through the use of a trust. You can do this one of two ways.

- **As part of your will.** Your will can contain a provision to establish a trust upon your death (called a testamentary trust). All funds flow into that trust. You name a trustee to handle the funds. This should **not** be the same person you named as guardian of your children. Your trust contains your instructions on how it is to be administered. You can make decisions on how to financially provide for your children and when they should ultimately receive their money.

- **Living trust.** Usually a better way to accomplish the same thing is with a living trust. It avoids probate, cares for you if you become disabled, and is difficult to contest.

Disabled children

Unlike minor children, many disabled children are never able to handle their own financial affairs. You can make provisions with a special type of trust that can be used to protect these children, depending upon whether or not you want to qualify them for government assistance.

EFFECT OF DIVORCE ON PREVIOUS PLANNING

If you and your ex-husband had a will, then you need to recognize the effect of your divorce on that will. In some states, it remains in effect, meaning your ex-husband could inherit your property. In other states, it becomes invalid, leaving you without a will. In either case, you need a new will or trust to pass your property the way you want, and to take care of any minor children.

Beneficiary designations

Many states have passed laws concerning beneficiary designations in retirement plans, annuity contracts, and life insurance policies. This law voids all beneficiary designations after a divorce when the spouse was named the beneficiary. This can be either advantageous or detrimental to you, depending on your side of the fence.

The exception to this is when there is a contractual agreement between the two of you. This can be in your divorce decree or a separate document. Just make sure there can be no misunderstanding of his intent to include you as beneficiary.

Don't settle for your husband's verbal agreement to make you beneficiary. You may lose those benefits. Get it in writing, and make sure all post-divorce designations are up to date.

ESTATE TAXES

Upon your death, you can pass $600,000 to your heirs free of federal estate taxes. If you are married, you can effectively double this exemption to $1,200,000, with proper planning. However, we expect the government to reduce these figures to $200,000 and $400,000 respectively within the next few years. These repercussions are discussed in Steve's book.

The best way to handle the estate tax problem, if you are married, is the use of a trust. As in the above situation, either type of trust will work, but we prefer a living trust.

If you still have an estate tax problem, you can reduce the size of your estate through gifts or the purchase of life insurance in an irrevocable trust to pay estate taxes. The latter can reduce the cost of your estate taxes by up to 90%.

Guidelines

✓ *Prepare a will or living trust to indicate your wishes.*

✓ *If you have minor children, consider a trust.*

✓ *If divorced, protect your money from your ex-husband.*

✓ *Make sure your beneficiary designations are up-to-date.*

✓ *If you anticipate estate tax problems, put life insurance in an irrevocable trust or have your children own it.*

Part Three

Investment Basics

Chapter 26

Why Can't I Leave All My Money In The Bank?

Most of the money in this country is in the banks, savings banks, and credit unions. These financial institutions provide a high degree of safety, reliability, and convenience. They are a fine place for your cash reserves as well as some of your longer-term savings. However, these institutions are not the place to accumulate wealth.

Financially successful people don't let their money rest in a bank long. If they do, it is in small amounts. Financially troubled people, on the other hand, leave everything there forever, because they're afraid of taking **any** risks.

Let's start out with a basic fact: **you won't get rich putting your money in the bank.** Of course, you won't lose your money, either. It will just get reduced by taxes and inflation.

What's wrong with money in the bank? Nothing, within limits. Everyone needs to have some money in the bank. The problem is that if you have too much there, you are losing money unnecessarily to taxes, inflation, and low interest rates.

The first column of the following chart shows how 6-month CDs (certificates of deposit) performed over the past 20 years. Columns two and three reflect the taxes and inflation that reduced that yield. For illustration purposes, we assumed only a 35% tax bracket. That is actually much less than it was during that period. The top bracket was as high as 70%. Since you probably weren't in the top bracket all those years, 35% is a good compromise. The last column is the net return after taxes and inflation. It is what you really earned.

YEAR	CD RATE	LESS TAXES	LESS INFLATION	REAL RATE OF RETURN
1973	8.3	2.9	8.8	-3.4
1974	10.0	3.5	12.2	-5.7
1975	6.9	2.4	7.0	-2.5
1976	5.6	2.0	4.8	-1.2
1977	6.0	2.1	6.8	-2.9
1978	8.6	3.0	9.0	-3.4
1979	11.4	4.0	13.3	-5.9
1980	13.0	4.6	12.4	-4.0
1981	15.8	5.5	8.9	+1.4
1982	12.6	4.4	3.9	+4.3
1983	9.3	3.3	3.8	+2.2
1984	10.7	3.7	4.0	+3.0
1985	8.3	2.9	3.8	+1.6
1986	6.5	2.3	1.1	+3.1
1987	7.0	2.5	4.4	+0.1
1988	7.9	2.8	4.4	+0.7
1989	9.1	3.2	4.6	+1.3
1990	8.2	2.9	6.1	-0.8
1991	4.7	1.6	3.1	0
1992	3.5	1.2	3.2	-0.9
Avg.	8.7%	3.0	6.3	-0.6

Let's review what this chart reveals. First, the average 6-month CD rate during the past 20 years was 8.7%. That sounds okay so far. If someone had told you in 1973 that you could average 8.7% for the next 20 years in CDs, you probably would have been pleased. However, when we take taxes and inflation into consideration, the entire picture changes. Taxes ate up 3% of the earnings. That reduced the after-tax earnings rate to 5.7% of the investment.

Then inflation devoured an average of 6.3% of the investment. In other words, after inflation, you actually lost money keeping it in 6-month CDs. The average **loss** was 0.6%!

Compound interest

On top of lower rates, the other reason that people don't accumulate enough money is that they spend their interest. Albert Einstein, when asked man's greatest discovery, responded **"the power of compounding."** People who understand compounding make money; those who don't, don't.

> *When Belinda's husband died, she received $50,000 in insurance proceeds. Belinda was fairly young at the time, had a decent job, and didn't really need the money. She put it in a six-month certificate of deposit at her local bank. The bank deposited the interest from that CD into her savings account. When she wanted money, she simply drew it from her savings account. Her original $50,000 is still worth only $50,000 today.*

During that 13-year period, Belinda earned an average of 8.7% in the bank. She withdrew an average of $4,350 per year in interest. Over the 13-year period, that amounted to $56,550, all of which she spent. The $50,000 she invested, plus the $56,550 she withdrew, totaled $106,550. Had she allowed the interest to compound, she would have **$147,588** today.

Let's go another 13 years in the future and assume Belinda continues to earn 8.7%. Over that period, she will earn additional interest of $56,500. On the other hand, if she spends her interest annually, her original $50,000 will still be $50,000 after the second 13 years. As you know by now, it will be worth much less due to inflation.

Instead of spending the interest, she could have chosen to let her money compound over that 26-year period. As the following chart shows, had she done that, her original $50,000 would be worth **$437,460!**

	Interest Withdrawn	Interest Compounded	Difference
13 Years	$106,550	$147,895	$41,345
26 Years	$163,000	$437,460	$274,460

She could have had $274,460 more by reinvesting her interest rather than spending it. Belinda's $50,000 could have become nearly half a million dollars in 26 years. That is the value of compound interest!

"Saving"

You see, the average person does what Belinda did. They "save" their money, then they spend their savings. They watch pennies and blow dollars. They're penny wise and pound foolish. We hate to burst your bubble, but that's not saving.

"Saving" means the money is put away for long-term goals and allowed to grow. It is not put away to accumulate for vacations and furniture. While that may be important, don't count it as part of your "savings." Count only money that is put away for retirement and future investment. Most people want things today, so they spend any free cash they can get. That's what Belinda chose to do, and look at the earnings she missed.

Financially successful people realize the value of compound interest. It is this concept, more than any other, that you must understand to become financially independent, whether you earn 5% or 15%

Higher rates

The final important concept to grasp is the advantage of earning a higher rate of return on your money. Notice, we don't say earning higher "interest." There is a big difference between the two.

Too many people think in terms of how much interest they are earning. Your mind set is all wrong if, when looking at growth investments, you ask a financial advisor, "How much interest will I make?" You are thinking the way bankers want you to think. You assume that your money is going to grow in a straight line, the only variable being how fast.

However, that is not the way to create financial independence. You must take some risk. As the chart on page 134 shows, even when your money is in the bank, you are taking a risk. You risk losing money to inflation and taxes.

You must achieve higher rates of return than you are receiving in the bank. Belinda put her money in the bank. But there were a number of alternatives she could have chosen. Unfortunately, she was not familiar with any of them. Let's look at the results of other choices she could have made.

$50,000 INVESTMENT - 1980	VALUE - 1993	ANNUAL RATE
6-month CDs	$147,588	8.7%
High Grade Bonds	$238,195	12.8%
Dow Jones Utilities Index	$310,730	15.1%
S&P 500 Index	$340,688	15.9%
Dow Jones Industrial Index	$348,337	16.1%

The results of the investments outside the bank were unusually good during this period. They won't always do this well. In fact, there will be times when banks beat alternative investments. However, over time, diversified investments will outperform money in the bank.

Focusing on higher rates of return will help you accumulate more money and secure your financial future. In Belinda's case, by doubling her rate of return she would have more than doubled her money in just 13 years. Think of what could happen over a 30-year period!

Higher rates and compounding

The ultimate technique is to increase your rate of return and let your money compound. The following chart reflects an investment of **$100 per month** at 4%, 8%, and 12% for four different periods.

Years	4%	8%	12%
10	$14,725	$18,295	$23,004
20	$36,667	$58,902	$98,926
30	$69,405	$149,035	$349,496
40	$118,196	$349,101	$1,176,477

The following chart shows the results of a **lump-sum investment of $10,000** at 4%, 8%, and 12%.

Years	4%	8%	12%
10	$14,802	$21,589	$31,058
20	$21,911	$46,610	$96,463
30	$32,434	$100,627	$299,599
40	$48,010	$217,245	$930,510

These charts reveal the importance of making more on your money. Whether you are saving monthly for retirement or have a lump sum to invest, you <u>must</u> make your money work harder for you to stay ahead of the game.

THE CONCEPT OF RISK

Of course, many people don't want to take any risk. They prefer to keep all of their money in the "safety" of banks. That is because they don't understand risk.

Gail met with a broker about investing some money. He asked about her goals. "I'd like to make as much as I can without taking any risk." He asked if she was willing to take any risk at all. "No," she replied. "I can't afford to lose any of my money."

Gail is not unique. She, like almost everyone else, wants to make more without taking any risk. Well, it's just not possible. Everything has risk, even money in the bank! It's just that some investments have more risk than others, and some kinds of risk are more obvious.

If you don't want to risk any of your money, if you want no chance of loss at all, then we have the perfect investment: bury it in your backyard! Just make sure you leave a map for your kids.

Now, obviously, we are being facetious (although we know a couple who is actually proud of doing this). The fact is that an absolutely risk-free return doesn't exist in any financial investment. It doesn't even exist if you bury your money. You need to face reality: there is no place to invest your money that is 100% risk-free. Everything you do with your money involves some risk. The key to success, however, is to manage the risk within your particular goals and in **your** favor.

Every time you get into your car, you take a risk. Every time you walk out your front door, you take a risk. Every time you eat a meal, you take a risk. Yet, you do all of these. You just accept the risks and get on with your life. The same should be true with your money. There are several different types of risk that you must consider, whether you invest your money at your local bank or put it into the most speculative stock.

Risk of principal

The first risk is the loss of your principal. If you purchase 100 shares of Coca Cola, you understand that the value of that investment might go up or down. You may make money, or you may lose money. On the other hand, you know that if you deposit money in the bank, and keep within the insured limits of $100,000, your principal is safe.

The same is true of government bonds. As long as the U.S. Government can make the interest payments, and you hold the bonds until maturity, your money is safe. And let's face it. If the government ever defaults, then virtually everything else you own will be worthless, too.

It is reasonable to assume that there are places where you can invest your money without risking your principal. However, many people make the big mistake of thinking that risk of principal is the only consideration. This thinking separates those who have money from those who do not. The "have-nots" keep their money in guaranteed accounts. The "haves" invest part of their money for growth. That is because they understand that there are other, potentially more danger-ous, risks than loss of principal.

Inflation risk

Inflation is something we've heard about all our lives but don't really understand. Prices go up virtually every year. This is called inflation. The amount of inflation we have depends on many factors, such as strength of the economy, interest rates, raw energy prices, supply and demand, wage pressure, etc.

Whatever the inflation rate, it is always there. Sometimes it's bad . . . and sometimes it's worse! But it's always there, chipping away your buying power.

Inflation is measured by the Consumer Price Index (CPI), which is a "basket" of goods and services. Over the years, the inflation rate has been very volatile. In 1979, for example, the inflation rate was 13.3%. In 1992, it was "only" 3.2%. But don't fall into the "only" trap. Any inflation is dangerous. It's just that politicians think it's great when inflation is lower than it was the previous year, so they make "only" sound like a great achievement.

It is important to consider inflation for two reasons:

- Investing your money "safely" means receiving lower interest rates than other alternatives.

- Inflation eats away the value of the interest you receive, which means your buying power on that money shrinks each and every year.

The chart on page 134 shows what inflation does to savings. Let's look at it a little closer. If you earn 4% in the bank, and prices go up by 4%, then you lose! Here's why: taxes and inflation. If you deposit $10,000 in a 4% certificate of deposit, you will have $10,400 at the end of the year. Assume you want to purchase a $10,000 car in January, but decide to wait until the end of the year. By that time, inflation of 4% will have pushed the cost of a new car to $10,400. At first glance, your interest of 4% kept pace with the 4% inflation rate. However, you have to pay taxes on the $400 interest. So your $400 is worth only $280 (30% tax-bracket). Therefore, you only have $10,280 after taxes for a car that costs $10,400. That is how inflation eats at your purchasing power.

Sue looked forward to retirement from her school system. Every month the school withheld some of her earnings for her retire-

ment plan. Her husband had worked in a factory before his death. She received some life insurance proceeds and his retirement benefits, which she invested in CDs. She retired in 1970 on a small pension, which was enough to provide her with a comfortable retirement. By 1993, lower interest rates had reduced her income from the CDs. Her pension adjusted slightly with cost-of-living increases, but prices between 1970 and 1990 more than doubled. While $800 a month was more than adequate in 1970, it didn't go very far in 1993. Now she wishes she had done something else with her money.

Ronald Reagan said that **inflation is the cruelest tax of all.** It is always there, creeping in and stealing part of your money. Inflation doesn't discriminate. It doesn't care whether you make $10,000 a year or $10,000,000 a year. It just continually nibbles away at your money. If you are not careful, it will devour every penny you have, until you end up like Sue . . . with too little money and too much month.

The actual impact of higher prices depends not only on the rate of inflation, but your age, as well. The younger you are, the greater the impact, the more you must plan.

Assume your goal is to have $2,000 per month of retirement income in today's dollars. Look how much you will need in the future to buy what $2,000 buys today, assuming a 6% inflation rate.

YEAR	EQUIVALENT OF $2,000
2004	$3,582
2014	$6,414
2024	$11,487
2034	$20,571
2044	$36,840
2054	$65,975

Scary, isn't it? In 2034, you will need to earn $20,571 **per month** to buy what $2,000 per month buys in 1994. It doesn't take a financial genius to realize that if you don't plan for the impact of inflation, you will be in serious financial trouble.

Therefore, if you are going to achieve your financial goals, you must take some risk. Let's move on and learn about some alternative investments that have higher "perceived" risk than money in the bank. We put perceived in quotation marks because investments contain risks that can be reduced by proper use and education.

Guidelines

- ✓ *Keep your emergency funds, money for short-term needs, and cash reserves in the bank.*

- ✓ *You need to go beyond the bank for investments that will grow to meet your future needs.*

- ✓ *Diversify for safety and an inflation hedge.*

- ✓ *Understand that inflation and taxes reduce your earnings.*

Chapter 27

What Should I Know About Bonds?

Bonds are debt obligations issued by governments or companies. The federal government, local government, and corporations all borrow money by selling bonds. When you buy a bond, there are several variables: **interest rate** (the percentage you receive); **maturity date** (the day your money is returned); and **safety** (the rating of the bond).

Ratings

Since it is virtually impossible for you to determine the safety of a bond, rating agencies, such as Standard and Poor's and Moody's, do this for you. S&P classifies bonds from AAA down to D. Moody's does so from Aaa to C. Our recommendation is to stick with bonds rated AAA (Aaa) or AA (Aa) only.

While the rating is not important with United States government bonds (they're all rated AAA), it is meaningful for bonds issued by corporations or municipalities.

Interest rate risk

The risk of default is not the only risk you face when purchasing bonds. Many people assume that bonds backed by the government are "risk-free," and to an extent they are correct. But while they are safe from default of principal and interest, they do contain interest rate risk.

Ruth purchased a $10,000, 30-year government bond that was paying 7%, or $700 per year. When a family emergency arose, she needed to sell her bond. By then, interest rates had in-

creased and new treasury bonds were paying 8.5%. That meant that anyone buying a new $10,000 bond would receive $850 interest. Ruth's was paying only $700. Therefore, the current value of her bond was no longer $10,000. In fact, she only received $9,200 when she sold it.

Had Ruth been able to hold the bond to maturity, she would have received $10,000. However, she didn't have that luxury . . . she needed the money. It can work in reverse, as well. Had interest rates dropped, Ruth would have received more than $10,000 for her bond.

GOVERNMENT BONDS

There are many types of debt issued by the government and its agencies. Let's look at some of the more popular.

Treasury Bills are issued in minimum amounts of $10,000, then in $5,000 increments. They are short-term in nature, maturing in 90, 180, 270, or 360 days. They don't pay interest directly . . . they are issued at a discount and mature at face value. For example, a one-year bond might be issued for $9,600 and mature at $10,000.

Treasury Notes are issued for periods of two to ten years. The minimum purchase is $5,000 for 2-4 year bonds, and $1,000 for 5-10 year bonds. Interest is paid semiannually.

Treasury Bonds are issued in minimum units of $1,000 and mature in 10 to 30 years. However, the only treasury bonds being issued today are 30-year bonds. Historically, the government has relied on these bonds to finance the bulk of its debt. The 30-year bond is called the "long bond."

Government agency bonds

Besides bonds issued directly by the government, there are obligations issued by government agencies, such as **Ginnie**

Maes, issued by the Government National Mortgage Association (GNMA), **Fannie Maes,** issued by the Federal National Mortgage Association (FNMA), and **Sallie Maes,** issued by the Student Loan Marketing Association (SLMA).

Ginnie Maes are the most common. They are mortgages guaranteed by the federal government. Since they are pools of mortgages, they pay both principal and interest, just as you do with your mortgage payment.

> *Jan purchased a $25,000 GNMA from her broker. At the time, the interest rate was 13%. She deposited her monthly interest checks and spent the money. The amount she received varied. A statement came with every payment, but she didn't understand it. Every so often, she received extra-large payments. She prided herself on her great investment. But after every large payment, her subsequent payments dropped. Eight years later, she stopped receiving any money. She called her broker. He explained to her that she had been receiving interest <u>and</u> principal over the years. She had spent it all, and had nothing left!*

Two things happened to Jan. First, part of every payment she received was principal, which she spent. To make matters worse, interest rates dropped. People refinanced their homes, paying off the old mortgages. That is why she received large chunks periodically. And as they paid off their mortgages, the original pool dropped in value, because principal was returned to her. Finally, nothing was left. As is all too common, Jan invested in something she didn't fully understand. (Obviously, she hadn't read our book!)

Savings bonds

EE Savings bonds are perhaps the best known government issue. They are currently issued for an original maturity period of 12 years in denominations starting as low as $50. The purchase price is one-half of the face value, so a $50 bond costs $25. Although the original term is 12 years, bonds can mature sooner if the current rate is higher than the minimum.

The maximum number of years bonds pay interest (called their "final maturity") depends upon their original issue date. Bonds issued before December 1965 reach final maturity in 40 years. Bonds issued December 1965 and after reach final maturity in 30 years. At that point, you can redeem the bonds or exchange them for HH bonds.

HH Bonds differ from EE Bonds in that they pay interest semiannually. Remember, EE bonds don't pay current interest - it is all deferred. You can exchange your EE bonds for HH and pay taxes only on the income you receive.

Upon the death of the holder, the bond automatically passes to the co-owner or beneficiary. If none was named, the proceeds go into the estate of the last co-owner to die.

You may change, add, or remove a beneficiary by completing Form PD-F-4000. If the beneficiary is living, you cannot remove him from E Bonds without his signature. His approval is not necessary on EE bonds.

For bonds issued after November 1, 1982, the interest earned is the higher of the guaranteed rate or the market rate. The variable rates are announced May 1st and November 1st of each year. Get the current rate by calling **1-800-4US-BOND** (1-800-487-2663). The interest rate on bonds held five years or longer is the higher of the market rate average or the minimum rate.

A note of caution. The minimum guarantee ends with the end of the original maturity. At that point, the new interest rate drops to the current minimum guaranteed rate or the current market rate, whichever is higher.

Beverly bought savings bonds in 1982 when the minimum guaranteed rate was 7.5%. She assumed she would always receive at least that amount. However, when the bonds matured in 1992, the minimum rate had dropped to 6%. By 1993, the minimum guaranteed rate was 4%. Her bonds were only earning

*the current market rate from 1992 on . . . which was far less than
7.5%.*

When the guaranteed rate drops, that doesn't mean that
is all you will earn. For example, in Beverly's case, although the
1993 guaranteed rate was down to 4%, she earned the market
rate average, which was greater, But she did not earn the 7.5%
minimum she expected.

TAX-FREE BONDS

Tax-free bonds are one of the last great tax shelters
remaining. Proper use of tax-free investments can make quite
a difference in your income. Let's compare the way two sisters,
JoAnn and Linda, handled their inheritance.

> *JoAnn needed additional income. She purchased a $50,000 CD
> paying 5%. Each year, she earned $2,500 interest, which she
> declared as "interest income" on her tax return. In her tax bracket,
> that resulted in $750 a year in taxes on those earnings. It never
> occurred to her that she really ended up with $1,750 after taxes
> ($2,500 minus $750 taxes), a return of only 3.5% after taxes.*

Like most people, JoAnn failed to consider taxes in her
planning. She never realized that she was making only 3.5% on
her money after taxes. All she considered was the 5% the CD
earned.

Understand one thing: **it makes absolutely no difference
how much the financial institution is paying you. The only
factor you should consider is how much you <u>get to keep</u> after
you have paid your taxes.**

It is no secret that the government wants more of your
money and will continue to raise taxes, just as they did in 1993.
That means that you must take steps to protect yourself if you
wish to reduce your tax burden.

JoAnn certainly didn't do that. She only looked at what her bank was paying. Let's look at how JoAnn's sister took advantage of tax-free income.

Linda, a resident of Ohio, purchased a $50,000, 6% tax-free bond from her broker. She received semiannual interest in the amount of $1,500. Since it was issued by her state of residence, the interest was free from federal, state, and local income taxes. She kept 100% of the $3,000 annual interest!

Look at the difference between JoAnn and Linda's income. Both invested $50,000. Both received the interest. But look at the bottom line: Linda kept **$3,000** after taxes and JoAnn kept **$1,750** after taxes. Linda made **71% more** than her sister on identical investment amounts. Of course, Linda's bond was subject to fluctuating values if interest rates changed, but she was well compensated for that. And it wouldn't affect her unless she sold her bond before maturity.

You can receive tax-free income by investing in municipal bonds, which are debt obligations issued by states, counties, or cities. They raise money for a variety of needs, from water facilities and road improvements, to new schools and hospitals.

Bonds issued by municipalities are free from federal income taxes. In addition, those by your state (or Puerto Rico or Guam) are also free from state and local income taxes.

Value of tax-free income

Let's look at the value of tax-free income. As stated above, one of the biggest mistakes most people make is failing to consider taxes in their calculations. When they receive 5% from their bank, they think that's what they're really making. As you know by now, that is not so. That 5% is reduced by the taxes they must pay on their earnings.

A solution, therefore, is to invest in tax-free bonds. You

should only buy tax-free bonds if you will earn more **after taxes,** not just because you hate to pay taxes. The deciding factor should be the after-tax yield.

Marian had $60,000 in CDs that were maturing. She called her banker who quoted 5% for a three-year certificate of deposit. She called the Federal Reserve and learned that 30-year Treasury Bonds were paying 7%. She called her broker and found out that AAA-rated 25-year tax-free bonds were paying 5.5%. Marian was in the 30% combined federal and state income tax brackets.

Let's look at her after-tax returns for the three choices.

	Bank	Government	Tax-Free
Rate	5.0%	7.0%	5.5%
Less: Taxes	1.5%	2.1%	-0-
Net Return	3.5%	4.9%	5.5%

- **Bank.** She would lose 30% of the 5% (or 1.5%) to taxes. Therefore, she would end up with **after-tax earnings of only 3.5%.**

- **Government bonds.** She would lose 30% of the 7% (or 2.1%) to taxes. Therefore, she would end up with **after-tax earnings of 4.9%.**

- **Tax-free bonds.** She would lose nothing to taxes. Her **after-tax earnings would be 5.5%.** She could keep it all!

At first glance, Marian would be better off with tax-free bonds. Remember from our previous discussion, however, that municipal bonds are not risk-free investments.

- **Interest-rate risk.** If rates are higher when she needs to sell her bonds, she will likely sell them at a loss.

Conversely, if interest rates have fallen when she sells the bonds, she will make a profit.

- **Liquidity.** Liquidity means the ability to get your money at any time without loss. While Marian can go into the bank any day and cash in her CD (although she will suffer an early-surrender penalty), it takes longer to sell a bond. She must call her broker to sell it for her. It will then take over a week to receive the check.

- **Default.** Although it's relatively rare, municipal bond defaults do occur. However, Marian can prevent this by buying **insured** bonds.

As you can see, this is not a clear-cut choice. There are many factors at work. Nevertheless, tax-free bonds are very appealing for the right people in the right situation. Those who are more concerned with income than liquidity will find them an excellent choice.

The following chart, which reflects the 1993 tax increase, shows the taxable return you would have to earn to equal a 5, 6, or 7% tax-free return. This includes federal tax rates only. If your state has a personal income tax, your taxable equivalent yield would be even higher.

Taxable Income Single	Taxable Income Joint	Tax Rate	Tax-Free 5% Equals Taxable:	Tax-Free 6% Equals Taxable:	Tax-Free 7% Equals Taxable:
$0-22,100	$0-36,900	15%	5.88%	7.06%	8.24%
22,101-53,500	36,901-89,150	28%	6.94%	8.33%	9.72%
53,501-115,000	89,151-140,000	31%	7.25%	8.70%	10.14%
115,001-250,000	140,001-250,000	36%	7.81%	9.38%	10.94%
250,001+	250,001+	39.6%	8.28%	9.93%	11.59%

For example, if you are in the 28% tax bracket and earn 5% in a tax-free investment, you will need to earn 6.94% in a taxable investment to end up with the same return. Conversely, if you obtain a 6.94% taxable return, taxes will take approximately 1.94%, leaving only 5%.

Investing in municipal bonds

Municipal bonds are excellent for those who want monthly income free from federal and state income taxes. There are three ways to purchase them.

- **Individual bonds** are purchased through brokerage firms. You receive interest semiannually, and your principal is returned when the bond matures, or whenever you sell it. Selling a bond before maturity means that you might lose money if interest rates rise, or make money if rates fall. Your risk is higher with individual bonds. That's why we recommend insured bonds.

- **Unit investment trusts** (UIT) are fixed portfolios holding a number of individual bonds. The bonds pay interest to the trust, which in turn pays the investors either monthly, quarterly, or semiannually. The UIT is an unmanaged portfolio . . . the bonds are not sold during the duration of the trust. Therefore, it is very important that the fund be insured. There are expenses built into the UIT, so the yield is slightly lower than that of individual bonds. But you do have the advantage of diversification and frequent interest payments.

- **Mutual funds** are a very popular way to purchase municipal bonds due to their diversification, professional management, liquidity, and affordability. Mutual funds are explained in detail in Chapter 29. Portfolio managers constantly monitor the fund, buying and selling bonds as necessary. There is comfort in the measure of safety provided by a broadly diversified portfolio.

Early redemption

One important factor about municipal bonds is that they are "callable." If the issuer wants to redeem them before maturity, they can do so by calling them at a predetermined price. This can cause problems for the purchaser, especially in times of falling interest rates.

> *Florence purchased a $25,000, 9.5% tax-free bond in 1984. In 1990, she received a notice that $10,000 of her bond was being "called" by the issuer. She contacted her broker and was told that the issuer was doing a partial redemption to refinance at a lower rate. She had no choice. She mailed in her bond and received a new bond for $15,000, along with a check for $10,500.*

In this situation, the investor has no choice. Municipal bonds were "called" in record numbers in the early 1990's due to lower interest rates. When your bond is called, you typically get more than face value. That's why Florence received $10,500 for her $10,000 bond. However, that is little consolation if you need current income and are forced to reinvest the money at lower interest rates.

CORPORATE BONDS

When considering government bonds, the risk of default is not a factor. While it is a minor consideration with municipal bonds, the risk can be neutralized by purchasing insured bonds. Corporate bonds, however, are completely different stories. There are corporations and there are corporations! There are the "blue chip" companies like Merck, Proctor & Gamble, Coca Cola, etc.; and the "not yet blue chips," like Wal-Mart, Apple Computer, etc.; and the "never will be blue chips" that we won't mention here. Suffice it to say that there is a world of difference between the top and bottom rungs.

When buying corporate bonds, more than with any other bond type, you **must** be concerned with ratings. If you are buying individual bonds, stay with AAA and AA ratings only.

Investing in corporate bonds

There are two primary ways to invest in corporate bonds:

- **Individual bonds.** Like municipal bonds, individual corporate bonds can be purchased through brokerage firms. You receive interest semiannually and receive your principal when the bond matures, or whenever you sell it. Remember, however, that selling a bond before maturity means that you could lose money if interest rates rise, or turn a profit if rates drop.

- **Mutual funds.** Mutual funds are the best way to purchase corporate bonds, but you still need to be careful. There are funds that specialize in quality bonds, and funds that invest in lower quality bonds. The latter are referred to as "high-yield" bonds, or sometimes as "junk bonds."

Guidelines

- ✓ *Realize that bond prices go down when interest rates go up, and vice versa.*

- ✓ *Consider tax-free bonds only if the <u>after-tax return</u> is higher than other investments.*

- ✓ *Use bond mutual funds if you want professional management, diversification, and monthly income.*

- ✓ *If you invest in individual bonds, do so only in bonds rated AAA or AA.*

Chapter 28

What Should I Know About Common Stock?

When a business owner needs money, there are two ways to obtain it: either borrow the money, or raise money by selling a portion of the business. The first method is done by borrowing from banks or selling bonds; the second is accomplished by selling stock.

> Diane started her own decorating business. She saved money over the years, and had enough capital to begin working out of her home. After four years, she decided that she wanted to expand so she could maintain an inventory of wall and floor coverings. She looked around and found a suitable building to rent. The only problem was that Diane didn't have the money to purchase adequate inventory. She went to her local bank. Like most people who really need money, she was unable to qualify for a loan. Finally, in desperation, she sold part of her business to an acquaintance. The good news was that she now had enough money to operate her business. The bad news was that she no longer owned 100% of the business.

Diane sold shares of stock in her business to her acquaintance. Major corporations do the same thing, only on a larger scale. When they sell stock to the public, they sell part of the company to investors.

The advantage is that they don't have to pay interest, since they are not borrowing the money. In addition, they never have to pay the money back. The downside is they dilute their ownership by giving others ownership in the company.

When you buy stock in Home Depot, you become a part owner of the company. If they have 10 million shares of stock outstanding, and you own one share, you are a 1/10,000,000 shareholder in Home Depot.

Reasons for buying stock

When you own stock, you can make money two ways:

- **Dividends.** Many companies choose to pay quarterly dividends, which are excess profits that the company distributes to shareholders. Faster growing companies pay less in dividends than more established ones. They would rather invest in themselves than pass profits to the stockholders. For example, Wal-Mart continues to expand by building more stores and filling them with inventory. This takes money. Why should they pay dividends when they can put that money to better use internally? Don't get hung up on dividends unless you need the income.

- **Capital gains.** The primary reason most people buy stock is not just to receive dividends, but to make money when the stock goes up in price. Therefore, you might buy shares of Home Depot, which pays virtually no dividends, because you hope it will go up in value.

Selling stock at a profit is not as easy as it sounds. Money managers are paid hefty sums to pick the right stocks. It is very difficult for the novice to do the same thing consistently. Since no one has a crystal ball to accurately predict the future movement of stocks, it is hard to know the best time to buy and sell.

Risk of buying stock

If you ask the average woman why she doesn't buy stock, it's because she doesn't want to take any "risk." People perceive the stock market as one giant slot machine. They think that after you sink your money in, you might make some money, but more than likely you will lose your shirt.

In a few cases, people with poor judgement do lose everything. But the stock market is not a black hole where your money disappears. Rather, it is the place where you have an opportunity for above-average gains.

There are several factors that can cause you to lose money in the stock market. Over the long run, the most detrimental factor is emotion - yours! To paraphrase Will Rogers, "Making money in the stock market is easy. All you have to do is buy low and sell high." Unfortunately, a great number of people do just the opposite.

One of the reasons for this is that they let their emotions get in the way. They get scared and/or greedy. Either one of those can result in significant losses. Together, they can be devastating. People get greedy and buy too much when the market's rising. Then they panic and sell when the price drops. Buying high and selling low guarantees losses.

Making money over the long run in the stock market is not as easy as everyone says. When the stock market does well for several years, everyone feels like a stock-picking genius. Well, anyone can pick stocks when the market is going up. It's the downturns and flat markets that reveal your true ability.

Another risk when buying individual stocks is lack of diversification. Most people can't afford a well-diversified portfolio of individual stocks. The fewer companies you own, the greater your risk. Diversification is like wearing snowshoes. With snowshoes you walk securely on top of the snow; without them you can easily sink.

The stock market vs. individual stocks

The stock market is made up of individual stocks.

Therefore, it doesn't help much to know that the market went up if your stock went down. You still have to be able to pick the right stocks.

Historically, the stock market has performed very well. If you compare investing in the stock market over the years, versus putting money in the bank, you will usually be better off in stocks. However, that doesn't mean that you will **always** be better off in the stock market, nor does it mean that the market won't do poorly in the short-term. There are ups and downs. Everyone knows about the stock market "crashes" in 1929 and 1987. And yet, in both cases, the market went on to new highs.

Jennifer, a single mother of two, received a small settlement upon her divorce. She met with a stockbroker and decided to invest part of that money in two growth mutual funds. Six months later, when she received a statement of her account, she calculated that she actually lost 2%. She called the broker, very upset because she was losing money. "I could have made more if I had just put it in the bank," she complained.

She was right. During that period, she would have done better in the bank. However, over the long-term, she can do better in stock funds. You can't compare an investment that will fluctuate over time, with money in the bank that doesn't. They are totally different.

The problem occurs when people look at the stock market from a short-term perspective. It is really a medium to long-term investment. You can't expect to **always** make more money in the stock market than you would at the bank on a month-to- month basis. But you can expect to do so **over the long run.** Remember that it is the end result that matters. **Focus on your goal, not on your journey.**

Six years later, Jennifer was again in her broker's office. Her children were in high school, so she was concerned about upcoming college costs. They compared her two growth funds, which she still owned, with the results she would have received by leaving her money in the bank. Their study revealed that she now had four times more money in her mutual fund than she would have had in the bank. She was so relieved that she had chosen to take a long-range approach.

Selecting good stocks

"How do I find good stocks?" That's the $64,000 question! Picking good, and we emphasize "good," stocks is an art in itself, one that few people ever master.

This book is not the place for a discussion on the intricacies of the stock market or how to invest. There are many excellent books on the subject. Nevertheless, unless you enjoy analyzing stock, you are going to have to rely on another party to pick stocks for you. Some of these are:

- **Stockbrokers.** Stockbrokers make money buying and selling stock. They receive commissions, so they are not necessarily impartial. Remember, whether you make or lose money, your broker will **always** make money. Brokers get many of their recommendations from their firm's research department. Unfortunately, the history of most research departments is not very good. So don't get talked into a stock because of the brokerage firm's "great" research department. Also, remember one thing about stockbrokers: if they were so good at **picking** stocks, they wouldn't be in sales, they'd be cruising the Caribbean in their yachts!

- **Newsletters.** There are hundreds of newsletters that provide individual stock recommendations. However, it's tough for newsletters to perform well over long periods of time. Just because somebody writes a newsletter doesn't make him or her a stock-picking genius.

- **Stock rating services.** There are several services that rate individual stocks. *Value Line Investment Survey*, for example, rates many different companies for their investment potential. Again, the reports are only as good as the person who reviews the company.

- **Magazines and newspapers.** Several publications contain articles on individual companies: the two financial daily newspapers, *The Wall Street Journal* and *Investor's Business Daily;* the major weekly financial newspaper, *Barron's*; and magazines such as *Forbes, Business Week*, and *Fortune*. Of course, the fact that a company is mentioned or recommended in any of these publications doesn't mean their stock is going higher. Take everything you read with a grain of salt.

- **You.** It is amazing how many people can find good stock bargains just by being aware of what people are buying and where they are spending their money. They recognize that a certain company is providing a unique product and decide it would be a good investment. While this doesn't always work out, it is much better than relying on somebody else's advice. It's amazing how people have made money using their own intuition and lost money by relying on others. Even the famed Peter Lynch, former manager of the Fidelity Magellan Fund, has often said that he got his best stock tips by listening to his wife and daughters after their shopping trips.

How to invest in the stock market

If you choose to invest in individual stocks, we caution you to make sure you know what you're doing. There are several avenues you can follow:

- **Full service stockbrokers** such as Merrill Lynch, Dean Witter, Shearson Bear Stearns, Prudential Securities, etc., provide a full range of services for their clients. You deal with stockbrokers who receive a commission based upon what their clients buy and sell. The commission rate is set, but the broker **can** give you a discount if he or she wants. The broker can help you with decisions, such as what to buy and sell, and when. Remember, the broker is a salesperson, not an analyst. He or she makes money whether or not you do. You also need to beware of brokers who buy or sell without your authorization, or who continually recommend buying and selling to generate commissions for themselves.

- **Discount brokers** such as Charles Schwab, Quick and Reilly, etc., provide no investment advice, but they can make some research information available. However, **you** must decide what stock to buy or sell, and when to do it. Their commissions are lower than those of full service brokers. There are also "deep discount" brokers whose commissions are even lower than those of the mainstream discounters.

- **Independent financial planners** sometimes handle individual securities. They may provide some research information, although generally not to the extent provided by full service stockbrokers. Their commissions fall somewhere between those of full service and discount brokers.

- **Direct purchase** from the company is a popular alternative. Although most companies won't directly sell the initial shares, some larger companies will reinvest your dividends in additional shares without sales fees. In addition, once you are a stockholder, some will even allow you to purchase additional shares directly from them without commissions. You must hold your shares in certificate form (instead of in a brokerage account) to do direct purchases.

If you want to invest in the stock market without worrying about making decisions on individual stocks, and if you want diversification and professional management, then we recommend mutual funds. They are discussed in the following chapter.

Guidelines

> ✓ *Only buy stocks with mid- to long-range goals in mind. They are not short-term investments.*

> ✓ *Be sure to investigate the company thoroughly before investing your money.*

> ✓ *Never buy anything from a stranger over the phone.*

> ✓ *Buy low and sell high. Don't panic when your stock drops.*

> ✓ *Don't invest all your money in just one company. Diversify.*

> ✓ *Don't give any broker the right to buy or sell without your prior approval.*

> ✓ *For maximum safety, buy stock mutual funds instead of individual stocks.*

Chapter 29

What Should I Know About Mutual Funds?

Mutual funds have become an extremely popular investment vehicle because of the increase in stock and bond prices over the past 10 years. As discussed previously, it is very difficult to choose individual investments on your own, especially since the markets are controlled by "the big boys." Therefore, we recommend mutual funds as a great way to invest.

A mutual fund is a unique type of investment company that receives money from individuals, then pools that money and invests it. The fund may invest in stocks, bonds, or other investments, depending upon its objective. Mutual funds are for people who, for one reason or another, don't want to take the risk or time to select stocks and bonds themselves, but would rather let professionals manage that for them.

There are three primary reasons why people invest in mutual funds:

- **Diversification.** If you own shares of one company, and that company's stock takes a big drop, you will suffer a major loss. However, if you own shares of a mutual fund that invests in hundreds of companies, then a similar drop in a particular stock should be insignificant.

- **Professional management.** We stated earlier how difficult it is to pick good companies on a continuing basis. Fund managers can't always do this either, but at least they have the resources to get information.

- **Affordable.** Unlike investments in individual stocks and bonds, mutual funds allow you to start with purchases as low as $25, although more and more are increasing the minimum to $250 - $1000. You may also make automatic drafts or additional contributions in amounts as low as $25.

TYPES OF MUTUAL FUNDS

There are as many kinds of mutual funds as there are classifications of investments.

Bond Funds

- **Government bond** funds invest in bonds backed by the United States Government. These can be Treasury bonds, bills, notes, and/or securities issued by agencies of the government, such as Ginnie Maes and Fannie Maes.

- **Tax-free bond** funds invest in municipal bonds that are free from federal income taxes. In addition, there are special state funds that invest only in securities issued by a particular state. That makes the interest free from state and local income taxes to residents of that state.

- **Corporate bond** funds invest in bonds issued by corporations. There are quality funds that invest only in higher quality bonds, and "high-yield" funds that invest in lower quality bonds.

Stock Funds

- **Balanced** funds invest in a combination of stocks and bonds. They provide growth opportunity with reduced risk.

- **Income** funds invest in companies (such as utilities) that pay high dividends.

- **Equity-income** funds invest in companies that are expected to provide growth in addition to paying dividends. They tend to invest in established companies that pay regular dividends.

- **Index** funds invest in the same stocks, and in the same percentage, as the various indices. Most index funds mirror the Standard & Poor's 500 Stock Index.

- **Growth** funds invest in companies with a good record of growth and potential for above-average returns.

- **Aggressive growth** funds invest in smaller companies that are expected to experience above average growth. These funds, while providing great upside potential, involve a larger amount of risk.

Specialty Funds

- **Sector** funds invest in companies in only one industry. For example, they might invest only in health companies, computer companies, or communications companies. Obviously, they provide great potential, but often at above-average risk.

- **Foreign** (International) funds invest in companies outside the United States. The largest holdings are usually in companies located in Japan and Europe, but that will change as the world economy expands.

- **Natural resource** and **precious metals** funds invest in companies engaged in the various aspects of natural resources (oil, gas, industrial metals) and precious metals (primarily gold and silver). Of these, precious metals funds are typically the most volatile.

HOW YOU MAKE MONEY

Mutual funds are only as good as the investments they make. They fluctuate in value with the stocks and bonds they own. If everything goes well, you make money from three sources: dividends, capital gains, and increasing share values.

Dividends

Companies in which the mutual funds invest pay interest (if they are bonds) and possibly dividends (if they are stocks) to the mutual fund. The degree of emphasis on dividends depends on whether the fund is a bond fund or a stock fund, and whether it is designed for income or growth.

- **Bond** funds invest in government, municipal, or corporate bonds, depending upon their objective. All these bonds pay interest to the mutual fund. When the fund receives this interest, they pay it to the shareholders and call it dividends. You may receive your dividends in cash, or have the mutual fund reinvest them in additional shares.

- **Stock** funds invest in shares issued by corporations. Some companies, usually the older, more established ones, pay dividends. When the mutual fund receives dividends, they pay them to the mutual fund holders, usually quarterly or annually. You may receive your dividends in cash or have them reinvested.

Capital gains

When the mutual fund sells the stocks or bonds in their portfolio, there is either a gain or a loss. The fund balances the gains and losses and pays you a "capital gains distribution." The amount of capital gains depends on the type of fund.

- **Bond** funds pay more in dividends than in capital

gains. Since bonds provide an income stream, capital gains are minimal.

- **Stock** funds, however, look for capital gains. Their primary objective is to invest in companies whose stock will increase in value. Although many of these also pay dividends, the main goal is capital gains.

Increase in value

People who aren't seeking income invest in mutual funds to achieve growth. Stocks have historically appreciated nicely, with obvious fluctuations along the way. Stock mutual funds are a way of participating in this growth.

BUYING MUTUAL FUNDS

Purchasing mutual funds is probably the easiest, least complicated way to invest. There are two ways to do this.

- **Buy directly** from the company. Many mutual funds sell directly to the public. These are called **no-loads,** because they don't charge a sales commission. You find the fund you want, call an "800" number, and ask them to send you information. You then complete the paperwork, send it back with your money, and voila, you're the proud owner of the fund. It is illegal for the phone representatives to provide investment advice unless they are licensed (virtually none are), so you are on your own.

- Through **investment firms.** On the other hand, you might not want to do it all by yourself. You may want some assistance. In this case, you go to a broker or financial planner. They are compensated by the mutual fund company. However, you really pay for their advice via a sales fee.

There are two types of funds sold by brokers: **front-end loads** and **back-end loads**. Front-end load funds charge a fee with each purchase, usually 3 to 6%, with a few charging as much as 8%. Back-end funds don't take anything out initially, but charge a little extra in the form of a service fee (called a 12b-1 fee) each year you hold the fund. In addition, they have a "deferred" sales charge, which means that if you sell it within the first five or six years, there is a decreasing sales charge on the redeemed principal only. For example, it might be 5% the first year, 4% the second, 3% the third, and so on until it disappears. Those fees don't apply to your earnings, however.

Given the choice between front-end and back-end loads, you are better paying up-front if you remain in the fund at least seven years. The sales charge is negligible in the long run.

PRICING MUTUAL FUNDS

Mutual fund shares are listed daily in the larger papers around the country. Some smaller newspapers list them only weekly. In addition, national papers like *The Wall Street Journal, USA Today,* and *Investor's Business Daily* have daily listings of mutual funds. When examining the mutual fund listings, you will see several columns:

FUND NAME	NAV	OFFER PRICE	NAV CHANGE
Kemper Growth	14.42	15.30	+0.17
Kemper Invst. Growth	17.92	17.92	+0.18
Janus Fund	19.58	NL	+0.14

- The **Fund Name** is listed under it's particular "family" name. A family of funds is a group of funds under the same management company, such as American, Fidelity, Kemper, Vanguard, etc.

- **Net Asset Value (NAV)** is the total value of the fund, divided by the number of shares outstanding. It is the true value of each share. Unlike stock, which trades at an arbitrary price, the net asset value of a mutual fund is its true value. It is the price you would get if you sold your shares at that time.

- **Offer Price** is what you pay for the fund. Look at the chart. With some funds, such as Kemper Growth, the offer price is higher than the NAV. That is a "front-end load" fund. Some, such as Janus Fund, show the letters "NL," which means "no load." You pay the net asset value when you purchase shares. The third type, Kemper Invest. Growth, shows the same number under the offer price and net asset value. It's an example of a "back-end" fund.

- **NAV Change** is the change in net asset value between the market close the day of the listing, and the previous day. The funds are priced at the close of business each day. The price that appears in a Thursday paper, for example, was Wednesday's closing price. The change is the difference between the close Wednesday and the close Tuesday.

Load vs. no-load

There has always been disagreement between advocates of load and no-load funds. This is something about which the two sides will never agree.

While nobody wants to pay a fee, that should not be your main consideration. Rather, you should concentrate on the performance of the fund. If you pay a fee and get good fund performance, then great. If you don't pay a fee and the fund doesn't perform well, you haven't saved anything.

Second, brokers and planners can provide valuable

assistance. If the advice you get is worthwhile, then it is worth the cost. Over the long-run, the effect of the fee is negligible.

Don't place so much focus on the fees that you lose track of your goal. Your concern should be the performance of the fund, after all fees and expenses. That is far more important than whether there is an initial fee.

Somewhere along the way, you have to pay, even with "no-loads." Since they don't pay commissions to brokers, they have to attract their money somehow. They do this by advertising heavily in financial publications. The cost of this, just like all fees, is born by the shareholders.

Doing it yourself

If you feel comfortable investing by yourself, then by all means do so. Go to your local library. Get a copy of *Morningstar*, which is a mutual fund rating service. Look at the annual mutual fund surveys in magazines such as *Money*, *Kiplinger's Personal Finance*, or *US News and World Report*. You will eventually see a pattern among the funds.

Once you have found a few that you would like to consider, call their toll-free numbers and ask for a prospectus. This document spells out all the information about the fund, including management fees, expenses, etc.

Make sure the fund's objective matches yours. For example, if you're looking for conservative growth, don't pick an aggressive growth fund. Once you've made your decision, don't panic if the market goes down. You will see fluctuation in the price of your shares, whether you like it or not!

Dollar cost averaging

If you want to accumulate money for the future, one of the best ways is by investing in growth mutual funds (or individual stocks) monthly. When you invest the same dollar amount regularly, it is known as "dollar cost averaging." With this method, you buy more shares when the price goes down and fewer shares when the price goes up. It is one of the reasons that people who invest monthly in retirement plans retire with significant savings.

Let's assume that you invested $100 per month in a mutual fund. Each month, you purchased as many shares as possible with your $100. Obviously, the lower the price, the more shares you purchased. Assume that during the first six months, your transactions looked like this:

Month	Investment	Price	# of Shares	Value
January	$100	$10	10.00	$100.00
February	$100	$8	12.50	$180.00
March	$100	$6	16.67	$235.02
April	$100	$5	20.00	$295.85
May	$100	$6	16.67	$455.04
June	$100	$8	12.50	$746.64
Total	$600		88.34	$746.64

You can see that after six months, you still had a profit of $146.64, the difference between the value ($746.64) and your investment ($600). This occurred even though your fund had dropped 50% by April, and still wasn't back to its original price by June. As dramatic as that gain may seem, it didn't even reflect additional shares from any dividends or capital gains. Dollar cost averaging is a great way to accumulate money and develop investment discipline.

Contractual plans

One poor method of purchasing mutual funds is a

contractual plan. In this program, you commit to investing a stated amount over a period of years. However, the fund is heavily front-end loaded with fees, with as much as 50% of the first year's payments going to expenses and commissions. Military members are special targets of these plans. Thankfully, few salespeople offer them.

Avoid these plans. Although you should stay away from contractual plans, realize that they differ from systematic investments (or dollar cost averaging). With dollar cost averaging, you make monthly investments from your checking account and can stop the bank-draft anytime without penalty. Don't sign anything that is going to commit you to investments that contain penalties if you stop putting in money. Make sure you understand the expenses before proceeding.

Guidelines

✓ *Use mutual funds for diversification and professional management. Diversify further using different funds.*

✓ *Choose funds whose objectives agree with yours.*

✓ *Plan to leave your money in stock funds for at least seven years.*

✓ *Use no-loads if you feel totally comfortable handling your own investment decisions.*

✓ *In the long-run, fund performance is more important than whether you pay a fee.*

✓ *If you can make monthly deposits, use dollar cost averaging to accumulate wealth.*

✓ *Avoid contractual plans.*

Chapter 30

What Investments Should Be Viewed With Skepticism?

There are several investments that may be inappropriate for you. Let's look at some:

- **Commodities and futures.** These are perhaps the riskiest of all investments. They sound attractive, because you can control a significant amount of gold, cattle, corn, etc., for a relatively small amount of money. **Avoid them.**

- **Options.** Options give you the right to buy or sell an individual stock or commodity at a certain price within a specified time frame. Next to commodities, they are the most speculative. **Stay away!**

- **Limited partnerships.** These investments haven't worked out as well as had been hoped. While a few may be beneficial in certain cases, in general they are probably not right for you. They are not very liquid. That means that you cannot get your money in case of an emergency or a change in plans. Although there is a resale market, the prices are usually a fraction of the original values.

- **Precious metals.** Gold and silver are okay as a small portion of your total portfolio. The best way to invest in these is by purchasing individual stocks or mutual funds that invest in precious metals. You can buy individual coins or bars, but you must store them. Do not buy gold and silver futures or options.

- **Direct solicitation.** This is not a product, but a way
  of doing business. Do not purchase anything over
  the phone from someone you don't know. There are
  operations nationwide that are designed to cheat
  people out of their money. They sell everything from
  oil wells to cellular phone franchises, wireless cable
  to free prizes (that always end up costing something),
  and low-priced stocks. They may tell you that you've
  qualified for a credit card, but they are just trying to
  drag information from you. **Just say NO!**

- **Time shares.** These are certainly not an investment,
  unless your objective is to lose money! A time share
  is a program where you buy a week's vacation at a
  resort with the option to trade for other locations.
  The problem is that they are overpriced and virtually
  impossible to sell. If you must own one, buy a resale
  for no more than one-third of the original cost.

Our best single piece of advice is: don't buy **anything**
over the phone from **anyone** you haven't worked with or met.
Don't commit to anything until you check it out. And definitely
don't send money in advance for anything and **don't give out
your credit card number** or **provide any personal information!**

Guidelines

✓ *If it sounds too good to be true, it probably is.*

✓ *Only deal with people you trust and in investments you
understand.*

✓ *Never invest if you feel pressured.*

✓ *If your instincts tell you not to do it, don't do it!*

✓ *Don't buy anything over the phone from a stranger, and
never give out any personal information.*

Chapter 31

Why Is Tax-Deferred
Growth So Valuable?

Tax-deferral is another type of tax-advantage. Unlike tax-free investments, in which the interest is never taxed, this method allows you to defer the earnings (and the taxes) until you make withdrawals. That is an important difference.

Nevertheless, there is a tremendous advantage in deferring the taxes on your earnings, especially considering the 1993 tax bill. This is especially true if you don't need current income.

Lucy had $50,000 in the bank earning 4%. Since she was in the 30% tax bracket, she lost approximately 1.2% of her 4% earnings to taxes. That meant she was earning only 2.8% after taxes. Lucy was 50 years old and felt she wouldn't need any income from that money until she was at least 65. She didn't want to buy tax-free bonds because she was afraid of losing principal if interest rates went up. She didn't want to take any risk, but she needed to net more than 2.8%.

Lucy's situation was not unique. In these days of lower interest rates, women are reaching out for higher returns. Unfortunately, most investments offering higher returns expose the investor to higher risk. Lucy, for one, didn't want to take **any** risk with her money.

What if Lucy can invest her money, virtually risk-free, but defer taxes on the interest until she withdraws it? Would that be much of an advantage? It sure would!

Look at the value of tax-deferring income at various interest rates over a 25-year period, assuming a 30% tax bracket:

Interest Rate	Tax-Deferred Value	Taxable Value	Tax-Deferred Advantage
4%	$133,292	$99,724	$33,568
5%	$169,932	$118,162	$51,770
6%	$214,594	$139,850	$74,744

You can see the definite advantage of deferring taxes!

Tax-deferred fixed annuity

Where is this investment available? In a "tax-deferred annuity." This investment (TDA for short) is like a tax-deferred certificate of deposit. You invest your money and it simply grows. The primary difference is that taxes on the interest in a TDA are not due until the money is withdrawn. Therefore, not only do you earn interest on your money, you also earn interest on the money you would have sent to Uncle Sam.

Earnings are tax-deferred because TDAs are issued by insurance companies, which operate under a special set of tax laws. President Bush tried to do away with the preferential treatment of annuities in early 1992, but was forced to drop his proposal when the opposition grew too strong. It is one of the few safe, tax-advantaged investments remaining.

Social Security benefits

In 1993, the amount of Social Security benefits included as taxable income increased. However, money accumulated in an annuity isn't taxable until you withdraw it. Not only do you defer income taxes on the interest, but you get to keep more of your Social Security benefits.

TDA vs. the bank

As a rule, tax-deferred annuities pay higher interest rates

than banks. The following chart shows Lucy's advantage if she had invested $50,000 in a TDA at 6% per year, instead of a $50,000 CD at 4% a year, fully taxable. Remember, she was 50 years old when she made the decision.

Lucy's Age	Tax-Deferred Accumulated Value	CD (Taxable) Accumulated Value	Tax-Deferred Advantage
55	$66,911	$57,292	$9,620
60	$89,542	$65,646	$23,896
70	$160,357	$86,189	$74,168
75	$214,594	$98,758	$115,836
80	$287,175	$113,160	$174,015
85	$384,304	$129,662	$254,642

She would have had a tremendous advantage by choosing tax-deferred growth over the CD.

Taking income

The argument against tax-deferred annuities is always, "That's great. But I'm not going to leave my money in forever. What happens if I need income?"

That's the beauty of tax-deferred annuities. With this product, you may start drawing your income anytime you want. Let's look at Lucy's situation and assume she begins taking income at age 75 and interest rates remain the same.

Lucy's Age	Tax-Deferred Accumulated Value	Bank CD Accumulated Value	Tax-Deferred Advantage
75	$214,594	$98,758	$115,836
Rate	6%	4%	
Income	$12,876	$3,950	$8,926

You can see that in 25 years, Lucy's income (based on current interest and tax rates) will be substantially greater by tax-deferring her money. The 6% tax-deferred annuity will pay her $12,876 annually, before taxes. The 4% CD will pay her only $3,950 annually, before taxes. That will be 225% more income!

Withdrawing the money

Another frequent remark is, "I'll get killed with taxes when I take all my money out." That is not necessarily true. Let's see what will happen if Lucy decides to take all the money out in a lump sum at age 75. Obviously, there will be no additional taxes due from the CD, since she paid taxes along the way. However, taxes on the growth ($214,594 minus $50,000) of the annuity will be due upon surrender of the contract. We'll even assume that by the time she reaches 75, her tax rate has gone up to 45%. (Everyone worries about taxes going up!)

Lucy's Age 75	Tax-Deferred Accumulated Value	Bank CD Accumulated Value	Tax-Deferred Advantage
Value	$214,594	$98,758	$115,836
Tax	- $74,067	0	
Net	$140,527	$98,758	$41,769

Even if she took all the money in one lump sum, which would be the worst alternative, and paid 45% taxes on the gain of $164,594, she would still come out ahead by putting her money in the tax-deferred annuity instead of the CD.

All is not rosy. Let's look at the possible disadvantages.

- Tax-deferred annuities are offered by insurance companies, so your money is only as safe as the company. We explained the way to judge insurance companies in Chapter 18.

- There are rarely front-end fees when you invest in an annuity. Instead, there are surrender charges for withdrawing principal in the first five to nine years. However, most companies will allow you to withdraw 10% of your principal annually, penalty-free. There are generally no surrender fees on earnings.

- There is a 10% IRS penalty for any earnings withdrawn prior to age 59½. First dollars out are considered earnings, not principal.

- Taxes on the interest do have to be paid at some point. However, that's not a real disadvantage because you have avoided taxes all the previous years.

Annuitizing

Another way to get money from an annuity is to "annuitize." That means you relinquish ownership of the money in exchange for lifetime income. Because this money is partially a return of your principal, only a portion of the income is taxable. However, we rarely, if ever, recommend this option.

If you decide to annuitize, you have several income options from which to choose. First, you can receive income as long as you live. The problem with that, however, is that if you die the first year, all the money reverts to the insurance company. Second, you can receive income for a stated period, for example ten years. The problem with that is if you live more than ten years, you receive no further income. Third, a compromise is income for life, with a guarantee for at least ten years. That at least allows your children to get something if you die within the first few years. The problem with this choice, however, is that you get less income than with the other options.

In any case, once beyond the guarantee period, your heirs never receive anything, including your original principal. That belongs to the insurance company. That is why we advise most people **not to annuitize.** Instead, just take monthly interest and withdraw part of your principal as needed. That way, your heirs will still receive the money upon your death and you will always own the principal in case of an emergency.

Tax-deferred variable annuity

A variable annuity is another form of tax-deferred annuity for those looking for growth and willing to assume more risk. In our example, Lucy didn't want to take any risk. However, some people like the idea of tax-deferred growth, but want more growth than traditional fixed annuities provide.

In a variable annuity, your money is invested in one or more different accounts. Choices include a fixed account (like a fixed annuity) plus several mutual fund choices, called "separate accounts." This gives you the opportunity to attain higher growth and diversification.

Of course, with that opportunity comes higher risk. Variable annuities have a unique benefit not found in any other investments. Upon death, the amount paid to your beneficiaries will be at least the amount you invested. It will be the **greater** of the amount you invested or the actual value. That means if the stock market drops before you die, at worst your beneficiaries will get your original investment back. If your investment increases in value, then your beneficiaries will receive that amount. Your heirs can't lose . . . as long as you die!

For this guarantee and the tax advantages, there are additional costs. Most annuities have an annual fee of $25-$30, plus general and administrative expenses in the 1 to 2% range. This reduces your yield. Nevertheless, good performance in the accounts will overcome the additional expenses.

Advantages & disadvantages

There are many advantages with tax-deferred annuities.

Tax-deferral makes money grow faster. Growth doesn't count against the taxability of Social Security, unless withdrawn. There is no risk of loss upon your death (assuming safety of insurance company). You may receive income whenever you need it. The death benefit avoids probate by going directly to the named beneficiary or beneficiaries. If the beneficiary is a spouse, the proceeds can be put into an annuity in the spouse's name **with no taxes due.** It can provide an income for life. There typically are no up-front sales charges. Income can be received (many companies allow up to 10% per year) free of company surrender charges, although subject to 10% IRS penalties if you are under age 59½. And, unlike an IRA, you can invest as much as you like in any year and let your money accumulate indefinitely.

There are also several disadvantages. The company imposes surrender charges if you redeem the annuity within the first five to nine years. You must choose a quality insurance company. Your gain is taxable when redeemed or upon death, if not left to a spouse. There is a 10% IRS penalty if earnings are withdrawn before age 59½. And you face a possible loss of principal in a variable annuity for money withdrawn before death.

Guidelines

- ✓ *The higher your tax bracket, and the longer your time frame, the greater the positive impact of tax-deferral.*

- ✓ *Use tax-deferred annuities to accumulate money for future needs.*

- ✓ *Use variable annuities if you are willing to accept higher risk for greater rewards.*

- ✓ *Do not "annuitize." If you need income, just make withdrawals.*

Chapter 32

What Should I Know About My Retirement Plan?

In the past, most employers totally funded their employees' retirement plans. They made all the contributions, while sometimes giving employees the option of additionally contributing their own money. However, all that has changed.

The burden has been shifted to employees to provide for their own retirement. Companies are reducing their own contributions while providing vehicles for their employees to set aside money. If you don't put away money for retirement, it won't be there. Thankfully, there are several good ways to do this.

If you want to retire with a large sum, the best way to do it is through your employer's voluntary retirement plan. The primary benefits are **before-tax contributions** and **tax-deferred growth**.

PRE-TAX SAVINGS PLAN - 401(k)

One of the best retirement plans available is a 401(k). You can defer part of your salary by having your employer deposit it into a special account. Your money goes into the account free of taxes, except for Social Security taxes.

This voluntary plan grows tax-deferred until you take distributions, preferably after age 59½. At that point, whatever you withdraw directly from the plan is taxable.

Contributions

Your employer's plan sets the maximum percentage of income you may defer, but it is subject to an IRS imposed dollar cap that increases each year with inflation. The cap in 1994 is $9,240.

In addition, many companies match their employees' contributions. For example, they might contribute $1 for every $10 you invest. The total contributions of the employer and employee cannot exceed 25% of your income, with a maximum contribution of $30,000.

Withdrawals

You may withdraw your money under certain circumstances. Generally, you may not withdraw funds until you reach age 59½ or retire. There are a few exceptions: if you leave the company, become disabled, show hardship, the plan terminates, the company is sold, or you die.

Hardship

If you meet certain IRS rules, you can qualify for the hardship exemption. This allows you to withdraw money for the purchase of a home, certain tuition payments, threat of eviction, and medical expenses. Always remember, however, that if you choose to use that money today, you lose both the money and potential growth on it for your retirement years. If you do qualify for a hardship exemption, you must still pay income taxes, plus the 10% IRS penalty if you are under age 59½.

Loans

Many plans give you the opportunity to borrow money. This is certainly better than taking a hardship withdrawal, because no tax is due on the loan. The maximum you can borrow is limited to $50,000 or 50% of your balance, whichever is less. However, if your account is worth $20,000 or less, you can borrow up to $10,000.

Your loan must be repaid over a five year period, unless you borrow to purchase a home, in which case you have 10 years to repay. You must establish a payment schedule and adhere to it. Otherwise, your loan becomes taxable. If you use the loan to purchase a home, the interest you pay is deductible. It is also deductible if you use the money for investment purposes. But don't do this. It's a bad idea.

If you leave your employer and have a loan outstanding, you need to pay it back. Otherwise, it becomes taxable.

Retirement

Upon retirement, you can withdraw your money (and possibly qualify for special averaging), or move it to an IRA rollover. The IRA rollover is normally more advantageous because it defers the taxes until you take income. Unless you need cash immediately, it usually makes sense to roll it over.

Under current law, if you receive the money directly, your employer must withhold 20% of it for taxes, even if you eventually move it into an IRA rollover. To avoid the tax, do a "trustee to trustee" transfer. In other words, have your plan trustee transfer it directly to a new trustee. Employers have special forms for this, as do investment companies and banks.

Pre-59½ distributions

Under normal circumstances, distributions taken before age 59½ are subject to the 10% IRS penalty. There are several exceptions, including: leaving your employer after the age of 55; your death or disability; leaving prior to age 59½, but taking "substantially equal payments" over your lifetime; or payments made as the result of a Qualified Domestic Relations Order as the result of your divorce.

TAX-SHELTERED ANNUITY - 403(b)

Tax-sheltered annuities are available for employees of tax-exempt organizations, such as hospitals and school systems. You may have part of your salary withheld and deposited to the account. Your employer may also choose to contribute.

Contributions

Generally, the maximum salary reduction is $9,500 per year. The employer may also contribute, but the total may not exceed 25% of your pay or $30,000.

Withdrawals

You can get money out of your plan under several circumstances. Generally, you may not withdraw funds until you reach age 59½ or retire. However, there are a few exceptions: if you leave your employer, become disabled, show hardship, the plan terminates, or you die.

Hardship

It's not easy to qualify for this exemption. The IRS limits the qualification to: purchase of a home, certain tuition payments, threat of eviction, and medical expenses. If you qualify for a hardship exemption, you must still pay income taxes plus a 10% IRS penalty if you are under age 59½.

Catch-up provision

If you have been with an employer for 15 years and didn't always contribute the maximum, there is a catch-up provision that may allow you to make additional contributions.

Loans

Loans are better than hardship withdrawals since there

are no taxes on loans. The maximum you can borrow is $50,000 or 50% of your balance, whichever is less. If your account is less than $20,000, you can borrow up to $10,000.

Your loan must be repaid over a five year period, unless you borrow to purchase a home, in which case you have 10 years to repay. You must establish a set payment schedule and adhere to it. Otherwise, your loan becomes taxable. If you use the loan to purchase a home, the interest you pay is deductible. It is also deductible if the money is used for investment purposes. But don't do this. It's a bad idea!

Retirement

Upon retirement, you can take money out of your 403(b) in cash (and possibly qualify for special averaging), or move it to an IRA rollover. The IRA rollover defers the taxes until you make withdrawals. Unless you need the cash immediately, it usually makes sense to choose the IRA rollover.

Under current law, if you take the money directly, your employer must withhold 20% for taxes, even if you eventually move it into an IRA rollover. To avoid the tax, do a "trustee to trustee" transfer. In other words, have your plan trustee transfer it directly to a new trustee. Your employer has special forms for this, as do investment companies and banks.

Pre-59½ distributions

Under normal circumstances distributions taken before the day you reach age 59½ are subject to the 10% IRS penalty. There are several exemptions, including leaving your employer after the age of 55; your death or disability; leaving before age 59½ but taking "substantially equal payments" over your lifetime; or payments made as the result of a Qualified Domestic Relations Order due to your divorce.

DEFERRED COMPENSATION - SECTION 457

State and local government employees may participate in a deferred compensation plan, known as Section 457.

Contributions

You may contribute 33⅓% of your salary up to a maximum of $7,500 annually.

Withdrawals

You may withdraw money when you leave your employer, reach age 70½, or qualify for a hardship exemption.

Hardship

Generally, you can withdraw money due to an "unforeseen emergency," assuming you can't get the money elsewhere. The IRS specifically **excludes** a home or education as a hardship.

Catch-up

An attractive feature of this plan is the ability to make up for previously missed contributions. Your limit is $15,000, up to three years in arrears.

Loans

No loans are available.

Retirement

What makes this plan unattractive is the fact that it cannot be rolled over into an IRA upon retirement. That means that you cannot maintain complete control over this plan after you retire like you can in the previous two. You must leave your money in the plan or take a cash distribution. If you do the latter, you cannot take advantage of special averaging.

THRIFT SAVINGS PLAN - CIVIL SERVICE

Civil Service employees have recently been able to participate in a voluntary plan, known as the Thrift Savings Plan. It is an integral part of the newer Federal Employees Retirement System (FERS). Your money grows tax-deferred until you take it out, preferably after age 59½. At that point, whatever you withdraw directly is taxable.

Contributions

FERS employees are permitted to contribute up to 10% of their salary (5% for Civil Service Retirement System employees) into the fund. In 1994, the maximum deferral is $9,240. The cap increases each year with inflation.

Government matching

The government matches employee contributions up to a maximum of five per cent. Even if FERS employees choose not to make contributions, the government still kicks in 1% of their salaries into the Thrift Savings Plan. There is no employer matching for CSRS employees.

Withdrawals

Although you can withdraw money from your plan under special circumstances, generally you may not withdraw funds until you have reached the age of 59½. Exceptions are: if you separate from service, become disabled, or die.

Hardship loans

The TSP program allows loans for certain situations,

including purchase of a home, education and medical expenses, and "financial hardship." But remember, when it's gone, it's gone. College or home purchases, for example, are not exactly unforeseeable events. Don't touch your retirement savings except for true emergencies, or you'll end up with nothing!

Retirement

When you retire, you can withdraw money one of several ways: you can take it in cash, receive an annuity, or transfer it to an IRA rollover. The latter is more advantageous because it defers the taxes until you make withdrawals. Unless you need the cash immediately, it makes sense to roll it over.

Under current law, if you take money directly, TSP must withhold 20% for taxes, even if you immediately roll it into an IRA. To avoid the withholding, you should do a "trustee to trustee" transfer. In other words, have your plan trustee (TSP) transfer it directly to a new IRA trustee. The National Finance Center supplies you with the forms.

Investments

You currently have three investment choices. The C fund is a common stock index fund; the F fund is invested in a corporate bond index fund; and the G fund is a short-term U.S. Government fund packaged especially for TSP. Money managers are periodically selected by lowest bid. Changes between investments are somewhat restricted, so stay abreast of current rules and "open seasons."

INDIVIDUAL RETIREMENT ACCOUNTS

Once extremely popular, IRAs (Individual Retirement Accounts) lost their luster when Congress eliminated the tax advantages for some people. Nevertheless, IRAs are still quite attractive.

Contribution

You may contribute 100% of your earned income, up to a maximum of $2,000 per calendar year into an IRA.

Deductibility

Your contribution may or may not be tax-deductible. To qualify for the deduction, you must meet certain criteria:

- If neither you nor your husband participate in a qualified retirement plan, you may deduct your $2,000 contribution, regardless of your income.

- If you (or your husband) participate in an employer sponsored plan, then you may deduct 100% of your contribution only if:

    You're single and your adjusted gross income is below $25,000. If it is above $35,000, you may not deduct anything. In between, you can deduct a pro-rata share.

    You're married and your adjusted gross income is below $40,000. If it is above $50,000, you may not deduct anything. In between, you can deduct a pro-rata share.

Withdrawals

Generally, you cannot withdraw money from your IRA prior to age 59½ without facing the 10% IRS penalty. However, there are several exceptions: death, disability, or systematic payout over five years or until age 59½, whichever is longer.

Loans

Forget it. You cannot borrow money from your IRA.

Any loan is treated as a distribution. You can't even use your IRA as collateral for a loan without jeopardizing its tax status and incurring the penalty. The only exception is that you can make withdrawals interest-free as long as you repay the money within 60 days.

Investments

When IRAs were first introduced, bank rates were extremely high. CDs were in the range of 15 to 16%! As a result, most of the money invested in IRAs went to banks and savings & loans.

However, all that has changed. The drop in interest rates, along with the great performance of mutual funds, has resulted in more money being invested in the latter. You may choose from several investment alternatives:

- **Banks and credit unions** all offer IRA accounts. Most of this money is deposited into certificates of deposit.

- **Brokerage firms** offer "self-directed" IRA accounts. This means that you can choose from a number of investments, such as stocks, bonds, partnerships, and mutual funds.

- **Mutual funds** have special custodian arrangements with various financial institutions. This allows you to invest your IRA money in mutual funds.

INVESTING YOUR RETIREMENT MONEY

Your retirement plan should have a variety of investment choices. Typically included are stock and bond accounts, a money market, and possibly your company's common stock.

We recommend that during your accumulation years, you invest most of your money in the growth accounts. Remember what we said about long-term growth: the stock market and mutual funds historically have outperformed most other choices over longer (10 years or greater) periods of time.

In addition, since you are investing monthly, if the value drops, that just means that you will buy more shares or units for the same amount of money. Actually, it is better for your fund to go down while you're contributing. That means you are buying at lower prices. You will be taking advantage of "dollar cost averaging" as discussed in Chapter 29.

Higher returns

Most people get too conservative when it comes to investing. They are afraid of losing money, so they pick the guaranteed accounts. **That is the worst mistake you can make.** You must achieve higher rates. Therefore, you need to invest your retirement plan in growth accounts. Don't panic over market fluctuations and sudden drops. In the long-run, you'll still be ahead.

Look at the difference between $100 per month invested at various average returns for 10, 20, 30, and 40 years:

Years	4%	8%	12%
10	$14,725	$18,295	$23,004
20	$36,667	$58,902	$98,926
30	$69,405	$149,035	$349,496
40	$118,196	$349,101	$1,176,477

If you are under age 40, you should be 100% in growth accounts. If you feel the need to be more conservative as you get older, you can start moving some money slowly from the growth to the fixed accounts.

Not participating

Having a voluntary retirement plan is one of the greatest privileges and benefits you'll ever have. Yet, most people fail to take full advantage of it. They are always waiting until they "have enough money" to invest. Face it. You will never have **enough.** However, if you don't participate, you won't have **anything** when you retire.

Again, it's a matter of priority. Most people choose to spend their money today rather than saving for tomorrow. We recommend the opposite approach. The difference is staggering.

When Megan, age 30, completed her first year of teaching, she became eligible for her system's 403(b) plan. It consisted of seven different accounts: some growth, some guaranteed, some in-between. She was already saving money each month by having it automatically deducted and deposited into her savings account at the credit union. In fact, she was saving over $300 per month. She liked that. It was safe, and she could get to it anytime she wanted. As a result, she turned down the 403(b), figuring she'd start it "someday."

Let's examine her decision **not** to participate in the 403(b) and see what it actually cost. To make the comparison fair, we must realize that the money in the bank goes in **after-tax,** but the deposit into the 403(b) goes in **before-tax.**

Therefore, if she takes $333 of her earnings and puts it in the bank, she really only has $233 of that savings after taxes (her tax rate is 30%). In addition, if the interest rate is 5%, she keeps only 3.5% after taxes. On the other hand, the full $333 goes into the 403(b), and all earnings are tax-deferred. Look at the difference:

Years	Bank CD 5% before tax	Retirement Plan 10% growth	Retirement Plan Advantage
5	$15,845	$25,789	$9,944
10	$36,181	$68,212	$32,031
15	$62,278	$138,019	$75,741
20	$95,771	$252,870	$157,099
25	$138,753	$441,834	$303,081
30	$193,916	$752,743	$558,827
35	$262,709	$1,264,281	$1,001,572

This example assumes that Megan invests $333 per month and does not even increase her investment as her earnings increase. The advantage in the tax-sheltered annuity is both obvious and significant. You are making a big mistake if you don't contribute as much as you can to your employer's retirement plan . . . **and leave it there!**

Guidelines

✓ *If your employer offers a retirement plan, jump on it!*

✓ *Participate as fully as possible . . . preferably contributing the maximum.*

✓ *Start participating today! You are never too young, nor too old, to begin.*

✓ *The more years until retirement, the more growth-oriented (aggressive) you should be with your investment choices.*

✓ *Don't be too conservative. That is the most common error made and the single reason that savers still don't have enough at retirement.*

Part Four

Application

Chapter 33

How Do I Set My Financial Goals?

Now is the time to apply what you have learned up to this point. In this section, you will learn various ways to meet your financial goals. Before you can meet your goals, you must set them. That is what this chapter is all about.

> Elizabeth was an administrative assistant earning $24,000 per year. She had $15,000 in credit card debt and three children to feed. She wrote in her journal, "I just finished paying my bills and I'm depressed. It seems like all I do is pay bills. I'm sick of it. I am going to get out of debt by the end of the year. That gives me 10 months to get everything paid off. I'm ripping up all my credit cards except one."

Goals are worthless unless they are specific. Otherwise, like Elizabeth's journal entry, they are just wishes and good intentions. The road to the poor house is paved with good intentions.

There are no right or wrong goals from a personal standpoint. However, there **are** right and wrong goals **if you want to be financially secure.** While we generally say that you should be comfortable with your goals, sometimes you need to be uncomfortable. As they say in sports, "no pain, no gain." Goals cannot be "pipe dreams."

Characteristics of goals

A goal, to be legitimate, must possess several characteristics. It must be **realistic, specific, manageable,** and **obvious** when accomplished.

When setting a goal, there are four questions you must

197

ask yourself. **What** is my goal? **When** do I want to achieve it? **How** am I going to achieve it? How will I **know** when I have achieved it?

Financial goal setting is no different from goal setting for a trip. For example, if we want to drive from Atlanta to Los Angeles, we can't just load up the car and drive out the driveway. Obviously, it is a long journey that will take 5-6 days and cover 3200 miles. We must have a definite plan that answers the four questions above. First, let's see how it fits our definition of a goal.

Our goal: drive to Los Angeles. Is it realistic? Yes. Is it specific? Yes. Is it in manageable units? It will be. Will we know when we have achieved it? Yes.

So our goal (to drive to Los Angeles) definitely meets the qualifications for a legitimate goal. However, before we leave, we still need to answer the four questions necessary to reach our goal. We need specifics, not generalities. Let's address each.

- **What is our goal?** To drive to Los Angeles.

- **When do we want to achieve it?** We want to leave Saturday morning and arrive by Thursday afternoon.

- **How are we going to achieve it?** This is where the work comes in. We have to get a road map and plan our exact route. Next, we have to find out the number of miles (3200) and divide it by the number of days we are going to travel (5.5). Therefore, we know that we have to average 580 miles a day. We will average 50 miles per hour, so we must drive 11½ hours for the first 5 days and 6½ hours the final day.

- **How will we know when we have achieved our goal?** When we see the "Welcome to Los Angeles" sign.

Setting your financial goals is just like setting travel goals. They must meet all the qualifications.

Realistic

Remember Elizabeth's goal to pay off her debts by the end of the year? Let's see how it fits the characteristics:

- Was it realistic? Not on her salary.
- Was it specific? Somewhat.
- Was it in manageable units? No.
- Will she know when she has achieved it? Yes.

Her goal does not qualify. While getting out of debt is a worthy goal, it is not realistic for her to pay off $15,000 worth of debts on a $24,000 salary. Instead, she must develop a schedule of payments that will allow her to pay off those debts within three to four years.

Specific

Your goal must be specific in nature. To live "comfortably" is not a goal. You can't define "comfortable." You must be specific and set landmarks to determine when you actually reach that goal.

Frances hated her job. She felt unfulfilled and unappreciated. She wanted to find a "better" job as soon as she could. She found a different job, but soon realized that it wasn't "better."

Most people want to better themselves. However, "better" is a relative term, not sufficiently specific to target. Frances should have listed the pros and cons of her current job, and listed the qualifications that her new job should have. Then, she could have found one that would fulfill her aspirations.

Time table

You must set a definite time frame on the goal. It can't be open ended.

> *Martha and Bill decided to set up a retirement plan. Their goal was to have enough money to retire when they were "ready." However, they never defined when that day would be. Therefore, when they were "ready," their money wasn't!*

A common mistake is setting goals without a specific date in mind. This makes it nothing more than an open-ended wish list. Martha and Bill should have set a specific date and worked toward that end.

Manageable units

You must break your financial goals down to manageable units. When you eat a steak, you don't shove the whole thing down your throat - you take small bites. You've heard the expression: "How do you eat an elephant? One bite at a time." The same goes for goal setting. You must break your goal into bite-size pieces.

> *Anne wanted her daughter, Caroline, to go to college. She started a savings account and deposited money "whenever she could." When Caroline was ready for college, there wasn't enough money in the account.*

Anne made a common mistake. She didn't target a realistic amount for her goal (college), nor did she calculate how much she would have to invest monthly to achieve it.

Obvious when accomplished

Not all goals are as obvious as the "Welcome to Los Angeles" sign. For example, being "comfortable" is not obvious enough to be meaningful. Make sure your goal could light up a marquee flashing "Congratulations! You made it!"

For example

- My goal is to pay off my Sears credit card.
- I have to pay the balance of $2200.
- I will accomplish this within 15 months.
- I will do this by paying $168 per month (including interest).
- I will know I have achieved my goal when I receive my bill from Sears with a zero balance.

Now you do it

1. My goal is to _____

   _____

2. I have to _____

   _____

3. I will accomplish this by _____

   _____

4. I will do this by _____

   _____

5. I will know I have achieved my goal when _____

   _____

Set some financial goals with definite time frames. If the ones we list are important to you, complete the appropriate time table. Feel free to add your own.

GOAL	PROJECTED COMPLETION DATE	ACTUAL COMPLETION DATE
Pay off Credit Cards		
Pay off Mortgage		
Begin College Fund		
Complete College Fund		
Begin Retirement Plan		
Retire		
Begin Savings Plan		
Build (Buy) New Home		
Pay off College Loan		

As you see, goals are more than wishes. They must be well thought-out, specific, and carefully planned. Therefore, to successfully achieve most financial goals you need to answer three questions. By what **date** will I achieve my goal? How much money will I **need**? How much will I have to **pay** (or save) each month to achieve it?

Retirement goals are a little more complicated. By what **date** do I want to retire? How much **income** (in today's dollars) will I need? How much will it be **worth** when I factor in inflation? What **rate** will I earn during that time? How much will I need to **invest** each month to achieve that goal?

Consequences

You must consider the consequences of all aspects of your goals. You must visualize the consequences of both **achieving** and **not achieving** your goals.

Let's say your goal is to invest $75 a month for your daughter's education. What are the consequences of both accomplishing that goal and not accomplishing it? If you reach your goal, she can go to the college of her choice. She can concentrate on her studies and make the most of her intellect without becoming sidetracked by financial burdens. That will enable her to get a quality job with a good salary because she will have the skills and education.

On the other hand, if you don't achieve that goal, what might happen? She might have to quit college and go to work. She might not go to college at all. She might have to attend a trade school or go straight to work. She won't have the education required for a really great career.

You get the picture. Fantasize about the consequences. Stick up pictures and notes that remind you of your goals. It will help you stay motivated.

Guidelines

✓ *Set definite, specific goals for yourself, both financially and in other areas.*

✓ *Your goals must answer: what, when, how, and have a landmark of accomplishment.*

✓ *You must break your goals into achievable small steps so you can maintain a sense of accomplishment.*

✓ *You must visualize the pain of not accomplishing your goals, as well as the pleasure of achieving them.*

Chapter 34

How Can I Get The Best Job?

Your ability to be financially secure depends on having sufficient income. Usually, that involves obtaining a new job or improving your current employment.

Women who have been in the workplace more than 15 years already lived the adage, "a woman has to be twice as good as a man to earn half as much." Pay scales are becoming more equitable in some career fields, but the glass ceiling is still firmly in place. Now the lament seems to be, "a woman has to be twice as good as her male counterpart to climb half as far up the corporate ladder."

Wherever you are on the corporate ladder, there are certain keys that will help you move up the rungs, not the least of which is your ability to be assertive. Since many widows and divorcees are suddenly plunged into the job market with little preparation, let's start at the beginning.

Displaced homemakers

When you have been out of the marketplace for years, it can be very intimidating to look for a job. You are competing with young people who seem to exude energy, self-assurance, and computer literacy. You may be lacking computer skills completely. Your other office skills may have become rusty or gone by the wayside with technological changes in office equipment.

The advances in technology, more than any other single factor, account for the problems you may be facing. In fact, this is so prevalent that there is a special label for women in this situation. If you are entering the work force after five years of homemaking, and have limited job skills, you are officially known as a "displaced homemaker." The biggest problems faced by displaced homemakers are low self-esteem, limited technical education (or outdated skills), and lack of child care.

Education

Education is the key to getting out of this rut. It is the best and fastest way to conquer low self-esteem and inadequate job skills. If you feel intimidated and out-of-step, enroll in a course or seminar for displaced homemakers. Most vocational and community colleges offer such programs. Some are free, others are very inexpensive. A variety of state and federal assistance programs are also available for displaced homemakers, some of which even provide free transportation to classes. An additional advantage of displaced homemaker classes is that you can learn about the best career fields in your geographic area for employment, job security, and pay.

Child care

The child care issue presents a number of problems which you must resolve in order to take even the smallest vocational step. Day care is available through special government programs, as well as for-profit centers. There are a number of competent people who keep children in their homes. You can barter or trade services with someone who will keep your children, or even swap child care times with a friend.

The problem that sneaks up on women is the need for alternative child care. Always have a backup. It's amazing how devastating this can be for women who are unprepared. And it's amazing how few prepare for the unexpected child care problems, especially when they are such a common occurrence in both school and the workplace.

SEEKING EMPLOYMENT

Once you are ready to take the plunge and actively seek employment, there are a few guidelines that should separate you from the rest of the pack.

Never ask friends and social acquaintances for jobs. The exception to this is if they are advertising a specific job for which you know you are qualified. In any other situation, this crosses the bounds of what is acceptable in business circles. Worst of all, it puts your friends on the spot.

You've been such a great friend, sticking with us through Carl's illness and death. Now I really need to go back to work and support myself, but I'm not sure what job skills I might have. Do you have anything I can do at your office?

This puts both you and your friend in an awkward position, and may damage your relationship permanently.

Ask friends and social acquaintances for advice about jobs. People love to give advice and show off their knowledge. They may or may not choose to provide the names of contact people. By simply asking for advice, you give them permission to provide as much or as little help as they are comfortable sharing. There is no pressure or obligation that can later come back to haunt your relationship if things don't work out.

I have a lot of experience with bookkeeping. Do you know of anyone who wants to hire a bookkeeper?

Don't tell your prospective employer that you were recently widowed or divorced. While you may gain some sympathy at first, it soon works to your disadvantage. The employer may begin to underrate your ability to handle the job. You may be discounted as being unable to cope with crisis. In addition, you may be perceived as likely to have excessive absences. Always be *very* businesslike in any job situation.

Use only realistic resumes. Too many "experts" advise women to think up every voluntary position they have ever held and shape a resume with all those experiences. Prospective employers often find this unprofessional.

> *I appreciate this interview, Mr. Smith. Here is my resume. As you can see, I have not worked outside the home for many years. But I have successfully handled many volunteer roles, as listed. I taught preschoolers in Sunday School for seven years, was a room mother for six years, led a Girl Scout troop for three years, and I have been teaching choir for elementary children for two years. I can handle responsibility. Oh? What position am I applying for? I'm interested in the salesclerk position that was advertised.*

Since the salesclerk position had no relevance to any of the "resume" skills, the resume was a waste of Sandra's time and the employer's. If you haven't worked outside the home, be straightforward and say so. Relate any skills you have to the job you are seeking.

If the job for which you are applying is an entry position, then having a prepared resume is neither expected nor necessary. Only bring information that is pertinent to the position for which you are applying.

On the other hand, your volunteer experiences can provide a credible background if they are related to the specific job that you want. Linda's interview shows a good use for a resume with volunteer skills.

> *Thank you for seeing me, Mr. Johnson. As you can see from my resume, I have established an excellent track record of skills that fulfill the requirements of this position. You need someone for telemarketing and to supervise a group of young people who must be picked up at the train station each evening and shuttled back after work. As president of the Parent-Teachers Organization, I was responsible for supervising individuals and committees, organizing schedules, and setting goals and time limits. I phoned each member at least monthly and contacted all prospects. I have also been responsible for carpooling youngsters on*

a daily basis for the past six years, without a single accident or problem. I'm sure you can see that I have the proven capability of handling this position.

While resumes should put you in the best light, they should be realistic and honest. Don't underplay your past achievements, but don't make yourself look overqualified for the job, either.

Use your own name. "Mrs. John Doe" is a social title, not a workplace name. Instead of titles, use "Mary Jane Doe."

Be positive about yourself. This is true before, during, and after interviews. You can talk yourself and others into believing anything. So be positive. Psych yourself up. Believe in yourself before the interview. Visualize yourself feeling confident, relaxed, and having an enjoyable conversation. During the interview, speak only in positive terms about yourself and others. Afterwards, pat yourself on the back for having completed the interview. If it didn't go as well as you would have liked, don't knock yourself. Instead, ask yourself, "What did I do that was good? What should I do differently next time?" Use every experience as a learning experience. Say, "I'm learning and I'm getting better."

Be professional. This is not a social call. Sit forward on the seat with good posture, legs uncrossed and knees together. Make eye contact with the interviewer. Speak clearly and distinctly, without rushing. Take a slow breath as you think about the question before answering. It gives you time to compose your answer, makes you appear thoughtful, and helps you relax. Speak loudly enough to sound confident. Avoid prattling small talk, boisterous laughter, and other party behavior. Keep your hands relaxed in your lap, using them only to emphasize your dialogue in natural gestures, without overdoing it. No hand flapping or waving. No repetitive noise-making gestures such as tapping, cracking knuckles, chewing and/or popping gum, snapping a pen top off and on, etc. If it is something your kids would do to drive you nuts, it will also irritate a prospective employer!

Dress for success. No matter what position you seek, the initial impression will be the most lasting. Being overdressed is just as bad as being too casual.

> **Do** wear a conservative, nice dress, skirt and blouse, or suit. Wear minimal jewelry that is conservative and traditional. Leave the distracting, distinctive personality items at home. Dresses or skirts make a better first impression than slacks. If you must wear slacks, wear the dressiest ones you have, preferably with a jacket. Make sure hemlines aren't too short, nor skirts too tight, so they won't ride up.
>
> **Don't** wear party outfits, sheer fabrics, anything with a low cut neckline, or wild colors and prints. This is the time to appear conservative, solid, and dependable. Don't layer jewelry, mix pins and necklaces, or have rings on every finger. Less is best. Don't wear anything that is tight or revealing, or that bares any body parts. Don't wear clothing that has not been freshly laundered and mended. Don't wear shoes that are unpolished or worn down at the heels. Employers find that attention to detail reveals a lot about prospective employees. Don't wear really bright or strange colors of fingernail polish; a natural, not too long, appearance is best. The "less is best" rule applies to makeup also. Don't get too heavy-handed when applying makeup before an interview.

Remember that time is money. Stick to the subject at hand. Answer questions completely, then hush. Don't get sidetracked into irrelevant topics. Respect the interviewer's time, and thank him or her for that time and consideration.

Make yourself available for further information. Be sure to offer a daytime number where you can be reached, or offer to call back at a pre-set time to see if there are any further questions. Show willingness to be available for additional information or for starting the job.

You do not need to be available in a familiar or sexual sense! This is called sexual harassment and is illegal. Don't put up with it for even a minute!

Newspaper ads

Your local newspaper contains many advertisements for jobs. Understand that these are just advertisements. The job may sound better than it actually is.

In addition, many employment agencies run ads for jobs that are not available. This is unethical, and in many locations, illegal. Unfortunately, it still goes on. They try to rope you in with an ad for a great job, tell you it has been filled, and then try to place you in another, less attractive, position.

Another problem with newspaper ads is that many companies advertise for management, but really are only looking for commissioned sales people. These companies may hire you for management, tell you they need money for fees, bonding, samples, etc., and only then tell you that you are in commissioned sales. Remember, if the offer sounds too good to be true, it probably is. **Don't pay any fees or expenses.** Legitimate businesses don't operate that way.

Employment agencies

Employment agencies can help you find a job. They make their money from fees paid either by you or the employer. Obviously, you would like to find a job that is **"fee paid."** That means the costs are assumed by the company hiring you. However, that is not always possible, especially for entry-level positions.

If you must pay the fee, do so only after you have accepted a job **and** gone to work. Preferably, pay it over time, so if the job doesn't work out, you can get the agency to locate a new one. They will certainly have more incentive to find you another position if their compensation depends on it.

Many agencies guarantee that they will place you again, free of charge, if the first job doesn't work out. This will give you some protection. There are many organizations (technically not employment agencies) that charge fees in advance for putting together a resume and finding a job. **Avoid them! Never pay a fee in advance!** You should pay no fees until you actually have a job.

Your salary/benefits package

Once you have a job offer, you need to consider the entire compensation package. This consists of your salary and any fringe benefits.

Obviously, your salary is self-explanatory. It is the amount of hourly, weekly, or monthly compensation you receive. In addition, you may get some benefits, depending on the size of the company. Health insurance and retirement plans are the two main benefits available. If health insurance is offered, and you need the coverage, make sure it's truly health insurance, not some type of reimbursement plan. Take advantage of any retirement plan and contribute the maximum.

MOVING UP THE LADDER

People won't notice your worth if you don't tell them of your value. Have you asked for a raise? Looked for a better paying job? Worked on a degree or taken special classes that might qualify you for advancement at work? If so, bring it to the attention of management.

Wanda tried to control her nervousness and speak calmly but firmly to Mr. Bracken. "I really enjoy my work, but I know I am ready for advancement. Since being hired three years ago, I have developed my on-the-job skills as well as taken classes on my own time. I have completed courses on word processing, spread sheets, and office management, and have assumed more responsibilities. I believe I deserve a raise that will reflect my added responsibilities and skills. My work record is excellent, with very few leave days taken.

Mr. Bracken cleared his throat, then peered at Wanda over the rim of his glasses. He could be so intimidating. "So, you are whining for more money?"

"No," replied Wanda. "I'm stating my increased abilities and job growth, and requesting matching pay. I am a valuable member of this firm and deserve a raise. I have given of myself and ask the same in return."

Wanda was prepared to state her own case in a business-like fashion. She anticipated browbeating and intimidation, and had practiced in front of the mirror at home for just such treatment. That part was very important.

Wanda knew her boss well enough to know how he would react. She wanted to be sure she was ready. She thought of everything he could say, every objection he could throw at her, and wrote them all down. Then she developed and practiced the answers so she wouldn't be caught off guard.

She stuck firmly to her demands. They were not unreasonable. As a result, she achieved them. She not only got the raise, but gained new respect from her boss. If she had not asked, she would never have received.

It's your company

One of the biggest mistakes people make is that they think of their job as just that - a job. They go to work, do the minimum required, and go home at night. As a result, they are unhappy, unfulfilled, and unable to advance in their current job.

Patty worked very hard her entire life. She had always enjoyed her work and done a good job. One day, her co-worker, Nancy, came to her in tears. "I lost my job," she cried. "I can't believe that after all the years I put in, they let me go. It just proves that this company doesn't care about its employees, they only care about their profits. You're crazy if you give your all for this company. Just do as little as you can. You'll probably get fired, too." Patty was in shock. They had worked together, and although Nancy was always complaining and often late for work, she seemed to do a pretty good job.

She thought long and hard about what Nancy had said. "She must be right," she said to herself. So Patty cut down on the work she was doing. She stopped working late, doing the little extra things she used to do. She got there right at nine and left the minute the clock struck five, no matter what she was doing. Finally, she was fired, too. She called Nancy. "You were certainly right. The company didn't care a thing about me, either."

Patty is a good example of what is happening in America today. It has turned into an "us versus them" mentality. All too often, people do just enough to get by, and then can't understand it when they get fired.

They have great excuses, however. "The company doesn't care about me. They are making me work harder. All the bosses are making money while they pay me a pittance. They keep cutting benefits. They are just in it for themselves." Please remember a few realities.

- If your employer doesn't make money, you don't have a job (unless you work for the government).

- You need them more than they need you. There are plenty of good people looking for jobs.

- They have to cut expenses to compete. Foreign competition, plus increased government regulation, are making it more difficult for businesses, especially small ones, to make a profit.

The solution is relatively simple: do more than is asked of you. Work for the company like you own it. Remember, if you have a bad attitude and get fired, only you will suffer, not the company. No one is indispensable. Put everything you have into it and be the best you can be. Your own pride in your work will give you job satisfaction that nothing can touch!

Guidelines

✓ *If you have been out of the workplace at least five years, or if your self-esteem is low, enroll in a displaced homemaker course.*

✓ *Arrange backup (emergency) child care before returning to school or the workplace.*

✓ *Dress and act professionally while seeking a job, as well as during employment. That will give you the best opportunity for advancement.*

✓ *Do your best and take pride in your job performance.*

✓ *Take advantage of training opportunities to improve your skills on an ongoing basis.*

✓ *If job advancement is not offered, actively seek it.*

✓ *Be careful when answering newspaper ads. They rarely are as great as they appear.*

✓ *Don't pay employment fees in advance.*

Chapter 35

How Should I Finance My Car?

Buying a new car is a very intimidating experience for most people. Financing it, although easier, is a mine field that can cost you a lot of money.

Buying

From an economic standpoint, it doesn't make sense to buy a new car. They are expensive and lose value quickly. In fact, the minute you drive it out of the dealership, it loses up to 30% of its value. The best buy on a car is usually one that is two or three years old. It will be much less expensive, and it should still be reliable.

Most people say, "Yes. But I don't want to buy another person's problems." That might have been a concern years ago, and it might still be so to a small extent. However, with increased quality control and longer factory warranties, buying a car with 20,000-25,000 miles on it is still a good idea.

If you must purchase a new car, shop around. Don't set your heart on only one car or model. That is how you get trapped. The dealer knows he has you if you only show interest in one specific model.

Review *Consumer Reports* to check the car's reliability. Get books that show the dealer's cost, so you can decide, in advance, the maximum you are willing to pay. Most libraries and banks have a book that lists car values, both new and used. Go in with a figure and stick with it. There are other dealers, and there are other cars. Shop for your best deal. Don't get stuck with add-ons. Forget special coatings, extended warranties, etc. They aren't worth the expense.

Financing

The dealer makes additional money by arranging the financing. However, this usually results in a higher rate. Don't finance with the dealer, even if he is using your bank. The rate you get directly from the bank should be lower than the rate offered by the dealer.

Don't take the optional insurance: credit life, accidental death, disability, etc. You will pay too much for too little coverage.

Finance your car at the lowest rate for the shortest period possible. Review our discussion in Chapter 12 on how to save money by financing over a shorter period. Don't forget, consider only the APR (annual percentage rate). It is the only figure that matters.

How do you solve the problem of not letting the dealer finance it for you? Simple. Go to your bank or credit union ahead of time and get a pre-approved loan. Tell them how much you expect to pay, and get approval for that amount. Then, when you make your best deal with the car dealer, you will already have your financing in place and they can't try to talk you into financing with them. One other point: **if you don't have your financing in place ahead of time, don't sign anything that binds you to purchase that car.**

Marilyn finally found the car she wanted. The dealer gave her what she thought was a good price. She told the dealer she wanted to go to her bank to get financing. He tried to talk her into dealing with them, but she didn't want to do that. She did say, however, that she would check with her bank to see how it would compare with his rates. She signed all the paperwork agreeing to purchase the car. When she went to her bank, she discovered she didn't qualify for a loan because of her poor credit history. She checked with other financial institutions, and they all said the same thing. In panic, she went back to the dealership. It turned out they couldn't get her financing, either. However, according to her agreement with the dealer, she had already purchased the car. The only thing they were waiting for was the money. She was stuck. The dealership bought the car back at a lower price and sued her for the difference!

Again, don't sign a purchase agreement if you haven't lined up the financing. Give the dealer a **refundable** deposit of $100 to hold the car, but that's it. Don't sign anything else.

Financing versus leasing

Automobile companies realized long ago that the only thing Americans care about is the monthly payment. As long as they can afford the payment, they will take the car. Leasing fits well into this "What is my monthly payment?" mentality. It allows you to get a shiny new car for lower payments. Unfortunately, it costs you more in the long run.

This is the way leasing works. You lease a car for two to four years for a fixed monthly payment. At the end of this term, you have two choices. You either give the car back and your payments end, or you buy the car from the leasing company at a predetermined price. In addition, if you exceed your mileage allotment, you face additional charges.

If you give the car back, then you have to start the process all over again. You gain nothing except the use of a car for several years. If you buy the car for the price stated in the lease, you have to come up with the money. If you don't have it, you have to get financing. Again, you gain nothing.

Cash vs. leasing vs. financing

Unless you enjoy driving a new car every few years and don't mind making payments for the rest of your life, leasing is a bad deal. According to *Consumer Reports*, April 1993, the total cost for a 1993 Honda Accord EX at 8.5% APR would be:

	LEASE	FINANCE	CASH
UP-FRONT COSTS			
Down Payment or Price	0	$3,676	$18,380
Fees, license	$450	$80	$80
Sales Tax	0	$919	$919
Total Up-Front Costs	**$450**	**$4,675**	**$19,379**
MONTHLY COSTS - 48 months			
Loan/lease payment	$305	$374	0
Sales tax	15	0	0
Total of Monthly Costs	**$15,360**	**$17,952**	**0**
OTHER COSTS			
Lost Interest @ 6%	0	$694	$3,473
Termination Fee	$400	0	0
Cost after 48 months	**$16,210**	**$23,321**	**$22,852**
Residual Value	0	$8,400	$8,400
YOUR TOTAL COST	**$16,210**	**$14,921**	**$14,452**

Although the "Down Payment or Price" column shows zero for the lease, many leasing companies do require a down payment. If so, it will result in "lost interest."

Paying cash is the most economical way to buy a car. Depending on how you could better invest your money, financing at a good rate is a close second. Leasing, however, is a distant third and should not be considered unless you plan to make payments the rest of your life.

Save in advance

If possible, save up for your next car and pay cash. **It's better to earn interest than to pay it.** Once you've paid off your current loan, put the same amount monthly into your savings, just as though you were still making car payments. When the time comes to replace your car, you should have saved enough money.

Check insurance rates

Many consumers are unpleasantly surprised when they discover the cost of insuring their new car. Sporty cars and small, lightweight cars are often much more expensive to insure: The model's safety/repair record is also a factor. We recommend checking the insurance rates **before** you get serious about a car. This can save you a lot of money in the long run.

Guidelines

✓ *Buy a car that is two or three years old, instead of the latest model.*

✓ *Take your time and shop around. Be open to other models. Drive the car and make sure you like it.*

✓ *If you purchase a used car, have it checked by a reputable mechanic.*

✓ *Don't buy add-ons, such as extended warranties, special coatings, etc.*

✓ *If you finance, do so for the shortest time possible, and never for more than three years.*

✓ *Don't lease unless you want a new car every few years and are willing to pay extra for the privilege.*

✓ *Check insurance rates before buying a car.*

Chapter 36

Should I Rent Or Buy?

Several years ago, this was an easy decision. Inflation was higher than it is today, real estate prices were going up, and income was taxed at higher rates. Back then, you could assume your home would increase in value. In addition, the income-tax deduction of mortgage interest had more value. All that has changed, although taxes are headed back up again.

Home values today are not increasing in most parts of the country. In fact, people across the country consistently report a significant drop in the value of their home. Although income tax rates are higher than they have been for the past five years, they are still relatively low, but rising.

So the questions remain. Should I rent or buy? Should I pay rent to someone else when I could pay my own mortgage and build equity, especially when so much of it is tax deductible?

Betsy was paying $425 a month to rent her apartment. A friend said she was wasting money and should buy a house. She looked around and found one she liked for $75,000. She could afford a down payment of $10,000, bringing her loan amount to $65,000. If she financed for 30 years, her monthly payment would only be $454.49, plus property taxes and insurance. The total monthly payment would be $580. She wondered, "Should I buy or should I continue to rent?"

The decision making process

Let's look at the <u>after-tax</u> implications. Mortgage interest is deductible. With monthly payments of $454, an average of $404 is deductible interest the first year. Her property taxes

220

of $100 per month are also deductible. Therefore, $504 of each monthly payment is a deductible expense on her income taxes. If you multiply $504 by her 28% tax bracket, you get $141.

Every month that Betsy pays $545 (mortgage payment plus property taxes), she saves $141 in taxes. The **after-tax** cost of the mortgage is really $404 ($545 payment, less $141 tax savings). That is just a little less than her monthly rent.

The choices look similar from a monthly payment standpoint. Betsy's decision must rest on other factors.

- She must pay approximately $2,000 in closing costs if she buys the house.

- She will probably want to buy new furniture and spend money decorating.

- Home values aren't appreciating now.

- She would have maintenance expenses on her home that are provided without extra cost at her apartment.

On the other hand:

- She doesn't like living in an apartment.

- The management isn't very responsive to complaints.

- She would like to own something instead of just paying rent.

- Eventually, when her loan is paid off, she would have no more monthly payments, a luxury she won't enjoy if she continues to rent.

Financially, it would probably make more sense to stay

in her apartment. Emotionally, however, she would like to move now. In Betsy's case, emotion won out. She bought the house.

As usual, decisions aren't black and white. There are emotional as well as financial factors to consider. The financial aspects weren't bad enough to make moving a foolish decision. Betsy was pleased with her new home.

The choice between renting or buying also hinges on whether real estate values will do as well over the next twenty years as they have in the past. There is some doubt about that. If you can rent a home or apartment that is comfortable, then do so until you're ready to settle down.

If you decide to get a mortgage, be sure to review Chapter 15, in which we discuss the best way to finance your home. The method of financing affects the affordability.

WOMEN IN TRANSITION

One of the immediate concerns of women who have just divorced or become widowed is whether to remain in their homes. There are several conflicting issues.

The first is the desire to maintain stability for the family, especially if children are involved. Death or divorce is traumatic under the best of circumstances, and very few are blessed with "the best of circumstances." In their desire to reduce the impact on children, many women try to stay put.

However, the flip side is economic reality. It is usually too expensive to remain in the same home and handle the mortgage payments, utilities, maintenance, and other living expenses. Statistically, divorced women see an immediate drop of almost 50% in their standard of living. Widows are often better off due to life insurance benefits.

In any case, it can be a costly mistake to try to remain in the same home. Trying to protect children from change, while a noble endeavor, can create additional problems if keeping the home causes severe financial pressure. As many Americans can attest, being "house poor" adds a lot of stress.

If you talk to your children and explain that you will all be more secure by moving to a place you can afford, they will cope with the change better. While children rarely like to move, it is easier if they understand the reasons.

Guidelines

✓ *Review Chapter 15 on choosing a mortgage for you.*

✓ *Evaluate the costs (including tax advantages) of buying vs. renting before making a decision.*

✓ *Consider the availability of affordable rentals in good neighborhoods or apartment complexes.*

✓ *Consider the potential maintenance expenses before buying a home.*

✓ *Don't try to buy or hang onto a house that you can't afford to maintain. It will make you miserable.*

✓ *Make an effort to be satisfied with what you can afford. It may be a lot less than what you're accustomed to, particularly after a divorce.*

✓ *It is more important to have security and independence than to impress others.*

Chapter 37

Should I Refinance My Home?

Mary Ann's original $50,000, 9% mortgage was down to $47,500, with a monthly payment of $402.31 plus taxes and insurance. She wanted to refinance and found a 7% mortgage with no points. The closing costs would amount to nearly $2,000, so she would need a $50,000 loan. Her new monthly payment would be $332.65, saving nearly $70 a month.

Is this worthwhile? It would cost her $2,000 to save $70 a month. Dividing the closing costs by $70 reveals it will take over 28 months to recover her costs. Since she plans to stay in the home for a while, it will probably be worthwhile. However, she still faces two negatives. Her loan amount returns to the original $50,000, and her loan term is again 30 years.

No-cost loans

A new type of loan available has no up-front expenses. The lender pays closing costs, which makes it very attractive. Although the interest rates are higher than traditional loans, the fact that you can refinance at no cost makes it appealing.

Make additional principal payments

Although Mary Ann could save $70 a month, her equity buildup from the previous years would be shot. The solution? Refinance, but continue to make the original $402 monthly payment. The $70 monthly bonus can directly reduce her principal. Thus, she will pay her mortgage in 18½ years instead of 30! The money she could save is incredible. Instead of paying **$69,554** in interest over thirty years, she will reduce that amount to only **$39,212** in 18½ years. She will save over **$30,000** in interest!

224

Pay credit card debt

Another good idea is to use the $70 monthly to reduce her credit card debt. The sooner she gets rid of her high-interest debt, the better.

Retirement plan

If Mary Ann participates in a retirement plan at work, she could increase her contributions by $70 per month. That would compound into a significant sum by the time she retires.

Invest it

If she does not participate in a retirement plan, and has no credit card debt, she might consider depositing $70 into a mutual fund each month. If she makes 8% after taxes, she will have enough money after 13½ years to pay the balance of her mortgage. Of course, there is a risk. To end up with 8% annually, she will need to average approximately 12% before taxes. Therefore, the "sure thing" is to prepay the principal.

Guidelines

✓ *Consider refinancing only if the interest rate is at least 2% lower than your current rate, and you plan to keep the home enough years to make it worthwhile.*

✓ *Unless you are refinancing to make the payments manageable, use the monthly "savings" to prepay the mortgage, pay off other debts, or invest for future needs.*

✓ *Make additional payments on your mortgage to reduce the amount of interest you will eventually have to pay.*

✓ *Review Chapter 15 for the advantages of a 15-year loan over a 30-year loan.*

Chapter 38

How Much Life Insurance Do I Need?

Selecting the amount of insurance you need is hardly an exact science. There are too many variables to make it little more than an educated guess, but we'll give it a try.

Single with dependents

You need insurance to protect your children. This chart provides an easy method to figure out the approximate amount.

1.	Annual income heirs will need upon your death	$
2.	Minus annual income your heirs will receive (Social Security, survivor's benefits, etc.)	$
3.	Subtract line 2 from line 1 for the total annual income shortfall	$
4.	The number of years until your youngest child reaches age 18	
5.	Multiply line 3 by line 4	$
6.	Debts to be paid at your death (mortgage, credit cards, car loans, etc.)	$
7.	College fund needed for your children's education	$
8.	Add lines 5, 6 & 7 to arrive at total amount of cash needed	$
9.	Subtract your cash, investments, retirement distributions, current insurance, etc.	$
10.	The amount of additional life insurance needed	$

The result is the approximate amount of life insurance

you should carry. No calculation is exact, however this will provide a reasonable estimate. We have not included inflation in the calculation, since we assume your current investments and eventual money from your life insurance will be invested at above-inflation rates of interest.

Don't leave insurance benefits (or any other assets) directly to your minor children. If the children's father will be caring for them, then you may want to make special provisions for any money you leave. Review Chapter 25 for a comprehensive discussion of leaving money to minors.

Married - insurance on husband

The calculation for married people is not as easy. Unlike a single person, whose obligation will end at some point, the surviving wife will statistically outlive her husband by at least seven years. Therefore, our calculation determines the amount of money it would take, invested at 8% after taxes, to support the surviving wife and children.

1.	Annual income you will need upon the death of your husband	$
2.	Minus annual income you will receive (Social Security, your job, etc.)	$
3.	Subtract line 2 from line 1 for total annual income shortfall	$
4.	Divide line 3 by .08 to determine money needed to generate shortfall	$
5.	College fund needed for your children's education	$
6.	Debts you want paid at your husband's death (loans, credit cards, mortgage, etc.)	$
7.	Add lines 4, 5, & 6 to arrive at total amount of cash needed	$
8.	Subtract your cash, investments, retirement distributions, current life insurance, etc.	$
9.	The amount of additional life insurance needed on your husband	$

This calculation assumes you want to live off the interest, rather than spend principal. This gives you an extra cushion to fall back on when prices go up and emergencies hit.

Married - insurance on you

Beyond covering your husband, there may be a need for life insurance on you, as well. This is appropriate if he would need to replace your earnings or obtain child care for several years.

The calculation depends upon whether you are working outside or inside the home. If you are staying home with small children, then your husband must hire someone to care for them. This is quite a strain for many families. Therefore, you need to carry enough life insurance (preferably term insurance) on you to cover the period until the children are old enough to stay by themselves after school.

1.	Annual income your husband will need upon your death	$
2.	Minus annual income he will receive from his job and any benefits	$
3.	Subtract line 2 from line 1 for total annual income shortfall	$
4.	Divide line 3 by .08 to determine money needed to generate shortfall	$
5.	College fund needed for your children's education	$
6.	Debts you want paid at your death (mortgage, loans, credit cards, etc.)	$
7.	Add lines 4, 5, & 6 to arrive at total amount of cash needed	$
8.	Subtract your cash, investments, retirement distributions current life insurance, etc.	$
9.	The amount of additional life insurance needed on you	$

Understand that these methods are not meant to be

precise. That is impossible, no matter how sophisticated the approach. At least it will get you in the ballpark.

Guidelines

- ✓ *Calculate your family's insurance needs, regardless of your marital situation.*

- ✓ *Full-time homemakers with small children need insurance coverage.*

- ✓ *Buy the cheapest term from a quality insurance company that can cover your basic needs.*

- ✓ *Review Chapter 18 on the types of life insurance.*

Chapter 39

How Much Should I
Set Aside For Retirement?

The answer to the title question is, "as much as you need to generate enough income for the rest of your life." Naturally, we can't tell you how much you need to set aside. But we can give you some rules of thumb if you **haven't yet started** systematic savings for retirement. The percentages reflect what you should invest each year. They don't take Social Security into consideration, but do factor in future inflation. Your retirement plan contributions are part of the percentage. If you start at the percentage shown, you may maintain that same percentage each year until retirement.

Age	Set Aside Until Retirement
20's	10-15%
30's	15-20%
40's	20-30%
50's	30-40%

We can hear you now. "How can I possibly do that when I can't even pay my bills?" That thinking will keep you from ever reaching your financial goals. You owe what you owe because of the lifestyle you have chosen. Yes, you might have been set back by death or divorce, but you are in control. It is up to you to provide for your future. It will take plenty of self-discipline, but you **can** do it.

Ouch Principal

Use the "Ouch Principal" to work up to your percentage. Begin putting smaller amounts into your retirement, **in addition** to paying off your debts. As the debts reduce and you become comfortable, increase the retirement contributions until you're back up to "ouch." Whenever that gets comfortable, "ouch" yourself again. Do this consistently until you reach your level. But remember, the longer it takes to reach your level, the higher percentage you will need to put aside.

If you don't participate in a retirement plan, then fund an Individual Retirement Account (IRA). Find a good mutual fund family and invest your money there. See Chapter 29. Stick with this plan and invest wisely. Then **don't touch it** until you retire. If you stay on track, you will meet or exceed your retirement goals. It's so simple, it's scary!

Professional planning

If you want more exact figures, meet with a financial planner. He or she can prepare a financial plan that will show you exactly how much you need to set aside for your retirement. In addition, in our workbook and tapes (see page 355), we will walk you through this process in simple steps.

Guidelines

- ✓ *Set aside a percentage of your earnings and invest it specifically for retirement.*

- ✓ *Do not touch that money for any other purpose, even if permitted by your employer's retirement plan rules.*

- ✓ *By sacrificing a little today, you won't have to sacrifice a lot in the future.*

- ✓ *Max-out your retirement plan first, especially if your employer matches contributions.*

- ✓ *Begin saving today. Do not procrastinate!*

Chapter 40

What Should I Do With A Retirement Distribution?

There are several circumstances under which you may receive a lump sum distribution from a retirement plan. For our purposes, retirement plans include 401(k), 403(b), Thrift Savings Plan, Pension Plan, Profit Sharing Plan, or an Individual Retirement Account (IRA). It is crucial to your financial security that you handle these properly.

- **Result of death.** If your deceased husband had a qualified retirement plan, you are entitled to his benefits. As his widow, you may be entitled to the first $5,000 tax-free as a death benefit. You may take the balance in cash and pay income taxes, or do an IRA rollover, which is described on the following page. This tax-free rollover provision only applies to the surviving spouse, not the children.

- **Result of retirement.** Once you retire from a company, you are entitled to your retirement benefits. Again, you can take them in cash or do an IRA rollover. If you take cash, all the money you receive is subject to income taxes. In addition, if you are under the age of 59½ (55 in certain cases), you will have to pay a 10% IRS penalty. This penalty does not apply if you can meet the IRS exceptions. If you were born on or before December 31, 1935, you may be eligible for five-year or ten-year averaging. This method reduces taxes on a distribution.

- **Result of divorce.** If you are entitled to your ex-husband's retirement benefits under a Qualified Domestic Relations Order, you may receive the money in cash or take advantage of an IRA rollover.

IRA ROLLOVER

Before deciding how to take a distribution, it is important that you consider all the methods available. There is a big difference in the tax implications for the various methods. Be sure you meet with a financial advisor who can help you decide.

We have referred several times to the ability to "roll" your retirement plan benefits into a special type of IRA account. This is called an "IRA rollover," which is available with most retirement plans. The primary exception is a deferred compensation plan, which does not allow rollovers.

When you receive a distribution, the choices are to either take it and pay taxes, or to roll it into an IRA and defer taxes. Unless you need the money immediately, the latter is usually the best alternative. Even when you roll your money into an IRA, you may still receive income and principal at any time. It just becomes taxable when withdrawn.

Don't confuse the IRA rollover with the normal IRA. The former is designed only to take distributions from qualified retirement plans, with no limits to the amount of money that can be rolled over.

Direct transfer

In the past, if you wanted to avoid taxes on a distribution, you had 60 days from the date you received it to reinvest it with a new trustee. That is no longer permitted. If you receive any of the money yourself, your plan trustee must withhold 20% for taxes.

The way to avoid this is by performing a "trustee to trustee transfer," in which the current trustee transfers the money directly to a new trustee. This is often called a "direct rollover." The 20% penalty does not apply when moving money from an existing IRA to another.

Although this law was passed to help the government collect money faster, it is beneficial. It keeps people from taking, and blowing, their retirement funds before retirement.

New trustee

You can choose to deposit your IRA among several financial institutions.

- **Banks.** If you move your retirement money to a bank, they will act as trustee at no charge.

- **Brokerage firms.** If you invest your retirement account in individual stocks and bonds, a brokerage firm will act as trustee. Most firms charge a fee for this; a few discounters do it free. This is called a "Self-Directed IRA."

- **Mutual funds.** If you invest in mutual funds, either the fund or a bank will act as trustee. Most charge a small fee for this; some do it at no cost.

- **Insurance companies.** If you invest in annuities, the insurance company will act as trustee. They normally do not charge a fee for this service.

When you choose your trustee, the investment choices (and earnings) are far more important than the custodial fees. It is better to pay a reasonable fee and get good growth, than to have no fees and earn only minimum interest. Keep your focus on the important issues. Review Chapter 26 on the importance of earning higher rates of return.

Lump sum or monthly income?

Annuitizing is the process by which you are paid a guaranteed monthly income from a retirement account instead of receiving a lump sum. We rarely, if ever, recommend this option. Here's why.

> *Margaret learned that her late husband had $100,000 in his retirement account. She had the choice of taking the $100,000 in cash, or receiving $651.23 per month the rest of her life, with a guaranteed minimum of ten years. She thought the income sounded good, since she would be guaranteed "an income she could never outlive." It never hit her until too late that her children would never receive any of the $100,000.*

The problem with receiving a lifetime annuity is that the lump sum magically disappears. If Margaret had wanted an income the rest of her life, she could have invested the money in bonds. At her death, her children would have inherited those bonds.

The only time we recommend a lifetime annuity is if the recipient is either mentally incompetent or cannot possibly handle the money without spending it all. Under normal circumstances, annuitizing is not a good choice.

INVESTING THE MONEY

Once you have received the money, you must decide how to invest it. Your decision should be based, among other things, on when you will need the money. Let's look at investment choices for income (if you need it now) and growth (if you won't need it for a number of years). The chapter in which we discuss each option is in parentheses.

Income

If you need income now, your choices are:

- **Banks** (Chapters 11 and 26).
- **Annuities** (Chapter 31).
- **Government Bonds** (Chapters 27 and 29).
- **Corporate Bonds** (Chapters 27 and 29).
- **Income Oriented Stock** (Chapters 28 and 29).

You will get the lowest return from the bank. However, the principal is guaranteed. Fixed annuities also guarantee the principal. The other choices will give you higher returns in exchange for somewhat increased risk. You can invest in the last three categories by buying individual stocks and bonds, or investing in mutual funds.

Don't forget that inflation will increase your cost of living. If you take all the income your account generates, nothing will be left for growth. Your income will fluctuate with interest rates, but you will lose all protection against inflation.

Growth

If you choose to leave all or part of your money for growth, there are several alternatives available.

- **Banks** (Chapters 11 and 26).
- **Stocks** (Chapters 28 and 29).
- **Bonds** (Chapters 27 and 29).
- **Annuities** (Chapter 31).

Once again, you will receive greater growth over time from stocks and bonds than from banks and fixed annuities. They can be purchased individually, through mutual funds, or in variable annuities.

Don't rush

Widows, especially, shouldn't rush to do anything. You don't have to make a decision right away. If your husband's employer wants you to take the money, then open an IRA rollover account in a mutual fund money market or at your bank and let it sit there until you are ready to make a clear decision. You do not have to jump into any long-reaching investment decisions immediately.

On the other hand, don't procrastinate forever or ignore the issue. That could ultimately leave you with little money to meet your needs. After a year or so, you need to begin exploring your options and looking into your financial situation and goals.

Guidelines

✓ *Don't feel pressured into making decisions about distributions soon after divorce or death. Give yourself a year or so to recover from grief before focusing on long-term finances.*

✓ *Invest your lump sum in an IRA to take advantage of reduced taxes.*

✓ *Do a direct rollover (transfer) from your qualified pension plan into an IRA to avoid the 20% withholding penalty.*

✓ *Invest for growth. The younger you are, the more growth-oriented you must be.*

✓ *Don't touch the principal. Let it grow to protect you against future inflation.*

✓ *Don't use any of your retirement money for non-retirement needs (home, children's education, loans to adult children, etc.).*

Chapter 41

How Do I Save For College Education?

With the increasing cost of college, it is more vital than ever to plan ahead for college education. This means that you must begin saving as soon as possible.

The first rule for obtaining college funding is to apply for as many grants and scholarships as you can. But that process doesn't begin until one or two years before college. By then, it will be too late to begin saving for college. Therefore, you need to begin saving and investing **now.**

Sacrifice Your Future?

A lot of people aren't going to like this, but we don't recommend putting your children's education first if it will strap you financially or jeopardize your future security.

Joan and her late husband felt very strongly about providing for their children's education. They wanted their boys to have the best. They thought that they should be able to go to college like their friends and not have to worry about paying for it. They counted pennies so the boys could go. Now Joan is a widow in her sixties with hardly any money. The money that could have provided for her security was spent on her children's education.

This situation is all too common. Since most people don't save far enough in advance for college, they have to "pay as they go." This often requires using all savings, drawing from retirement accounts, and taking a second mortgage or home equity loan. As a result, when their children are out of college, the parents end up starting all over again in mid-life.

Anita turned 52 the day she asked her financial advisor to handle

238

a $30,000 IRA rollover. When the advisor questioned her about her other investments, savings, and retirement benefits, she exclaimed, "This $30,000 is everything. Ben and I put three kids through college, and that used up all our savings. But now I'm ready to begin saving for myself so I can retire when I'm 62."

Anita is in an impossible situation. There is no way that she can save enough money on her salary to be able to retire comfortably in ten years. She may retire, but certainly not comfortably.

It is admirable to want the best for your children. However, sacrificing your future does not make sense, especially when there are so many scholarships, grants, and loans available. Any child who wants to go to college badly enough can get the money. Most schools bend over backwards to help motivated students get financial assistance and part-time jobs. They may have debts when they graduate, but they'll have their education, and you'll still have your future security.

Amounts to save

If you can plan for your child's or grandchild's education, the following chart will help you find out how much you must save. It shows the monthly investment you must make based on: your child's age; the four-year cost of college using $8,000 and a 6% inflation rate; and the amount you must invest each month at various after-tax rates to achieve your objective.

Child's Age	Cost For 4 Years	Invest @ 4%	Invest @ 8%	Invest @ 10%
3	$83,872	$302	$211	$175
6	$70,421	$331	$249	$215
9	$59,127	$382	$308	$276
12	$49,644	$482	$416	$387
15	$41,682	$746	$687	$660

Two facts are evident from this chart. The earlier you start, the better. And the higher returns you achieve, the less you must invest. The next logical question is where to invest. Before deciding that, you must first decide if you are going to put the money in your name, or your child's.

Many people recommend the latter. They say that since the child is in a lower tax bracket, it makes sense to put it in his or her name. But there is one important fact to remember. If you put money in a custodial account for your children, this money belongs to them the day they reach majority (18 in most states). That can be a frightening thought, especially if they take the money and join a rock and roll band - or worse! That is why we recommend that you keep the money in your own name. Also, financial aid officers consider money in the child's name 100% available for college expenses. But only a portion of the parent's assets are considered "available."

Where to invest

Now, where should you invest the money? You have several choices:

- **Banks.** You can buy certificates of deposit or put your money in a money market or savings account. You will receive a low rate of interest, but the money is insured up to $100,000 per person.

- **Savings bonds.** There is a break for savings bonds purchased in the parent's name after December 31, 1989 and used for college tuition and fees. The interest is tax-free if your modified adjusted gross income is under $44,150 (single) and $66,200 (married) at the time they are redeemed. The exemption reduces to zero if your income is over $59,150 (single) and $96,200 (married). These are the latest figures. They adjust annually for inflation.

- **Stocks or mutual funds.** For growth, you can invest in individual stocks or mutual funds. The advantages of mutual funds are explained in Chapter 29.

- **Tax-deferred annuities.** Annuities are one of the few investments (life insurance and retirement plans being the others) that are excluded as countable assets when applying for financial aid. The advantages of annuities are explained in Chapter 31.

Stocks, or stock mutual funds, are especially appropriate when saving for younger children. A monthly investment into a growth mutual fund should perform well over time. Obviously, there is more volatility, but as explained in Chapter 29, dollar cost averaging reduces risk and makes a lot of sense over a long period.

Once your child is within three to four years of college, you need to begin moving the money into less volatile investments. You don't want your entire fund to drop in value (in case of a bad market) when your goal is near.

Guidelines

✓ *Consider carefully how financing your children's education will impact your retirement.*

✓ *Don't sacrifice everything you've worked for to educate your children. They can take advantage of loans, grants, and scholarships, plus work.*

✓ *When saving for education, start as soon as possible and invest to earn as much as possible.*

✓ *Use growth investments until three to four years before the start of college, then phase into income-oriented (stable) investments.*

Chapter 42

How Do I Invest For Income?

If your goal is to receive income, you must first decide whether you want taxable or tax-free income. Remember, most investments are subject to income taxes, which reduce your current return.

Rate	3.00%	4.00%	5.00%	6.00%	7.00%
Less Taxes (30%)	.90%	1.20%	1.50%	1.80%	2.10%
You Keep	2.10%	2.80%	3.50%	4.20%	4.90%

The following chart shows the value of tax-free income. Locate your tax bracket in the left-hand column and follow it to the column that reflects your tax-free return. The number that results is what you would have to earn in a taxable investment to achieve the same return.

Taxable Income Single	Taxable Income Joint	Tax Rate	Tax-Free 5% Equals Taxable:	Tax-Free 6% Equals Taxable:	Tax-Free 7% Equals Taxable:
$0-22,100	$0-36,900	15%	5.88%	7.06%	8.24%
22,101-53,500	36,901-89,150	28%	6.94%	8.33%	9.72%
53,501-115,000	89,151-140,000	31%	7.25%	8.70%	10.14%
115,001-250,000	140,001-250,000	36%	7.81%	9.38%	10.94%
250,001+	250,001+	39.6%	8.28%	9.93%	11.59%

Tax-free income

If you decide that you want tax-free income, then your

242

choices are limited to tax-free municipal bonds purchased one of three ways. The chapter relating to the discussion is in parentheses.

- **Individual Bonds** (Chapter 27).
- **Unit Investment Trusts** (Chapter 27).
- **Mutual Funds** (Chapter 29).

We prefer mutual funds or unit investment trusts for the average investor, because they offer diversification, professional selection, and monthly income. However, if you have a broker who can get you good individual bonds, and you accept the risks involved (reduced liquidity, no diversification), plus you don't mind receiving income semiannually, then you can go in that direction. Just make sure the bonds are rated **at least** AA by Standard & Poor's or Aa by Moody's.

Taxable income

If you need income, and taxes are not a problem, there are four primary vehicles for you. The chapters relating to the discussion of each category are in parentheses.

- **Banks** (Chapters 11 and 26).
- **Government Bonds** (Chapters 27 and 29).
- **Corporate Bonds** (Chapters 27 and 29).
- **Income Funds** (Chapter 29).

Remember that banks offer the lowest interest rate, but provide the greatest stability and liquidity. If you invest in government bonds, you can use bond mutual funds or purchase individual bonds. If you choose corporate bonds, we prefer the diversification and professional management offered by mutual funds. Income funds provide a mixture of dividend paying stocks (such as utilities) and bonds. Remember the effects of fluctuating interest rates.

Guidelines

✓ *Diversify among different investments, even if your goal is income.*

✓ *Look for the best <u>after-tax</u> returns for your particular situation.*

✓ *Examine the risks of each type of investment, including those offered by banks.*

✓ *Try not to spend your principal, especially in your younger years. You will need protection against future inflation.*

✓ *No matter how old you are, you always need some money invested for growth.*

Chapter 43

How Do I Invest For Growth?

If you decide you need growth, either because you are young and saving for retirement, or older and trying to offset inflation, there are several investments from which to choose. The chapters with complete discussions are in parentheses.

- **Banks** (Chapters 11 and 26).
- **Stock** (Chapter 28).
- **Annuities** (Chapter 31).
- **Mutual Funds** (Chapter 29).

Banks provide the lowest return and least protection against inflation over time. We recommend that you consider growth mutual funds. Tax-deferred annuities (either fixed or variable) can be an especially good investment if you don't need current income.

The percentage of money you need in each investment will depend upon your age and risk tolerance. If you know you need growth, but don't want to take too much risk, consider mutual funds that invest in blue chip stocks, utilities, or income vehicles. If you are willing to take more risk, then look at a variety of growth funds.

If you are not comfortable making your own decisions, then you should work with a financial planner or stockbroker. He or she can help you decide how to best invest your money.

Asset allocation

One method of determining how much you should invest in each category is known as "asset allocation." It is a way of diversifying your assets among a variety of investment products. How you should allocate your assets depends upon your age, goals, risk tolerance, etc. The following chart shows how women of different ages might allocate their assets. Notice that as their ages increase, more money is invested for income and cash than growth.

Name/Age	Growth	Growth + Income	Income	Cash
Betty/30	70%	20%	0%	10%
Amy/40	60%	15%	10%	15%
Beth/50	35%	35%	15%	15%
Jane/60	15%	15%	50%	20%

This is merely an example and not meant to be applicable in all cases. Your financial planner or broker can help you allocate your assets the way that is best for you.

Guidelines

✓ *Invest in tax-deferred investments for retirement or long-term goals.*

✓ *Diversify among various categories of investments.*

✓ *Use mutual funds to get maximum diversification, affordability, and professional management.*

✓ *The younger you are (or more long-range your goals), the more aggressive you should be.*

✓ *Never put "all your eggs in one basket."*

Chapter 44

How Much Risk Should I Take?

There's no pat answer when it comes to risk, because there are too many factors involved. No matter where you put your money, there is always some risk. While the risk to your principal is minimal in a bank, you do suffer loss of buying power due to taxes and inflation. You can protect your buying power by investing in the stock market, but there you face risk of principal. You can receive higher rates of interest in bonds, but you face interest rate risk.

The key to managing risk is being aware of the kinds of risk and your tolerance for each. The various risks and investment choices are explained in Chapters 26-31. Let's see where you stand.

On a scale of one to ten, with **one** being "I totally **disagree**" and **ten** being "I totally **agree**," rate the following.

_____ I am willing to assume higher risk for higher rates of return.

_____ I am willing to tie up some of my money for at least five years, if it means earning higher rates of return.

_____ I am willing to accept fluctuations (increases and decreases) in the value of my investments, if it means higher long-term returns (6-8 years).

_____ I would like to reduce the amount of taxes I am paying on my savings and investments.

_____ I am concerned about inflation eating away the value of my money.

If you scored a five, then you want your money instantly available and risk-free. Therefore, 100% of your money belongs in savings accounts and money market accounts at your bank, with no more than $100,000 in any one institution!

If you scored six or higher, then you need to become familiar with the investment choices beyond savings accounts. The chapters in Part III - Investment Basics, cover the wide range of choices available.

The higher your score, the more important tax-advantages and growth become in meeting your goals. For example, if you scored 50, most of your money should be in tax-sheltered growth. In between those extremes, your money should be diversified among the investments that reflect your score.

Guidelines

✓ *There is no right or wrong answer when it comes to risk.*

✓ *Some risk is not necessarily bad.*

✓ *Accepting higher risk will usually result in higher long-term rewards.*

✓ *Don't be overly conservative or overly aggressive.*

✓ *Make sure your investments meet your risk tolerance.*

Part Five

Upheaval

Chapter 45

Why Do I Feel So Out Of Control?

The financial aspects covered thus far are vital to your future welfare. However, if you are consumed by grief, you can't make proper financial decisions. This section deals with working through grief, toward the ultimate goal of moving forward both financially and emotionally.

Both widows and divorcees experience grief. A widow mourns the death of her husband. A divorcee mourns the death of her marriage. While their circumstances are different, they share many of the same grief symptoms.

We have found that although both experience grief, they are not very tolerant of each other's situation. Widows say, "Well, at least you had a choice. Your husband didn't just die." Divorcees say, "Well, you were lucky. I wish mine had died. At least widows collect insurance benefits."

Nevertheless, the grief process is similar. It is a trip down a road marked by anxiety, fear, inability to sleep (or sleeping too much), and overwhelming sadness. There is often very intense anger and possibly even thoughts of suicide. Women experiencing traumatic grief worry that they are becoming mentally ill. Though all the components of "going crazy" are there, it is really just part of the grieving process. This may be difficult to believe, but **it will pass. You are OK.**

Counselors say that emotions travel at half the speed of events. So expect your emotions to be one of the slowest aspects of grief to heal.

If suicidal thoughts or similar feelings become dangerously overwhelming, then seek professional counseling. Often, though, it is enough to have a close friend or clergy who is a good listener. Talking really does help.

This "crazy" period can last for many months or longer. If the death was a result of suicide, it is even more traumatic for the widow. Guilt and anger can become overwhelming.

Everything reminds you of your grief - even a TV commercial or song on the radio. Since you are so preoccupied with your situation, it is perfectly normal to begin to resent others for going about their usual routines and complaining about comparatively petty concerns.

All of a sudden, everyone around you is an "expert" on grief. You are either ignored, pitied, or have acquaintances butting into the most intimate details of your personal and financial life. It can be totally infuriating.

Hallucinations are not unusual. They can occur at the most unexpected times, and seem totally real.

> *Laura let the book fall to her lap as the TV rerun caught her attention. This had always been their favorite show, the one they watched in bed just before turning out the lights.*
>
> *She heard his laugh and, startled, looked across the bed. There was Jim! His eyes crinkled and sparkled as he laughed. He ran his fingers through his hair, in that familiar gesture that he so often unconsciously did to push the hair back off his forehead. Even the scent of his cologne was so familiar and comforting.*
>
> *Then, just as suddenly he was gone. She was really alone, yet she still felt his presence in the room.*

The hallucinations are difficult to explain to others, but they can be very comforting. In a way, it's a good sign. It is a chance to remember your husband realistically. For example, if you have been feeling intense anger and abandonment, you might hallucinate a loving scene. If you have been feeling overwhelmed with guilt, you might hallucinate a situation when he made you angry, and you felt unappreciated. It all works together to help you regain balance and a more realistic memory of your marriage.

Ailments

Some common physical discomforts are headaches, digestive problems, and aching arms or legs. You may find that you have insomnia, which leaves you feeling exhausted and barely able to make it through the day. You may find it difficult to breathe and have the sensation that "an elephant is sitting on your chest." You may wake with your fists clinched or a sore jaw from grinding your teeth.

I don't know what's wrong with me. I go to bed exhausted, but wake up by 3 with my mind going full blast. For the rest of the night, I can't stop thinking. But during the day, I can't think at all. I feel helpless, hopeless. I don't feel like myself at all. I can't concentrate or make decisions. I don't want to do anything.

Irritability, inability to concentrate, and restlessness are typical. Appetites frequently change. You may eat everything in sight, or you may not be able to do more than pick at food. Sometimes everything seems to taste funny - like there is a metallic taste in your mouth.

Patterns

Your eating pattern is off. All the other physical and emotional stresses are going on. It is more important than ever to eat right whenever you can. Try to avoid greasy, sugary, or fatty foods. Eat fruits, vegetables, proteins, and other foods that supply as much nutrition as possible. If there are a few times when only a milk shake seems digestible, then go for it. But don't make it a steady diet! A poor diet will only complicate everything else that is going on, and make it worse.

I felt so tied up in knots that my stomach rebelled at the thought of food. If I was distracted by the TV, I could nibble all night. So all I ended up eating was junk food, which made me feel worse. Finally, I started pretending that my mother was tailing me through the grocery store. It may seem silly, but it worked. Every time I picked up an item, I'd pretend that Mom was either praising or criticizing my decision. It sure improved the quality of food I was buying. I'd still nibble at night and skip meals, but at least I was eating the right foods.

Surely eating and sleeping problems are enough to endure. But no! Muscle tension, constant fatigue, and even allergic reactions are common. Some people have acute anxiety attacks, including dizziness, shortness of breath, trembling, heart palpitations, and a weak, quavering voice. Constant tearfulness might make you want to avoid interacting with others. A few women have even been known to cease menstruating for as much as a year, due to the effects of the stress.

Stress

The ten most frequently reported stress sensations by people in grief counseling are:

- Tightness in the chest.
- A hollow feeling in the stomach.
- Tightness in the throat.
- A dry mouth.
- Lack of energy.
- Muscle weakness.
- Oversensitivity to noise.
- Shortness of breath.
- Depersonalization ("Nothing's real, including me").
- Inability to concentrate.

Is it any wonder that all professionals and "experienced" widows recommend postponing major decisions until later? That first year is so stressful just trying to cope from day to day, let alone trying to make difficult decisions.

My job at this time is to be like water, not wood. I need to go with the flow, not try to be firm and resilient.

If you were in the hospital with double pneumonia, no one would expect you to pack up and move. They wouldn't expect you to make major life changes. Yet the new widow or divorcee's whole life has just been turned upside down. Her body, brain, and emotions constantly betray her. Yet, society expects her (she thinks) to go about her normal activities, plus make all sorts of new decisions.

Ann Kaiser Stearns, in *Living Through Personal Crisis* said:

Water, as it freezes and the molecules expand, has the power to burst steel pipes wide open. Likewise, frozen emotion assumes a power out of proportion to its original nature. In the middle of a very harsh winter it's wise to see to it that the water flows fairly regularly through your home plumbing system. Similarly, during the harsh seasons of grief, it is best to keep the channels open so that hurtful feelings are freely expressed. Frozen emotion, like a frozen pipe, has the potential for causing unexpected problems.

Guidelines

✓ *When grief is fresh, concentrate on coping and emotional healing.*

✓ *Do not make any unnecessary decisions during intense grief, particularly financial decisions that can wait.*

✓ *Be gentle with yourself. Cut yourself some slack and lower your expectations for a while.*

✓ *Cry freely and talk out your grief to provide some needed release.*

✓ *Try to eat healthy foods when the stress is intense.*

Chapter 46

What Is The Grief Process?

Sometimes it helps to know what to expect in advance, especially during the worst times. Just knowing the key passages of grief might help you realize that it is not an endless agony . . . there is a light at the end of the tunnel.

There are certain stages through which everyone passes in the grief process: shock, denial, anger, bargaining, resignation, and acceptance. Let's explore those stages through the personal journals of two of our friends. They share their experiences with you as they move from stage to stage.

One of the women is **widowed.** We'll call her **Wanda.** The other is **divorced.** We'll call her **Debbie.** Their entries appear throughout this chapter.

It would be wonderful if you could move straight from one stage to the next, knowing that by the time you complete the sixth stage, your healing and grieving would be finished. Sorry! It just isn't that simple.

> *Working your way through grief is like trying to push a marble across the sidewalk with a strand of cooked spaghetti. It veers and wiggles and backtracks. The path is totally unmanageable. But with enough patience, you'll eventually succeed.*

Grief weaves from one stage to the next, then back again. Sometimes, two or more dynamics may be rocking you simultaneously. There is no consistent completion of one stage followed by movement to the next.

You may reach the point where emotions subside, you

have a great night's sleep, and wham! . . . a song on the radio brings it all crashing back down.

The stages

Shock is the initial stage. It appears to be a medical state that allows you to function as if in a trance, carrying on your daily living with no emotional impact. Then, just as suddenly as it appears, it disappears.

My mother has always been a strong person. When my father died, she didn't shed a tear. She carried on with unbelievable strength. She took care of all the arrangements and greeted the guests when they arrived. During the funeral, she just sat there, stoically. A few days later, after everybody had left, it hit her like a ton of bricks.

Denial (I'm OK!) is the initial state of unreality. Shock has gotten you this far, but you still can't adjust to the idea of what has happened.

Wanda: I'm doing fine. I keep a job list and just check off each item as I complete it. There is so much to do. I'm worried about our children's reactions, but I'm doing fine.

During this stage, words of comfort and reassurance that "you did the best you could" go right over your head. Advice goes in one ear and out the other. It's too early for you to open up with supportive friends. You'll need them later.

Debbie: I sat at the kitchen table one night. Dirty dishes were everywhere. The boys had long since gone to bed. I didn't even know what time it was. "He's coming back," I kept thinking to myself. "He's just playing one of his stupid jokes. He's not going to leave the boys and me alone. When I wake up in the morning, he'll be right there."

As denial wears off, you may begin to feel numb. Since it is so difficult to accept the loss of your husband, the numbness allows the reality to gradually sink in. This is one way in which your mind and body protect you as you grieve.

Anger (Why me?) is probably the most frightening for various reasons. For the widow, there may be tremendous guilt. You never expected to feel angry - it's so sudden. Yet, be assured it's universal. It's important to express it: anger submerged and turned inward becomes depression and fear.

> *Wanda: Sometimes I just feel irritable and out of sorts for no reason. I'll get angry with anyone or anything at the drop of a hat. Worst of all, I'm angry with Bill. I'm so mad at him for dying and leaving me all alone. We had so much to look forward to, and he ruined it all.*

On the other hand, the divorcee might be surprised how bitter and angry she really is. Divorcees have enough anger to go around, but most is aimed at their ex-husband. However, anyone within shouting distance can be a target, especially children.

> *Debbie: I feel like a war veteran. Tommy (ex-husband) is the enemy. He always seems to anticipate my every move. I stay awake night after night, formulating battle plans to defend myself. Now I'm exhausted and get angry at the slightest provocation. I have to stop taking it out on the kids.*

Bargaining is the "if only" stage. For widows, it is especially severe in instances of suicide or sudden death, such as heart attack or stroke.

> *Wanda: I can't stop thinking about what I should have done. With Bill's high blood pressure and stress at work, I should have done things differently. I feel so guilty for letting him have a heart attack. If only I had stayed home and gotten him to open up and talk to me. If only I had stopped serving fried foods and insisted that we walk together. If only I had stopped using salt and insisted that he eat right, he'd still be here today.*

For divorcees, bargaining can be seen in thoughts of how they might have been "better wives."

Debbie: I wonder if this is all my fault. Tommy always said if I had put him first, our marriage would have been better. Maybe he was right. Maybe I should have quit my job and prepared suppers on time. Maybe I could have saved our marriage. I went back to him twice, but I could never please him. If only I had found a way to be better . . .

Resignation is a stage of achievement and progress, yet it is a difficult one to leave. It is very hard to reach this point, yet once reached, many women slip back into earlier stages.

Wanda: Marlena and I chatted away as we walked through the park. Suddenly I burst into tears. "He's gone. Bill is really gone, and it hurts so bad. Before, it seemed like a bad dream. But now it hits me right in the face. Sometimes I feel so alone and empty, and I don't think I can go on. Other times I think I have to keep struggling because I would want Bill to be proud of me. But he's not even here to see."

Debbie: Even with the TV blaring, the room still seems so empty tonight. Although I'm in my own apartment, it feels so strange to be on my own. I finally realize that Tommy and I will never get back together. Heck, he's already seeing some girl he went to high school with. I guess I'd better get used to planning my own evenings. I need to get on with my life.

This is the dynamic of grief that can really bog down and turn into depression. There is an emotional tug-of-war constantly taking place, which can be triggered by just a word or thought. You might be laughing over lunch with a friend, then find yourself dissolving into tears.

One therapist tells grieving women:

We grow out of grief slowly . . . like an onion skin. One layer at a time.

Because of all the emotional swings, this is the best time to get involved with a support group or seek counseling. Some women resent the suggestion of counseling. Others appreciate having a support person who can give a different perspective and help them get a handle on things.

> Wanda: I know I need to talk with someone, but Mom always said only crazy people go to counseling. She said our thoughts are personal and they are nobody's business. She used to worry that someone would find out and talk about us.

> Jennifer finally talked me into seeing a therapist. I can't believe how much better I feel. I probably cried half the time, but I told her things that I wasn't even aware of myself. It was the best thing I've ever done. I can't wait until our next appointment.

Acceptance is the final stage of grief. At this point you can finally make decisions or comments without first saying, "He always used to . . ."

> Wanda: I went over to Amanda's house for a luncheon today. Olivia mentioned passing my house and not seeing any broken down cars in the driveway. Then she blushed and acted as if she'd swallowed a pickle. There was total silence around the table. I started laughing instead of crying. Soon everyone joined in. I told her that I had all those cars towed away. When I was backing out this morning, I realized how nice it was to have the whole driveway free. I miss Bill, but those cars were a nuisance.

Now it's time to put aside the mask and freely express emotions. It's also time to quit idealizing your lost mate and begin to accept the bad as well as the good memories. Sometimes this may happen in your sleep, in the form of dreams.

> Debbie: I called Tammy and asked her to go to the mountains with me this weekend. I finally decided to stop moping around and go do something. We just got back and we had a great time!

Though you may slip back into one or more of the other stages, you finally have a sense that you can survive. It is possible at last to find some contentment in the present.

This is the time to begin making the financial decisions that were postponed during your earlier grief. Now you can think about whether to move, change jobs, or make other lifestyle changes.

Just remember that decisions are best made on your good days, when you feel in control. If a bad day slips up on you, don't feel pressured to make an uncomfortable decision. Wait if possible. Likewise, try not to make major decisions on anniversaries or other special days that may be difficult.

The longer the symptoms of grief are suppressed, the longer and more painful the healing/grieving process becomes. The sooner you open yourself to the continuation of life, the sooner you can heal. It's like using a balm to heal a wound, versus refusing any aid. The latter just prolongs the soreness and severity of the wound.

Guidelines

✓ *Cry to release emotions, don't let them build.*

✓ *Avoid playing the martyr, victim, or superwoman role.*

✓ *Refuse to feel guilty or dwell on everything you either did or didn't do.*

✓ *Spend time with people. Share your thoughts and feelings.*

✓ *Stick to routines, especially if you have children. Get out of bed, have regular meals, and get dressed every morning.*

✓ *If working, continue your job.*

✓ *Avoid amateur "experts" who undermine, belittle, or butt into your personal life.*

✓ *Refuse to let your parents or in-laws take over for you.*

✓ *Avoid complaining constantly, especially around your children.*

✓ *Don't blame God and cut all ties with your church or synagogue.*

✓ *Don't spend all your time in the house. Get out and at least take a walk around the neighborhood.*

✓ *Find something to laugh about every day, no matter how hard it seems.*

Chapter 47

How Can I Pull Myself Out Of The Pits?

The situation you find yourself in is common. Unpleasant, but completely normal. It happens to most women at some point in their lives. How you deal with it is key to your future well-being.

It is encouraging for us to see how many widows and divorcees have coped with their grief recovery. We thought you'd like to know some things they have done to help themselves. While we recommend professional help as needed, you might try a few of these methods yourself.

Feelings

One therapeutic tool involves getting a broader view of what is going on. You can help yourself gain this prospective by stating: I feel _____ about _____ because _____. For example:

I feel angry that Jim died of a heart attack, because we never had a chance to enjoy any days of retirement and travel together.

I feel furious that Mike died and left me with all these bills, because I've never had to deal with finances and I feel overwhelmed.

I feel angry that John dumped the kids and me and left us with nothing!

I feel sad and vulnerable about being alone at night, because I've never been alone nights and it is terrifying to me.

This simple exercise will help pull into focus the real

issues that are grating on you, and give you insight into the things with which you need to deal. Interestingly, it is not always the obvious that is bothering you.

Practice relaxing

Take some time to defuse the accumulated stress that makes you so tired and sore. We're not talking about body building or a massive aerobics program. We are saying, "be nice to your body."

Take 10 to 20 minutes per day to relax. Sit in a comfortable, quiet room. Close your eyes and consciously relax all of your muscles. You might get a tape of the ocean, or whatever is soothing for you. Relax your body from the top down. Feel the tension leave your head, then your shoulders, down your arms, and out your finger tips. Inhale and exhale slowly through your nose. Focus on one thing - a lake, a waterfall, a beautiful sunset at the beach. Feel the tension run down your chest, slowly down your thighs and legs, and out your toes. Enjoy being at peace with yourself. When you are finished, slowly open your eyes and adjust to your surroundings. Then snap yourself out of it and get back to work. You'll feel much more relaxed!

For quickie stress breaks, breathe in slowly to the count of four, hold for four, then exhale slowly to the steady count of four. Some people use little phrases instead of counting.

I am (inhale) . . . in God's hands (exhale).

No person or thing (inhale) . . . can get me down (exhale).

Use whatever works for you, but be sure to relax and to exhale completely each time. Exercise can work wonders, too. Try a brisk 10 minute walk first thing in the morning, during your lunch hour, or in the evening.

At least four times a week, develop an exercise routine that lasts for 30 minutes. It can be slow, stretching exercises, or aerobics. It can involve using exercise equipment, or a combination of those warm up exercises that you hated in P.E. (toe touches, knee bends, twisting at the waist). It can be brisk walking, or it can be slow jogging. Do whatever you want, as long as you move and do **something**.

Journaling

Journaling is the act of recording your thoughts or feelings on paper. As such, it is an invaluable tool. Simply get any sort of notebook and start writing a little every day. It doesn't have to be fancy, grammatical, or even logical. Nobody will see it but you.

Find a quiet spot and start writing. Write everything and anything that comes to your mind. Sadness. Happiness. Anger. Just let it flow. Journaling will prevent the problems that come from keeping everything bottled up.

The simple act of writing also helps focus thoughts and anxieties. It provides a record of what you are going through. Later in your grief recovery, you can look back on it to find strength and progress.

Journaling is a way of always having a friend nearby who just listens, without criticism or comment. That friend (your journal) is there even in the wee hours of the morning when sleep is impossible and your mind refuses to "turn off."

Much of our research on widows came from Hospice, bereavement support groups, and individuals who graciously shared their journals. In every case, it was the first time they had shared their journals with an outsider. What a privilege on our part to have the trust of these caring people!

Why would people share something so intimate? The

common thread was that every individual wanted their own suffering to be used to help others. They felt that by sharing themselves with us, and ultimately you, that it could help you through your pain.

Isn't it comforting to know that people you will never meet are willing to share their innermost thoughts for your benefit? That is the beauty of support groups and friends who have "been there." Someday, your journal might enable you to help someone else who is suffering.

Dear John

Another idea, similar to journaling, is writing letters to your spouse. While some feel this is just playing games, others find it very comforting and helpful. You can personalize your feelings straight to him, then burn it, stick it in your journal, file it, or whatever.

Sometimes these letters are loving, as this one from a widow:

Dearest John,

Could it really be three weeks since you left me? It seems like just yesterday. How can the world keep going when I am frozen in time? The sun shines. People go about their business. And I feel like I've been swallowed by a huge, dark storm cloud. Why don't others see it?

Sometimes I find myself talking to you as though you are still here. I miss you so much. I'd love to just touch you one more time, to feel the strength and warmth of your arms around me. Then I could gather the strength to get hold of myself.

At other times I get so angry with you for leaving me. How could you suddenly be gone when the kids and I need you so badly? There's so much to be done, and so much of it is new and frightening. You always took such good care of everything. Now there's only me. Why couldn't you have gotten well? Did you really try to fight for life?

The nights are so long and lonely. I can't sleep. I miss having you beside me. I even miss your snoring. Imagine that! But the worst part is the vision of your heart attack, right here in our bed. It replays over and over in my mind, and I can't block it out. The desperation and helplessness, calling 911, the sirens, the medical equipment . . . the shock that nothing could save you. I really loved you, and I always will.

However, sometimes letters are not so nice. Another widow wrote this letter to her husband six years after his death. Notice the anger that's still there.

Bobby,

I hate you for what you did to me and to our children. I resent it to this day the fact that I had to sacrifice time my children needed and deserved because you were too sorry to work and provide your share. When you died, you left us with nothing, not even happy memories.

You were a sick, sorry SOB. You made no provisions for our needs or the future of your children. I hate you because I hated caring for you and providing for you. I would not and could not ever take care of another man. The past is past, but you did a terrible job on me emotionally. You manipulated me and made me feel responsible for you. Now, today, I know we are each responsible for ourselves. You died, but we never resolved anything.

This shows the importance of letter writing. In the case of the second woman, she harbored resentment a number of years after her husband's death. That resentment affected her relationships with other men. Divorcees also harbor a lot of resentment, as the next letter illustrates.

Dear Ken,

I hate you. I hate you. I hate you, you stupid jerk. You were such a big shot, weren't you? Well, you're not now. You're nothing but a jerk. I hate you and your kids hate you. I hope you're satisfied. But do you know what? We're better off without you. At least now there's some peace and quiet in our home. We don't have your stupid ranting and raving to worry about. The kids and I can enjoy ourselves without having to worry about aggravating you. What a pleasure.

Writing a letter will allow you to express very intimate thoughts. You might want to put your really strong, frightening feelings into letter form, to be sure that it's separate from your journal. You may choose to share your journal at some point and you might be uncomfortable recording your strongest emotions in it. Everyone is different. Do what is best for you. But getting it off your chest will help you heal.

Why should I reach out to others?

Reaching out to others is a wonderful way to increase your own healing. That is one reason support groups are so helpful. They allow you to model after people who are survivors and learn their survival secrets. However, there is also a great healing power in feeling important, needed, accepted, and understood.

Support groups

A bereavement group for widows, or a support group for divorcees, can be so helpful. All the participants "have been there," so they are not intimidated by tears. Nor are they threatened by your desire to cling to the past. That is a natural part of grief, too. They can even help you laugh again.

Just like people, support groups come in all sizes and shapes. Hospice is a wonderful organization with a presence in areas. They have trained counselors, support groups, and a variety of other services. Hospice is acclaimed for its work with the dying and their families, but many people don't realize it is equally involved with the bereaved. You can reach their national organization at (783) 243-5900. Another group that is frequently recommended by widows is AARP - WPS (American Association of Retired Persons - Widowed Persons Service).

The first months, or even the first year of bereavement, is not a time when you can expect to function as a "normal, consenting adult." This is another reason support groups are so important. You can bounce your confusing dilemmas off others and reach better conclusions.

Friends, family and clergy

First, get rid of the thought that you are a bother! People need to be needed. Your friends, family, and clergy really do want to be there for you. They will receive joy and other intrinsic rewards by providing you with someone with whom to talk. The clergy have had special training in grief counseling, all in preparation for the day when they can serve in that capacity.

You've probably heard the old adage, "A joy shared is twice the joy, a sorrow shared is half the sorrow." This has never been more true. It will help you so much to share your sorrow. It will lift some of the weight of your grief, while not overburdening your confidante.

As mentioned earlier, someone who will listen is one of the greatest helps. Treasure that person! Go for walks together, pick up the phone, invite them over. Talking is one of the most beneficial things you can do - even if it only consists of two words and five minutes of crying.

Many offer pity, others offer advice or reassurance. Even more don't know what to say, so they shy away and leave widows and divorcees feeling shucked-aside.

So many want to help: "Let me know if there's anything I can do." Then they never repeat their offer and you feel too uncomfortable to ask for help.

Assume that people are sincere, and do ask for their help. If you don't feel like going to the store, ask one of the volunteers to pick up some things the next time she goes. Perhaps one could babysit while you take a long walk.

Parents and in-laws can be the greatest help in the short-term, yet create the most difficult problems in the long-run.

Marsha checked herself in the mirror for the tenth time. She had to march downstairs and be firm with Bob's parents. It was time to move ahead.

She had been so grateful when they took over the funeral arrangements, then brought Marsha and the kids home with them. They took care of everything, but after about a month, Marsha felt pulled to return home.

The kids needed their friends and routines. They were beginning to complain, and she needed to be among the familiar household items that she and Bob had treasured together. Besides, she was beginning to feel more like a 13-year-old than a responsible adult. It was grating on her nerves.

Once family members take over, invisible threads begin to constrain and bind. The children become the living link with the deceased, so family members want to cling to the children. Your own parents may have resumed the parenting role because they see you as weak and vulnerable. They love you and want to help, but that love may cripple you in the long run if it undermines your own self-esteem and independence.

Professional counseling?

Deciding whether to seek professional counseling is a very individual decision. Remember, we are physical, emotional, and spiritual beings. The medical doctor is not the only practitioner who can help us. There is no shame or embarrassment attached to needing physical health care. Likewise, there is certainly nothing wrong with needing help emotionally or spiritually.

If you are unable to cope with your normal routine for

over a week, or you are having frequent suicidal thoughts, or if you feel severely depressed, then make an appointment to see someone **today**! A counselor can help you start coping sooner. It's ridiculous to suffer and force yourself to endure needless pain. You are already suffering enough.

> *I was embarrassed to go to the clinic until they said to me, "Seeking a counselor or therapist is like a trip to the dentist. You have a problem that hurts. So you walk in, get examined, and learn what is going on. Then you can receive treatment and get on with your life. Most people ignore their emotional state until it becomes a huge, gaping cavity. Then they need a root canal. If you catch emotional problems early, you may only need a few months of therapy. At that point, you can check your progress and see if you need to continue. However, if you ignore those problems, therapy could take years." Now I'm not embarrassed. I'm proud of myself for getting the help I need.*

You should not be deterred from choosing therapy because of the cost. Most communities have mental health services that work on sliding scales, even for free. Many medical schools and colleges also provide low cost mental health services.

If you feel desperate but can't get an immediate appointment with a therapist, call Hospice or a similar organization. They probably can help you make the right contacts for prompt professional help.

Dealing with bitterness

Divorcees, especially, are filled with bitterness and anger. As with grief, this is a long-term healing process. Studies show that half of all middle and upper-class women make hostile remarks about their ex-husband a year and a half after the divorce is final.

Five years later, almost a third still express a great deal of bitterness toward their ex-spouse. Nearly half still lack social or psychological stability. It's a long process.

The really sad part is what happens to the ultimate victims of the bitterness - your children. They are frequently used as weapons by bitter, estranged parents. They are the ones who most often hear the angry, hostile remarks. Somehow, they often feel responsible.

Please try hard not to use your children as the recipients of your hostility. It undermines their feelings of security and love, and lowers their self-esteem. It leaves them hurt and angry, without an acceptable outlet for their own fears and frustrations.

In addition, using your time and energy being bitter and angry hurts you more than it hurts your ex-husband. How is he damaged? Is he the one immobilized by anger? Is he the one who is miserable from your rage? Of course not. **You** are the one who is hurt by it. Let go of it. Get on with your life. Your future is ahead of you.

Guidelines

✓ *Make a list of people who volunteer to "help anyway I can - just let me know." Call on them as needed.*

✓ *Be kind to your body. Try to eat right, get some exercise, and build time into your day to pamper yourself. You need it now more than ever!*

✓ *Don't bottle up your feelings. That leads to depression.*

✓ *Join a support group to get reinforcement and encouragement from people who really understand.*

✓ *Keep a journal.*

✓ *Get professional help right away if you need it, particularly if you are having suicidal thoughts.*

Part Six

Special Concerns

Of Divorcees

Chapter 48

How Do I Prepare For Divorce?

On the Richter Scale of life, divorce comes in as the third greatest quake . . . surpassed only by death of a spouse and loss of a child. It's no wonder that it creates so much tumult and aftershock.

I'm in total shock. Jim told me we needed to talk. I knew he wasn't real happy, but I didn't think things were that bad. He said he wants out. He claims there isn't another woman, but I don't know if I believe him.

Divorce is filled with all kinds of emotions, guilt, and second-thoughts. "Is it my fault? Could I have done more? What could I have done differently? Did I pay too much attention to the kids?"

There is probably plenty of blame to go around, but that's in the past. If, in fact, divorce is inevitable, then it's time to move forward and protect yourself.

Should I do it?

If you are considering a divorce, but haven't yet made the decision, we don't envy you. It's not an easy decision. Many questions may be running through your head.

- If there are children involved, how will they cope?
- Can I afford it?
- How will my friends and family react?
- Will I have special religious problems?
- Can't I just work harder to resolve our marital problems?

- Who really wants the divorce, my husband or I?
- Will the two of us be civil or will we go to war?
- What will people think of me?
- Can I handle living on my own?
- How do I know that divorce won't be worse than marriage?
- Is he really that bad?
- Do I want to spend the rest of my life without him?
- Do I want to spend the rest of my life with him?
- Do I want to live the next 10 years like I've lived'the past 10 years?

You can drive yourself crazy trying to think this thing through. One scary fact remains: you really don't know what is going to happen until it happens. All you can do is prepare yourself as much as possible, and go into the process with your eyes open. This section will help you do that.

FINANCIAL REALITIES

Money has been well documented as one of the major causes of divorce. It is also the primary problem after divorce.

Statistics reported on CNN in May 1993, revealed that as of 1989 (the year the study was performed) there were 4.5 million divorced women age 45 or older. There were over 1.6 million divorced women over the age of 65. One fourth of all divorced women subsisted at the poverty level.

Consider that for every two marriages recorded, there is one divorce added to the records. This indicates that half of all marriages now end in divorce. Other data supports these findings. The odds of divorce are even greater in marriages when at least one partner marries for the second time.

This supports a variety of other research over recent years. For example, women who divorce after 18 years of marriage fare the worst. They tend to be "displaced homemakers," defined as women who have been out of the work force for five years or more and lack the proper education and skills. As a rule, they are from upper-middle class marriages. Within the first year after divorce, their living standard typically drops to less than half what it was while married. Yet their ex-husbands' standard of living typically zooms 222%, probably because they're not paying their child support or alimony. Among no-fault divorces, women tend to experience a 73% decline in standard of living while men experience a 42% increase.

Who is getting divorced? One out of every six adult Americans is divorced. The highest incidence is now among long-duration marriages. It used to be more common among short marriages of very young, immature people. Not anymore.

Experts predict that half of all marriages involving baby boomers will end in divorce. As society becomes more accepting, and as women's roles are redefined, we will see an even greater increase in divorce rates.

Reality

Statistics are just numbers. It doesn't matter that the chance of rain is only ten percent if it rains on your backyard barbecue. What you experience is the only thing that matters. That is the most relevant statistic of all.

From a woman's standpoint, the easiest financial recoveries are among young women in their 20's and 30's with no children. Typically, they have had short marriages, good educations, and well-established careers. Unlike their mothers, they have been working their entire lives, therefore they are better prepared for what lies ahead. Unfortunately, those well-prepared women represent a tiny minority of the total population of divorced women.

Families headed by single women have increased tremendously, and have become the fastest growing segment of American poor. One-third will never rise above the poverty level.

It's no wonder women become angry and bitter. While they often feel better about themselves after the divorce, their lives are much different. During the marriage, many entertained friends, took vacations, and exchanged expensive presents at holidays. Now they often find themselves alone with the full burden of childrearing, barely enough money to get by, and very little else. There is no money or time for vacations. Arrangements have to be made to take care of the children during their school breaks . . . adding to the guilt that already pounds in their heads.

Holidays become dreaded reminders of their change in status. No longer can they send the presents that were once their trademark. Receiving presents becomes equally uncomfortable. In reality, it is more difficult to receive than to give - especially if you are unable to reciprocate in equal value, if at all.

Face it. Life after divorce, as well as the divorce itself, can be hard on your self-esteem. This is true whether or not you initiated it. Now is the time to take stock of yourself. Look for your good points. Choose ways to pull yourself together, building self-confidence and self-esteem along the way.

LAYING THE GROUNDWORK

If you are still in the preliminary stages, or just considering divorce, we strongly urge you to go to the library and bookstore to obtain some books on the subject. Become aware of what lies ahead and ways to handle the problems you will face.

The most important challenge is gathering all the

information you can, so you can go into the divorce with your eyes wide open. That means getting a handle on your financial situation, because finances play a major role in any divorce.

Paperwork

Even if nothing else seems to be in your corner, be sure you have the right paperwork. You may never need all of it, but knowing where it is located is the same as having an insurance policy.

Susan and Jane were talking over a cup of coffee at McDonald's. It had been years since the former classmates had made time to see each other, yet they were still as close as ever.

"Thanks so much, Jane. I really appreciate you letting me store some things at your house. Your idea of allowing me to use your address for deliveries is great."

Susan sipped her coffee then continued. "Things just aren't getting any better with Greg. We tried marriage counseling, but he'll never change. It's just a matter of time. He's dragging me down with all this debt he keeps taking on . . . we can barely keep up with the minimum payments. He was so angry when I refused to co-sign that last note. I don't even know why businesses continue to lend us money."

Pausing to blot the tears, Susan took a deep breath and revealed her plans. "I know this marriage is on its last legs. I'll start moving my clothes, some household things, and copies of all our financial papers to your house. He probably won't even notice. I've set up my own P.O. Box and bank account in Summerville. He never goes there. I know I have to establish my own credit before we get a divorce, or else his debts will prevent me from ever having a decent rating. I've had my lawyer draw up a form saying that I will no longer accept responsibility for any loans Greg gets. With your help, I will be able to make a clean break and get on my feet."

Susan may still have some problems getting out from under the marital debt, but she's on the right track. If more women would make definite preparations **before** leaving their marriage, the transition would be much easier.

You've heard, "There's more than one way to skin a cat." Well, having proper documentation puts you in control by providing you with the necessary information to back up your claims. It can also help provide guidelines for setting up a new budget and determining your monthly expenses. Most divorcees underestimate their expenses. This is especially critical to substantiate your need for alimony or child support.

Top 10 ways to cover your assets

The following is a checklist of documents and information you need to have, along with additional lines for items you think are important. Check each as you obtain the information.

_____ A complete inventory of your household goods, preferably by video, and notes as to value and purchase date. Check your insurance files for these.

_____ Personal and business tax returns for the past several years. If your husband used a tax preparer, that person is required by law to keep copies for three years. Otherwise, call the IRS (1-800-TAX-FORM), and request Form 4506 (Request for Copy of Tax Form). This form need not be signed by your husband, assuming the two of you filed a joint return. The IRS charges $4.25 for this service. Processing time is approximately ten days to two months.

_____ Financial statements from banks and loan applications. Often things that are overlooked when filing taxes are somehow remembered when proving credit worthiness.

_____ Prenuptial agreements, or any other agreements showing how assets or income are to be split.

_____ Business and home accounting records, including

bank statements, ledgers, budget books, check registers, etc.

_____ Copies of notes payable to you, by you, or outstanding credit card bills.

_____ Deeds or contracts.

_____ Personal or business insurance papers.

_____ Statements from brokerage firms, mutual funds, partnerships, or other investment records. This includes appraisals on any collectibles (antiques, jewels, hobby or sports collections).

_____ A copy of your ex-husband's pay stub, pension agreement, profit sharing plan, or other retirement program.

_____ _____

_____ _____

_____ _____

This information will provide a world of data that will help you with your divorce. Knowledge is power. The more facts and figures you have, the more power you will have. Your goal is to know every detail about your finances. This will put you in a position to challenge anything your husband says.

Tax returns

Use your tax returns to help create a financial statement. This can then be entered on the forms in Appendix A. By using your tax return, you can gather a tremendous amount of information about your family's finances. Obviously, the tax return shows the income you and your husband have received from your employment or business. Beyond that, it tells a lot about how much money you have in various investments.

You are required to report interest and dividend income on your tax return. If the total is over $400, you must list each financial institution on Schedule B of your tax return. By reviewing that form, you can determine the sources of interest and dividend income. From that, you can get an approximate value of the investment itself.

For example, if you received $400 interest from the bank, you can assume you have $10,000 in that account. How? By dividing the interest you received by the estimated interest rate, you arrive at the investment amount. In this case, dividing $400 by 4% (.04) gives you $10,000. Do this for each entry to figure out how much money you actually have. The same can be done with dividend income. In addition, if you had profits and losses from the sale of securities (stocks, bonds, and mutual funds) or real estate, they are shown on IRS Schedule D.

However, a tax return doesn't reveal everything. The value of your home and other real estate doesn't appear, nor does information about your husband's retirement accounts. Everything else will have to be obtained during the deposition phase of the divorce process, unless you have access to that information.

Checkbook records

You must calculate your estimated living expenses. Just going after an arbitrary amount of alimony or child support is not enough. Sit down and do a complete budget. Again, the forms in Appendix A will help you in this area.

Do not puff up the figures because you think you "deserve" more. That can come in negotiations later. You don't want to become the greedy, bitter, divorcee stereotype. Divorce is a numbers game, and like anything else involving money, it should be businesslike and unemotional. You will get a lot further that way.

That doesn't mean you shouldn't stick up for your rights. Be tough and fight for every penny. Just back up your demands with reasonable statistics and figures.

Home sweet home

There are many decisions you must make, the first of which is where to live. Since continuity is so important for children, the custodian of the children is often advised to keep the marital home. That is why some divorcees recommend enrolling preschoolers in a nearby day care center before the divorce . . . to set a precedent for maintaining the same school district.

However, staying in the marital home is typically too costly. If it was tough affording your lifestyle when you were married, maintaining that level after divorce will be almost impossible.

Don't be in too big a rush to ask for the home. There are heavy maintenance costs involved with home ownership. You'll have upkeep, property taxes, and utilities. It may add up to more than you can handle. If you can't afford it, you will be forced to sell your house. In rough economic times, there is no guarantee that you can sell it, let alone get a good price for it. That can dissolve any equity very quickly. In addition, you face foreclosure if you can't keep up the payments. So don't rush into this. Know your figures and find out for yourself if this is a burden you can handle.

You have a conflict to resolve. On the one hand, you want to stay in the same home to maintain continuity for your children. On the other hand, doing so would probably place tremendous financial burdens on you. If this is the case, it would be best to move, but try to do so within the same school district. A "building" just isn't worth the emotional and financial cost. See Chapter 36 for a deeper discussion of this issue.

Family

Moving in with friends or family members can certainly help reduce costs, but at the same time it opens a host of new problems.

> *Jana rubbed her aching temples with stiff fingers. She breathed deeply, hoping to calm the tension that was causing her to tremble with barely suppressed anger. Mom had been so good to invite Jana and the kids to move in with her after the divorce. It seemed like such a good way to save money and get a little sympathy and nurturing until she could get back on her feet.*
>
> *Ever since, though, she had felt more like the child than the mother! "Jana, pick up your room before you go to work. Jana, surely you're not going to let Mark go to bed without a bath. Jana, you really need to spend more time with Sue and not let her watch so much TV. Jana, Jana, Jana . . . !" This was nearly as bad as her marriage. It seemed as if she'd have to "divorce" her mom, too.*

Newly divorced people are especially vulnerable immediately after the proceedings. It is a very difficult time to establish other new relationships, which are required if you do move in with someone. Parents tend to take over and expect you to fit back into old relationship patterns. Friends soon begin to feel taken advantage of and resent their lack of privacy.

If possible, strike out on your own. Renting a house or apartment will give you the freedom to change your mind about where you want to live as you adjust to your new circumstances. You may find that living close to your job, your children's school, or even shopping is more important than you had realized. Proximity can also reduce your costs drastically, especially if you live in a fairly large city and can manage without a car.

Whether you rent or buy, take time to discover what your new budget can handle before making a long-term commitment to living quarters. Consider the costs of maintenance, yardwork, insurance, transportation, utilities, etc. Think especially about safety.

LOOKING AFTER MYSELF

Much of what you need to do will depend upon the relationship you maintain with your ex-husband. If you can get along, great. Unfortunately, what begins as an amicable divorce often winds up as World War III.

Some people have pleasant, no-fault divorces. Both parties put the kids first. Both seek to be more than fair with the other, and assets are fairly and equally distributed. This is a rare situation.

More often than not, divorce is a nasty mess with scars that may never heal. You end up facing harsh new realities that seem impossible to handle. While you will typically obtain custody of the children, your standard of living may drop significantly while your ex-spouses's increases astronomically.

You need to protect yourself. Chances are, your husband is more familiar with your financial situation than you. That puts you at an immediate disadvantage! However, if you begin by gathering the information listed earlier in this chapter, you will be on your way to evening the odds.

You can take it with you

The rule of thumb leaving your marriage should be: **fight for a fair settlement.** "Fair" is the important word here. Too frequently mistakes are made on both sides: one party is usually too willing to fold first.

Often, the wife just wants to escape from the marriage. She doesn't demand enough - she only wants out. She doesn't want to appear greedy, nor further anger her husband and cause possible retaliation. So she leaves pretty much empty-handed, and regrets it down the road.

> *Carla was so glad to finally be free and on her own. She willingly left everything behind. Who would have ever guessed how much money it would take for just a few basics? The credit card was maxed out with purchases for the kitchen and some linens. It would take months to pay that off before she could even consider buying a bed or table. Just thinking about everything she left behind (dishes, cookware, supplies and furnishings) made her ill. He'd never use half the stuff, and she couldn't afford to replace it.*

Women often don't account for the value of all their wedding gifts, hand-me-down furniture, and other household goods that were picked up along the way.

If it's too late to try to retrieve household goods, and money is tight, then spend time at garage sales and thrift shops. Useful and often high quality items can be found at very reasonable prices simply because people want to upgrade or avoid moving household items. Always try to get the best possible quality for the least possible cost. If that means buying used items, then so what? Even if it's new, it will be "used" as soon as you get it home.

Take the first offer?

It is interesting to note that, commonly, the first offer the husband makes to his wife is the best, especially if he initiates the divorce. He feels guilty. He just wants out, and he will pay any price to get out without a big hassle.

The wife, on the other hand, feels hurt, angry, and betrayed. She may be determined to get every penny she can. She wants to "take him to the cleaners" (punish him for what he's done to her), her emotions get in the way, and the fight is on.

The longer the fight continues, the worse it becomes. You both allow your anger to get in the way of meaningful negotiations. You need strangers (attorneys, judges, and juries) to settle your arguments, and you both lose.

You must face reality: huge settlements are rare. In many cases, the husband doesn't pay anyway, even if alimony and child support are awarded. So save legal fees if at all possible and come to an equitable settlement.

Alimony and child support

Far be it from us to tell you how much alimony and child support you deserve. Everyone's situation is different.

This is something you should not handle yourself. You need a qualified attorney. There is a lot of money at stake and many years ahead. Shortchanging yourself now can make a world of difference in the future.

Getting the proper amount of alimony and child support is a game that you must play to win. The field of play might be your attorney's office or the court room. Somebody will win and somebody will lose.

If you have custody of the children, you especially need to be tough. Your children's welfare is at stake. This involves strategy and negotiation. Don't give in. Don't let up. Don't depend on voluntary increases later. Do insist that child support payments increase with your ex-husband's pay. Get it in writing, and do it right the first time.

Debt and divorce

Generally, you are responsible for your personal debts, your husband for his. However, in most states, both of you are equally responsible for debts **you both signed** for during the marriage. Your divorce decree should specify who is responsible for these joint obligations. In some cases, you can be held responsible for charges you made on his card, and vice versa.

Regardless of who incurred the debts, keep a list of all of them. It's also a good idea to get some distance from your ex-husband (and his debts) by establishing your own post office box, etc., prior to the divorce.

> *I thought I was so smart. The divorce decree clearly stated that the car loan, personal loans, and credit card loans were Dave's responsibility. Then I started getting harassing phone calls and warnings from the companies he owed. I explained that they needed to talk to him. The debts were his debts, and our divorce decree even stated so. But they said they didn't care, that I was still responsible because I was on all of the accounts.*

> *I couldn't believe it. My lawyer said they were within their rights. My only recourse would be to get Dave's wages garnished, but my credit would still be ruined unless I made sure they were paid. I couldn't sleep well until I knew every last penny of those old debts had been paid off.*

Understand that your **divorce decree** is an agreement between you and your ex-husband. The **loan agreement** is between you (along with your ex-husband if you both signed) and the lender. Those are two separate documents. The credit card company isn't interested in your divorce decree and is not a party to it. All they care about is who is legally responsible for paying them, and that is governed by the loan agreement.

That is why you must be careful before co-signing any loans. Doing so makes you equally responsible for **all** the debt, not just your portion.

If you are planning to get divorced, destroy all credit cards and write letters to the companies advising them that you will not be responsible for future charges. Send the letters "Certified Mail - Return Receipt Requested," so you'll know they were received. And keep copies of all correspondence. Divorce is difficult enough without having to make extra payments.

Life insurance

Alimony and child support involve a significant amount of money over the years. If your husband dies while liable for support, it will cost you dearly. Therefore, include a provision in your agreement requiring him to purchase a term insurance policy on himself, with you as beneficiary. The amount should total the lifetime aggregate of the payments he is required to pay. If you can't get him to pay the premium, then you pay it. Purchase level or decreasing term insurance only at the lowest premium available. Review Chapter 18.

Retirement plans

If he has a significant amount in a retirement plan that was earned during your marriage, you should be entitled to a portion of it. Make sure you, or your attorney, obtain this information. He should receive periodic (usually quarterly) statements that provide the value for his accounts. Get a copy of the latest statement. Otherwise, have your attorney demand it during the deposition and discovery stage of the proceedings.

Health insurance

COBRA, the Consolidated Omnibus Benefits Reconciliation Act, might force your ex-husband's health insurance company to provide benefits to you, at your expense. Rules change annually, so check current regulations.

Eligibility. If your husband worked for a company with at least twenty employees and participated in a group health plan, you are probably eligible for continued health insurance after your divorce, as long as you are a "qualified beneficiary" and your loss of coverage was a "qualifying event," which includes divorce.

Length of coverage. You are entitled to coverage up to 36 months if the qualifying event was divorce.

Premium. The premium the employer charges you can be no more than 102% of the premium the employer pays for current employees. However, if any qualified beneficiary is disabled upon qualifying, then the cost can go as high as 150% of the normal premium.

Social Security

Review Chapter 23 for a complete discussion of Social Security benefits. There are a number of ramifications of divorce, including the number of years you were married. Make sure you understand your benefits.

Guidelines

✓ *Before the divorce, gather as much financial information as possible. Keep copies of <u>all</u> related papers.*

✓ *Establish your own mailing address, checking account, and credit.*

✓ *Insist on keeping your fair share of household items and joint property.*

✓ *Negotiate for alimony and child support. Don't get greedy, but don't get "taken to the cleaners," either.*

✓ *Check into your benefits from retirement plans, social security, health care, life insurance, etc.*

✓ *Complete a financial inventory and set up a realistic budget.*

✓ *Try to live independently, but don't make any long-term commitments right away.*

✓ *Protect your children from the fray of divorce.*

Chapter 49

How Is The IRS A Third Party In My Divorce?

The IRS (Internal Revenue Service) is frequently called the third party in divorce. Most people never even consider the tax effects of divorce. For starters, your tax status will change from "Married Filing Jointly" to "Single" or "Head of Household." Your taxes may increase simply because the deductions and allowances are different in those categories.

Head of Household

Tax-wise, it is better to claim Head of Household status rather than Single. Many divorced couples split the children (at least on paper) so each can file as Head of Household. This is not proper under the law. To take advantage of this filing status, you must meet all of the following criteria:

- Be legally unmarried (or legally separated) at the end of the year.

- Maintain a household (pay more than half the cost of maintaining this household) for your dependent child.

- This household must be the primary home for you and your child.

- Be a U.S. citizen or resident alien for the entire year.

Deducting children

If you have dependent children, they can be claimed as

exemptions. However, you and your ex-husband cannot both claim them. The determination is made as follows:

- **Support.** The parent who provides more than half the support of the child may claim him or her. Normally, this is the custodial parent.

- **Special Agreement.** If both parties agree, the non-custodial parent may claim the child by filing Form 2120 with the IRS.

Unpaid taxes

If your ex-husband hasn't been claiming all of his income for tax purposes, or if he has been padding his business expenses, you may have a real dilemma. If you say nothing, he will pay less alimony or child support because he has lower income. If you "blow the whistle," you also trap yourself.

When you sign a joint return, you are equally liable for the taxes. However, there are limited circumstances that may free you from liability. Generally, if you had no knowledge of any misrepresentation, and the tax due is over $500, you may be relieved of liability. There are some special rules that you must meet in order to qualify for this. We recommend seeking the advice of a tax consultant.

Property split

Another important tax consideration occurs when property and assets are split during the divorce. It might be wiser to transfer appreciated property to each other (change the name on deeds or titles) rather than sell the assets and split the proceeds. This is because the sale of appreciated assets creates income tax implications, whereas transfer of title does not. Examples of assets that might fit into this category include the house, real estate, stocks, bonds, and collectibles.

Retirement plans

If you receive your husband's IRA as a result of your divorce decree, it can be transferred into your own IRA, with no tax liability. Once you remove the money, however, it is subject to normal IRA tax treatment.

If you receive a portion of your husband's employer sponsored retirement plan under a "Qualified Domestic Relations Order," you don't have to pay income taxes on that money, provided you roll it into your own IRA. If you don't do a rollover, then you must pay income taxes on it. In addition, if you are under the age of 59½, you must pay a 10% IRS penalty. Review Chapter 40 for a complete discussion of rollovers.

Guidelines

✓ *Be aware of the importance of your filing status.*

✓ *Be aware of tax implications when splitting property.*

✓ *Transfer any retirement money received in the settlement into an IRA.*

Chapter 50

Can I Depend On Alimony and Child Support?

The days of permanent alimony are long gone for all but a handful of women. If you can get alimony for a few years, consider yourself fortunate. Put that money to good use.

Latest research shows that few women receive alimony for more than five years. Most who get it at all receive it for two years or less. Judges tend to take the attitude that women should be self-sufficient within a few years.

If you need additional education to become established in your desired field, use your alimony for that. Begin immediately. It can be very hard to collect if he quits sending payments, so don't waste a dime. Preparing for a better job, as Martha did in the following case, can be one of the best investments you'll ever make.

I wasn't shocked that my husband wanted a divorce, but I wasn't prepared for it, either. I spent most of my years at home, caring for the family. I didn't have the skills to support myself. I certainly didn't want to go back to work doing menial tasks. I was awarded alimony for three years in addition to child support. I decided I had to do something quickly before the alimony stopped. I met with a counselor at the vocational school and decided to take accounting. I received financial assistance to pay the tuition while the alimony paid my bills.

I felt a little funny going to school with all those young people, but they really respected me for what I was doing. When I finished, I got a decent job. But I am now self-sufficient and feel good about what I did for myself. I never felt like I was capable of doing anything when I was married. Now I know I can do anything I want.

Martha made great use of her alimony. Louise, in the following excerpt, did not choose as wisely.

As I look back now, I guess I was kind of stupid. I never was good with money, and I was so damn mad at Dick for leaving me. I moped around, thinking about what I should do, but never doing it. I just collected the money and spent it on the kids and me. Now it has stopped and I am really in trouble. I'm tired of living on food stamps, but I don't know what else to do.

There is value in being a productive person. Martha took steps to better herself. As a result, she felt good about what she accomplished. Her self-esteem bloomed.

Louise did the opposite, and her self-esteem dropped even lower. Both made choices, but they went in opposite directions. You can see the difference.

The best possible investment you can make is your education. Enter one of the many programs available through vocational and technical schools. Financial aid is available for anyone who needs it. There is no excuse for not doing it!

Tax implications

Alimony is taxable income for the recipient and tax deductible for the payer. No taxes are withheld. Since you will probably change your tax filing status from "Married Filing Jointly" to "Single" or "Head of Household," expect your taxes to increase. The taxes are stiffer in your new category, assuming your income level remains the same.

If you receive alimony, you will probably have to pay quarterly estimated taxes. You do this by sending in your tax payment along with Form 1040-ES, Estimated Tax for Individuals, by April 15, June 15, September 15, and January 15 of each year. Failure to do this may mean that you have underestimated your taxes for the year, possibly resulting in your having to pay interest and penalties.

Child support

Child support is neither taxable to the recipient, nor tax deductible for the payer. That is the good news for you if you are receiving it.

Now the bad news. Despite statistics showing that the typical husband's standard of living increases after divorce (while the wife and children's decline), collecting child support is a real problem. It is very easy for men to get away with not paying, because the laws are seldom enforced. In fact, 60% to 80% of court ordered child support is never paid. None! Ever! That is not only tragic, it's criminal! How can fathers rationalize dumping their children this way? One newly divorced and bitter man justified it this way at a divorce support group.

> *You've got to be kidding! I'm allowed to see my children 90 minutes out of each month. For this privilege I'm supposed to pay $750 a month?! She's got to be dreaming!*

While some men remain excellent, caring fathers after the divorce, most do not. They feel just as divorced from the children as they do from the children's mother. They feel no personal or moral obligation to protect and provide for their children.

Fortunately, laws and attitudes are changing along with technology. As computers, computer networks, and communications improve, enforcement officers are becoming more willing to assist in finding those who refuse to pay child support. In addition, states are required to have a code of minimum uniform child support standard that is tied to the father's gross income. Check your state's laws to determine the amount to which you may be entitled.

Assistance

Many states have already established cooperative

information networks to help in tracking down delinquent parents. This makes it much easier to trace people using drivers license numbers, social security numbers, work records, and other similar types of information.

If your ex-husband moves out of state, the Uniform Reciprocal Enforcement of Support Act (URESA) can help locate him. This network even includes U.S. Territories. **For a complete state by state listing of Child Support Enforcement Agencies, see Appendix B.**

Another helpful agency is the Association for Children for Enforcement of Support (ACRES). Their address is 1018 Jefferson Avenue, Suite 204, Toledo, OH 43624.

Check with your congressional and state representatives. Laws are constantly changing. They might be able to help.

Even the IRS can be your friend on the child support issue. If all else fails, the IRS can withhold refunds from men who are delinquent in their child support payments. You may want to give them a call if this is a problem. They will send you the appropriate forms.

Guidelines

    ✓ *Do not count on alimony or child support as your main source of income.*

    ✓ *If you receive alimony, invest that money in your future by using it to enhance your job skills or to further your education.*

    ✓ *Insist on regular child support payments. Follow through with enforcement agencies listed in Appendix B whenever payments cease.*

Chapter 51

How Can I Deal With The Pain?

Anyone who has lived through divorce can tell you that this is one of the most shattering, disruptive events of their lives. Researchers score only the death of a spouse or child higher in terms of impact.

Divorced women are people in pain. Even years later, they long for someone to verify their status, to tell them they are accepted "as is." They wish for understanding and a little sympathy for their side of the story.

Our society has an abundance of **advice** givers, but very few **care** givers. Even in churches, it is hard to find sympathetic pastors with whom you can share your hurt, anger, bitterness, and confusion.

Crisis

Recent divorcees are people in crisis. Crisis is really something that happens within us, rather than to us. Since you are already under tremendous strain, more things seem to go wrong.

Crisis breeds more crisis. You are already stressed and exhausted, and this makes you more prone to accidents, career upheaval, and financial emergencies. As Murphy's Law states, "Whatever can go wrong, will go wrong." It has never seemed so true.

The Chinese word for "crisis" has only two characters. The first character means "danger." The second means "opportunity." To work through crisis constructively, you must see both aspects.

Conflicts

Most divorcees never considered the possibility of divorce. Many were taught that divorce was wrong, or not even an option from a religious standpoint. This results in tremendous guilt and unresolved internal conflict.

When you are in conflict with yourself and your own beliefs, you tend to think others are judging you by the same standards by which you judge yourself. That is manifested greatly by guilt. Your self-esteem is at an all time low. Physically you may be rundown. Your assumptions about what others are thinking snowballs in your mind. You begin to feel paranoid about what others are thinking.

> *I don't know if I'll ever be able to go back to church. I felt like everyone knew about the divorce and they all blamed me. I might as well have gone naked with a huge scarlet letter hanging around my neck - a "D" for divorced. I felt so uncomfortable the whole time, like everyone was staring and talking behind my back. I'm sure they all felt sorry for Walt. They probably think I wasn't a good wife and it was all my fault.*

> *It's almost funny. We have a real active single's group at church, and I always thought it would be fun to join them. I never heard anyone criticize those people. But now that I'm the divorcee, everything seems so different.*

The sad part is that this woman, like so many others, is about to cut herself off from the one group that will nurture and love her, because in her paranoia, she feels so threatened. It doesn't have to be the church. It may be your running club, country club, etc. Whatever the social support group, you probably perceive them as judgmental and threatening.

Are you the divorcee or the divorced? It really doesn't matter to society. Yet you probably think it does. You feel that everyone else is judging and blaming, so you cut off ties and hide. You would rather reject than be rejected.

Survival

Most women are terrified by divorce because they are uncertain of their ability to make it on their own. It has been encouraging and amazing to interview so many women who have actually grown through their divorce. In fact, women fare much better than men in many areas. Are women survivors? You bet! Can you make it? You bet!

True, men usually walk away with more money, but money isn't everything. (It just makes everything else a whole lot easier!) Men suffer more depression after divorce and have a harder time seeking help from others. Women tend to be uplifted, almost exhilarated, by having the decision behind them. They are much more inclined to open up to others, thereby receiving nurturing and support.

Men suffer physical problems and develop negative lifestyles that are damaging, such as smoking, drinking, and overeating. Their sexual activity changes (plenty or none). Women generally start trying to take better care of themselves.

Adjusting

In our experience, women reported very little problem with having to handle additional tasks. On the other hand, men complained of spending significantly more time doing personal and household tasks. Most women understand this phenomenon completely . . . they were already doing <u>everything</u> before the divorce!

I always hated those Enjolie perfume commercials. The woman would sing something like, "I can bring home the bacon, fry it up in a pan. And never, never let you forget you're a man. 'Cause I'm a woman . . ." It just made my blood boil. I did all the shopping, cooking, laundry, housework, and child care. I took the cars to the shop, paid the bills, sorted the mail, and did the yardwork. I worked and brought home almost as much money as he did. For Pete's sake! What did I need him for? He was just another child to care for!

Women have always been told that they are the weaker sex; that they can't handle problems; that they need a man to fall back on. However, our conversations with divorced men and women reflect just the opposite. It is the man who needs someone else. That is why they rush to get remarried - they just can't stand living alone.

Things are not easy for divorced women, but the opportunities are great. You are in a position to be your own person - to do the things that you want to do, without anyone else's approval. Take advantage of it. You'll feel better for spreading your wings and flying.

Look ahead

Pat yourself on the back for making a decision and following through on it. Many women in bad marriages wish they had the courage to be more like you.

Quit second-guessing yourself. Now is the time to look ahead and focus on healing the hurts. Focus on moving forward with new goals and expectations. Stop looking back!

As a beginning driver, I tended to look in the rear view mirror frequently. I always wanted to know if someone was gaining on me or getting near my blind spots. Of course, it was distracting and gave my dad some near heart attacks when I'd lose sight of where I was supposed to be going.

"Keep your eyes on the road ahead of you!" my dad always said. "You can't go forward successfully when you spend all your time looking in the rear view mirror. Focus ahead, and just steal a glance at the rear now and then."

You are at a major turning point in your life. If you keep looking back and second-guessing yourself, you'll go nuts.

Give yourself credit for having made the best decisions possible under the circumstances. Move forward and get on with life.

Living for today

There are people who live in the past, those who live for today, and those who live for tomorrow. Those who live in the past say things like, "I remember when . . ." "If only I had . . ." "I used to be able to . . ."

Those who live for tomorrow say, "One day I'll show him . . ." "I can't wait until _____ happens. Then everything will be okay." "When the children grow up . . ."

People who live for today speak in the present tense. They live fully, making plans and carrying them out. Forget the past! It's gone! There is nothing you can do about it. Don't dream endlessly about things that may never happen. Instead, use your energy to get the most out of today. It is the only place to be.

Guidelines

- ✓ *Expect more things to go wrong when you are in crisis, and be on your guard.*

- ✓ *See the opportunity (the positive) as clearly as you see the danger (the negative).*

- ✓ *Don't isolate yourself from your support groups. Give them the chance to accept the changes in your life.*

- ✓ *Be proud of the courage you have shown and the decisions you have made.*

- ✓ *Don't second-guess yourself.*

- ✓ *Live in the present, but plan for the future.*

Part Seven

Special Concerns

Of Widows

Chapter 52

What Will Happen Now That I'm A Widow?

Shock is such a merciful thing. The first few weeks after his death, you were able to just keep going. So many decisions to make! Yet, you somehow made all the arrangements.

Quickly and efficiently the funeral home was selected. A thousand questions were answered to provide the right information for the news releases and the funeral. People were notified. Others seemingly appeared out of the woodwork and were so supportive.

The casket, flowers, cemetery plot, special funeral requests . . . everything just clicked by with hardly any time for thought, tears, or fears. You somehow mechanically got through the necessary motions. Now, just about everything is a blur. Guilt and sadness are now taking root, overgrowing and choking out each new thought.

Paula slowly rocked as the insistent voices of her adult children washed over her. She felt so detached, yet vulnerable.

Once again a sigh broke through, using up every ounce of her strength. It felt like an elephant was sitting on her chest. How could it be so hard to even breathe, much less make decisions? Everything seemed so overwhelming!

The nights were terror-filled, with flashbacks of those final days, mixed with a sharp awareness of new noises and frightening aloneness. She kept thinking, if she had just acted faster, everything would have been different.

At night, her mind raced as rapidly as her pulse, while she prayed

for blessed, numbing sleep and rest for her aching body. She
had never, ever felt so awful. Paula had always thought of grief
as sadness. But how strange that it really felt like fear. And pain
. . . indescribable pain!

Was Paula going crazy? Would this last forever - the pain, confusion, total exhaustion, eating problems, guilt?

Though she felt completely unique and alone, Paula's experience was typical of many new widows. As her story illustrates, the shock and robot-like ability to make decisions soon departs. Initially everything seems unreal. In that stunned state, new widows are capable and surprisingly unemotional.

Within a few weeks, those supportive friends and family members begin to return to their own lives. Emptiness, confusion, and true grief set in with a vengeance. Widows report, "at first you can't start crying; then later, you can't stop crying."

Don't move too fast

Friends and family want to help. Unfortunately, they often make things worse. The first months are **not** the time to wipe every trace of your husband from your life. The hurt will be there whether those items remain or not. In fact, those little physical reminders are actually helpful. They provide a link with your spouse that can be very comforting.

After the funeral, Paula's adult children wanted to help ease her
burden. They wanted to be as efficient and helpful as possible
while they could be with her. They were ready for Paula to make
decisions, or allow them to make them. They wanted to dispose
of their dad's clothes, clean out his office and workshop, and
remove every trace that might further upset Paula. Perhaps she
should go ahead and move in with one of them, or at least get rid
of that big old house.

There was so much to do and so little time. Soon they were
frustrated beyond belief with Paula. Why did Mom just sit there

rocking, totally ignoring their suggestions?

In time you will be ready to discard his things, but for now just leave them alone. Widows who get rid of everything right away, or return from the funeral to find that this was already done by an overly-zealous friend, have a much rougher time.

Paula said it felt like an elephant was sitting on her chest. Some women say they feel like a wool blanket is stuck in their throats. Others report the sensation of a time bomb ticking and wildly throbbing in their chest or stomach.

These are all normal, common reactions to fear and grief. They are symptoms of your body warning you that things aren't right. You are not ready to function like your old self. Take it easy!

Even Ph.D's. are reduced to a fourth grade functioning level after a major crisis. You can't expect to be your normal self for a while. Go with the flow! Until you can swallow normally, breathe without having to consciously think about it, and concentrate on your thoughts, all nonessential, non-immediate decisions should be postponed.

Length of marriage

Research reveals that young widows experience more physical symptoms during mourning. Widows of long, extremely close marriages tend to have the most prolonged grief. After all, it took many years to achieve that closeness. It only makes sense that it will take a long time to "let go."

As rough as grief becomes, it is the older widower, not widow, who has the highest incidence of suicide. During the first 20 months of bereavement, three times as many widowers as widows commit suicide. This also points out the importance of seeking professional help when your emotional state is too rough to handle, or when suicidal thoughts are constant. This is especially important if a history of emotional problems already exists.

Women have a real inner strength and resilience from which to draw. Although they have problems along the way, women pull through better than men, many of whom never recover.

An evening news television broadcast in April 1993 did a story on emergency room admissions. They found that 34% of all "heart attack" admissions turned out to be panic/anxiety attacks. Since these attacks are not unusual among recent widows, you can imagine the added anguish and embarrassment that many suffer.

Vulnerability

Funerals are very public events. The local newspaper lists pertinent information, which helps not only mourners, but also those unscrupulous souls who want to take advantage of you. Wills have to be probated, which makes every detail public record. Creeps seem to come out of the woodwork!

Homes have been broken into during funerals. (Be thankful for that friend who missed the funeral in order to stay at your home to guard it and prepare the meal.) Unethical salespeople have items such as Bibles embossed with the name of the deceased and try to sell them to grief-stricken family members. Devious companies send COD (cash on delivery) packages "ordered" by the deceased. Amazingly, these are usually accepted and paid for without question. Con men even pose as IRS agents.

Protect yourself

Always ask for identification. Leave unknown visitors outside your locked door while you call their office to verify their information. Do not be concerned about "hurting their feelings." Instead, protect yourself.

> *You wouldn't believe how nice people were to step forward and offer advice. I thought they all really cared about me. It turned out that most of the advice helped them more than it did me. By the time I figured out what was happening, I was very hurt, humiliated, and angry. Then I was afraid to trust anyone.*

You may have problems with professionals such as lawyers, realtors, insurance agents, stockbrokers, and bankers trying to rush you into making snap decisions. Don't! Handle only the required business at hand, and postpone any other decisions until you are ready to cope with them.

There is no reason you should continue to work with anyone who pushes you, talks down to you, or with whom you feel uncomfortable. Just because he or she was the right person for your husband, that does not make him or her the right person for you. You deserve respect and acceptance of your wishes.

Darkest hours

Despite our desire for pat answers, there is no timetable for grief. Each woman has to go through it at her own pace. There are, however, some basic landmarks that apply to the majority.

The first six months are by far the most difficult. If you are journaling, you may need to write daily. Finally, things become less intense, but selected events still rock the boat. Sarah's journal entry tells of one such experience.

> *It's been four long months since Allen's death. I'm still trying to straighten out the health insurance and hospital charges. Today, when I was on the phone with the hospital business office, I commented that it has been four months since his death. Then I started to break down. It hurts more than anyone could begin to*

imagine. I prayed the Lord would use me to help others get through their mourning.

Special holidays, birthdays, anniversaries, and the numerical date of death each month tend to be more difficult. Sundays are also especially hard for many widows.

When holidays or Sundays seem especially lonely, remind yourself that 4½ billion people on earth are feeling the same way. That is how many have currently survived a loss similar to yours. According to the Bureau of Census, by 1992 there were over 11 million widows in the United States alone. That fact won't alleviate the pain, but at least there is comfort in knowing you're not alone.

As time goes on, each death anniversary is anticipated with dread. Sometimes the anxiety begins weeks before the actual day. One widow recorded the following journal entry at the first anniversary of her husband's death:

> *Until now, I have really felt that I was healing. But since Wednesday (the anniversary of the day that death was declared imminent), I've felt worse than ever. It must be due to reliving Ed's last days. The flashbacks keep reappearing, along with the fear and pain.*

She made the following journal entry at the second anniversary:

> *It seems each time I tell myself I feel I am near complete healing - Whamo! I am down. It's almost as though during that utter pain, through the tears and crying, I am spewing out the grief - almost like labor pains. I can't stand it at the time, but when it passes, although I'm utterly exhausted, there is a feeling of relief.*

Often, the fear of the approaching date is far worse than the actual date. As mentioned earlier, the deeper and longer the relationship, the more difficult and longer the healing. The pain at the anniversary can be severely excruciating, just as grief was in the first few months. It can cause low energy and physical symptoms all over again.

One widow had urologists and other specialists perform tests to discover the cause of her illness. The doctors conclusions: the energy loss was emotional due to her husband's death, which is quite common among widows around the anniversary date. She did have a minor infection, but the stress and emotional state blew the symptoms out of proportion.

Normal routine

Return to your familiar surroundings and old routines as soon as you feel able. Routines actually reduce stress and make the bereavement process easier. They increase stability, which is especially important at this time.

Routine is a lot different from packing your days so full of demands that there is no time to think. Exhaustion increases stress, as do any new changes in lifestyle. Pace yourself realistically.

This is not the time to change jobs, return to the work force, retire, or move. Each of those things adds more stress, resulting in many of the physical and emotional problems previously discussed. Even a vacation right away can emphasize your change in marital status and make you feel worse.

Force yourself to get up and get dressed. Also make yourself get out of the house daily, even if it's just for a walk to the mailbox or a trip to the store. Don't isolate yourself.

> *Mourning is the necessary process of getting back on life's track after being jolted from its road. It includes leaving behind what I need to discard, keeping what I need to hang onto, and being able to tell the difference. It is something that I must endure.*

In sifting through all the information and memories, the widow needs time alone to think, as well as time to share with others. Mostly, she just needs time. Time heals. According to a Chinese proverb: "Patience is power; with time and patience the mulberry leaf becomes silk."

Most people don't experience a sense of victory over grief for at least four years. Every day that passes is an achievement and a step forward. Though the grief and pain will return to toss you about from time to time, they will gradually loose their power to overwhelm.

Guidelines

✓ *Do not make any immediate decisions that can wait until you are in a better frame of mind.*

✓ *Don't get rid of your late husband's personal belongings immediately following the funeral. It may take months, or even years, before you are ready.*

✓ *Beware of people who take advantage of your vulnerability.*

✓ *Expect your mourning to prolong in proportion to the length and closeness of your marriage.*

✓ *Return to your normal routine as quickly as possible; it will actually make things easier.*

Chapter 53

What Must Be Done Immediately?

After the death of a spouse, it's hard to know what to do next. Your head becomes so clogged with questions that it's hard for answers to find any space. After the funeral, most widows find themselves at a complete loss trying to separate the immediate priorities from the decisions that can wait. Then, they begin to feel guilty for thinking of "selfish" things.

When Frank died, I was in shock. All I could think of was, "What's going to happen to me?" All kinds of questions went through my mind. "Will I lose everything to taxes? How will I pay my bills? Where's the money going to come from? Where are all the records? Will I lose my home? Will I have to go on welfare? Will I have to move in with my children?" I felt so guilty thinking only of myself so soon after Frank died. I felt so all alone, like a child whose parents had abandoned her on a door step.

Although Maggie felt guilty for her thoughts, she was not unique. It is normal to feel abandoned and alone after the loss of your husband. Some women are like children in that they've been cared for all their lives. It's a shock to suddenly be handed full responsibility.

The guilt you may suffer at your perceived selfishness is not unusual, either. Most women have been taught to feel guilty anytime they think of themselves. The fact is: you are responsible for taking care of yourself, and thinking of your needs is the best way to start.

Your top priority is to get your life in order. You may be entitled to a number of benefits. Some of these have a limited application period. If you wait too long, they're lost forever. In the next chapter, we tell you how to apply for survivor's benefits. First, let's look at changing the titles on your husband's assets.

Your husband's will

Appendix A contains a financial inventory form that will help you as you process your finances. In your search for information, hopefully you will find your husband's will or trust. If not, call your attorney. He or she might have the original.

His will or trust contains instructions for passing his property. If he didn't have a will or trust, then he died "intestate." That means that his property will be divided according to the laws of your state. If he owned property in his name, his estate must be **probated.** That's the process of paying his debts and changing the titles of his property. Whether you have to go through probate is determined by the ownership of his assets.

- **His name alone.** If your husband owned property in his name, it should be changed to the person or persons named in his will (or according to the laws of your state). This property must **go through probate.** While use of an attorney for probate isn't required, it usually makes the process easier.

- **Joint tenants.** If the two of you owned property as "joint tenants" or "joint tenants with rights of survivorship," the property will pass **free from probate.**

- **Joint bank accounts.** As a rule, joint bank accounts are titled in your name "or" his. That means that either party can withdraw the money. Sometimes, the bank may freeze the accounts.

- **Tenants in common.** This differs from "joint tenancy" in that it does not automatically pass to the surviving party. If the words "joint tenants" (or something similar) don't appear after your name (Mary Smith and John Smith, Joint Tenants), then his half of the property will pass according to his will or your state laws. It must **go through probate.**

- **Life insurance benefits.** If life insurance benefits are paid to a named beneficiary, they **avoid probate.** The instructions for obtaining this money are included in the following chapter. If the benefits are paid to his "estate," then they pass either according to his will or by intestacy, and must go through probate.

- **Retirement plan benefits.** If retirement plan benefits are paid to a named beneficiary, they **avoid probate.** The instructions on obtaining this money are included in the following chapter. If the benefits are paid to his "estate," then they pass either according to his will or by intestacy, and must go through probate.

- **Living trust.** If your husband had a revocable living trust, and property was titled in the name of the trust, then the property can be changed to the name of the beneficiary **free from probate.** This can be easily accomplished without an attorney.

Changing titles

Regardless of ownership, titles must be changed. You can handle the bank accounts with your local branch. Changing real estate titles is easiest with the assistance of an attorney.

If there are stocks, bonds, and mutual funds, you can handle these yourself or with the assistance of a broker or planner. This can be rather cumbersome, so seeking the assistance of a professional usually makes it easier. The information required to change securities depends upon the form of ownership.

- **Joint tenancy.** You need a stock or bond power

(which you can get from a brokerage firm), affidavit
of domicile, a death certificate, and a letter setting
forth your instructions.

- **Tenants in common.** You need a stock or bond
  power (which you can get from a brokerage firm),
  court appointment as executrix, affidavit of domicile,
  and letter of instruction.

- **Husband's name.** If he had stocks and bonds, it is
  easiest to open an estate account at a brokerage
  firm. For this, you need a copy of the court appointment, affidavit of domicile, and death certificate.

Safe deposit boxes

Safe deposit boxes may be frozen until after the estate
is settled. Technically, you are supposed to contact the bank
right away. Many widows, however, recommend removing
everything from the box before notifying the bank. Many have
found themselves unable to get to important documents.

Credit cards

Many widows are concerned when they realize that all
the credit cards were in their husband's name. They feel lost
without credit. The widows we interviewed recommended
leaving the credit cards alone and continuing to use them as
before. This may not be entirely legal, but it is certainly a
common practice. Widows of retirement age may never have
established their own credit. If their current cards were
canceled, they might be unable to get new ones.

> *When John died, all the credit cards were in his name. I realized
> that I couldn't qualify for credit on my own. Therefore, I continued
> to use his cards for six years. It was just the easiest thing to do.*

We don't necessarily recommend this. Instead, begin to

establish credit in your own name. Although you may have been the one to pay all the bills over the years, existing credit records that are in his name will not help at all toward establishing your own credit. Department store cards are usually the easiest to obtain. In addition, you can use secured credit cards described in Chapter 13.

HEALTH INSURANCE

Women who have been covered with health insurance by virtue of their husband's employment can face a rude awakening after his death. With the health insurance crisis, obtaining your own insurance can be costly, and sometimes impossible. However, all is not lost. There are government regulations that might force your husband's employer to extend coverage to you at your expense.

Let's look at the provisions under COBRA, the Consolidated Omnibus Benefits Reconciliation Act. Note that most of our discussion assumes that the husband was the covered employee under group insurance. If you are covered as an employee, then the same provisions apply to you. Rules change annually, so check current regulations.

Eligibility

If your husband worked for a company with at least twenty employees, and he participated in a group health plan, you are probably eligible for continued health insurance after his death. It depends on whether you are a "qualified beneficiary" and if the potential loss of coverage was a "qualifying event."

Qualifying event

A qualifying event is an occurrence that would have left you without benefits had the government not required the employer to continue your coverage. Included as a qualifying event is the death of the employee.

Qualified beneficiary

If the qualifying event is due to death, then you and your dependent children who were part of the plan on that date are qualified beneficiaries.

Length of coverage

You are entitled to coverage for 36 months if the qualifying event was death.

Premium

The premium the employer charges you can be no more than 102% of the premium the employer pays for current employees. However, if any qualified beneficiary is already disabled, then the cost can go as high as 150% of the normal premium.

Generally speaking, you must apply for coverage within 60 days of death. Sometimes, however, the time can be extended. This is something you need to take care of as soon as possible.

Guidelines

> ✓ *Find out if an advocate is available to help you.*

> ✓ *If your husband owned property in his name, contact a lawyer to begin the probate process.*

> ✓ *Access the safe deposit box and at least three months of living expenses before notifying the bank.*

> ✓ *Keep your husband's credit cards, but plan to establish one or two in your own name later.*

Chapter 54

How Do I Apply For Survivor's Benefits?

One of your most pressing priorities is to apply for survivor's benefits. You won't have the luxury of completing the grief process before starting out on this difficult path.

Even if you have your own income and feel that you can get along without benefits for a while, don't wait. Many benefits are permanently lost if you do not apply within the appropriate deadlines. The easiest way to do this is with the assistance of an advocate.

Advocates

Consider yourself fortunate if your late husband's employer has an advocacy program. You will be assigned an advocate, who is a person trained to guide you through the maze of applications and responsibilities required immediately after a death.

That person will usually contact you right away and explain the program. Everyone we have talked to said their advocates were absolutely wonderful.

If no one comes forth, ask about an advocate program. Your local Hospice may have information available. The union, the retirement association, or another organization may offer such a program. Since they have probably not been given your name, you will need to seek them out. NARFE (National Association of Retired Federal Employees) has a volunteer advocacy program to help spouses of federal employees.

Funeral homes are generally reported to be extremely caring and helpful. Reports we received from widows gave us a warm, fuzzy feeling about the funeral industry ... far different from those exposés in the 1970's. They are also very good about working out financing arrangements and helping to organize immediate tasks.

Checklist of important documents

The following documents may be necessary to obtain survivor's benefits. If you gather the information and documents immediately, it will be a tremendous help in easing the process of applying for benefits. Keep them with the completed financial statements contained in Appendix A.

_____ Death certificate. Get as many as you think you are going to need, and then double that number. On the one hand, you don't want to pay for more than you need. On the other, you don't want to keep going back, especially if the court house is not convenient.

_____ Social Security numbers of each family member.

_____ Birth certificates - one copy per family member.

_____ Marriage license.

_____ Certified discharge if your husband was a veteran.

_____ Will or trust documents.

_____ Life insurance policies.

_____ Mortgage or loan insurance policies.

_____ Accident insurance policy.

_____ Health records/health insurance information.

_____ Credit card information.

_____ Employee insurance or benefit documents.

_____ List of husband's past employers - some benefits might still be available.

_____ Professional organization or union papers.

_____ Tax related documents.

_____ Bank records, safe deposit box contents, brokerage Information, stocks or bonds, other statements.

All of the above items represent business that will need to be handled immediately. Fix a file, briefcase, or box and keep all the listed information handy until everything has been filed and completed.

Warning

One of the immediate priorities is to file for benefits. Let us give you a warning here. When phoning or visiting the appropriate offices, you will likely encounter unhappy people in stressful jobs. You probably will find them terribly insensitive. Large bureaucracies (most notably, government agencies) are especially guilty.

People tend to have their worst days on Mondays and Fridays, and to be at their best in the mornings. Therefore, make your contacts in the mornings from Tuesday through Thursday. That will leave you feeling "free" on Mondays and Fridays, when you are probably under more stress anyway.

Shannelle blew her nose, then managed a shuddering sigh to regain her composure while she laid the tissue on the growing pile in her lap. Even sharing yesterday's phone call to the VA with her support group was painful. But at least they understood.

"The first woman acted like I was a leech on the government! I

was so humiliated after it had taken me days to get up the courage to call. Then she kept asking if I had copies of the paperwork and proof of our marriage! Proof! I have four kids to support, and a stack of medical bills. Who does she think I am?

"Anyway, after grilling me and asking for Darrell's date of death over and over, I was in tears. Then she had the nerve to switch me to another department. I had to tell my story all over, from scratch.

"Once more, I had to repeat Darrell's date of death. I was rapidly using up every ounce of energy and stamina I could muster. Then they switched me again! I must have talked to six different people, repeating every painful detail, before someone finally said they could process the claim."

Since it is their job to screen requests and make sure only valid claims are met, they may put you on the defensive and make you feel like you're under attack. Many widows have agonized over this.

Since most people are not intentionally hurtful, it is pointless to hold grudges against them for the insensitivity they display and the pain they inflict. The only one who gets hurt by that anger is you! Pitying them removes their power to hurt you, and puts you in a more positive frame of mind. For example:

That poor woman on the phone. She probably has so much stress in her own life that she doesn't even realize what she sounds like. Instead of being angry, I'll just feel sorry for her.

Sample script for requesting benefits

If you file for benefits on your own, it is helpful to prepare a written script. That way you can practice it in front of the mirror. Having a script also helps you dissociate from the information - you're just reading off a piece of paper rather than dragging the information from your gut over and over.

Hello. I'd like to speak to someone in personnel about survivor's benefits please.

Hello. This is _____ calling. I'm calling to request survivor's benefits. My husband, _____, passed away on _____ (date).

He worked for your company from _____ to _____. His Social Security number was _____.

Do I need to make an appointment to come in to file for survivor's benefits, or can you send me the forms?

What paperwork do I need to have with me (or enclose)?

Are you the correct person to call if I have questions, or can you give me the name of the person who handles this?

Thank you for your help. Good-by.

Veterans' benefits

Depending on the extent of your late husband's veterans' entitlement (based on service, injuries while on active duty, etc.), you may be entitled to a funeral expense allowance, a marker (or marker allowance), and survivor's benefits for yourself and any dependent children. All veterans are entitled to a burial flag and burial in a national cemetery. Call (800) 555-1212 for the toll-free number of your regional VA office.

Review the sample script before calling. Be prepared for insensitivity. We have heard numerous complaints from widows who have encountered rudeness from VA employees.

Be sure to have the following documents on hand when you call or go to the Veterans Administration office:

- Service Serial number and/or Social Security number.
- Marriage license.

- Children's birth certificates.
- Discharge papers.
- Death certificate.

The deadline for all burial benefits is two years after burial. It's best to consider two years the maximum for any applications. Also, don't expect benefits to arrive right away. Six weeks is reasonable; over a year is a bit long.

> *When my father died, we requested a headstone from the VA. A month after burial, it still had not been placed. Six months, nine months, a year went by. We called the VA and the cemetery at least monthly. After a full year, the VA put a tracer out . . . and discovered that it had been in a storage room at the cemetery for months. We were furious with both the VA and cemetery, but never found anyone who would take responsibility for the slip-up.*

Social Security

You may be eligible for a $225 lump sum payment from the Social Security Administration. In addition, dependent children may also be eligible for benefits. If you are disabled or already of retirement age, you may be eligible for some additional benefits.

Read the sample script earlier in this chapter before calling. Be prepared for insensitivity on the other end of the phone. Again, it's better to be pleasantly surprised by a courteous, sensitive person, than to unexpectedly be given a rough time.

Chapter 23 contains a basic discussion of your entitlements. For exact information, call the local Social Security Administration office. Do not wait until you have every possible item of proof. They can begin the process and tell you what else is required once things get started. Try to have the following information available before calling or visiting:

- Husband's Social Security number.

- Your Social Security number.
- The Social Security number of each dependent.
- Your children's birth certificates.
- Proof of your age, if over 62.
- Death certificate.
- W-2 forms for the past two years.

Two years is also the maximum deadline for applying for survivor's benefits with the Social Security Administration. By the way, that is two years after death, not burial, unlike the VA. This is also an appropriate time to request any Medicare benefits to which you may be entitled.

Employers

Call the personnel department of your husband's last employer. You may want to do the same for previous employers, just in case there might be some benefits available. If possible, review his employee benefits handbook, if one exists. Before calling, have the following information ready:

- Husband's Social Security number.
- Your Social Security number.
- W-2 forms for the past two years.
- Husband's most recent pay stub.
- Death certificate.

Retirement and pension plans

You are probably the beneficiary of your husband's retirement savings and pension plans. The employer will provide the proper documents for claiming these funds.

Be aware that the vast majority of retirement plans can be "rolled over" into your own IRA. This is by far the best choice, since the money will continue to grow tax-deferred, and no taxes will be due at the time you put it into your own name.

If you instruct the trustee to mail you a check directly, they must withhold 20% for taxes, so you won't get the full amount. That is true even if you plan to immediately reinvest the money in an IRA yourself. Do a direct rollover (transfer from trustee to trustee; you never see the check), or just ask them to hold it in your name and Social Security number until you are ready to work with a trusted financial advisor.

If your husband had his own retirement plan (Simplified Employee Pension Plan, IRA or Keogh), you need to find a recent statement and original application. The beneficiary is clearly stated on the application. If you don't have a copy, call your financial advisor or the trustee (bank, mutual fund, etc.) of the plan. Most statements have the phone number printed on them. They can send you the necessary forms for claiming that money. The same thing is true of any annuities or private pension (insurance) plans that your husband may have had.

You do not have to decide at this time exactly how you are going to invest the money. It is enough to just notify the trustee and have it placed in your name. You can move the money into your IRA later. However, if you are desperate for the money, by all means request it right away. Just be aware of the 20% tax bite. Review Chapter 40 on the proper ways to handle a retirement distribution.

Annuity payments

When you go to collect benefits from insurance companies or your husband's retirement plan, you may be given the choice of receiving a lump-sum payment of the entire benefit or receiving annuity payments for life. Never take the annuity payments . . . always take the lump-sum. Here's why.

Annuity payments for life are a great deal for the insurance company. They pay you income as long as you live, usually with a minimum guaranteed period of 10 years. Upon your death, the payments stop and your heirs get nothing. It is much better to take the lump-sum and invest it for income. If you ever need part of the principal, you can get it. Upon your death, the balance goes to your children. If you are given this option, **always** choose the lump-sum, unless you feel you can't manage the money.

Civil Service

If your husband was a Civil Service employee for at least 18 months, you may be entitled to benefits. Contact the personnel office. They can direct you to the appropriate department, or put you in touch with an advocate. Be sure to have your husband's full name and Social Security number handy. They will provide you with all necessary claim forms.

Military benefits

If your husband was active military, you should have an advocate working with you now. If he retired after September 21, 1972, you need to contact his branch of the service for his Survivors' Benefits Plan. They will require his full name and Social Security number.

Other possibilities

If your husband was a member of a credit union or had loans at any financial institutions, check with them for possible insurance or death benefits. Also check with your bank, after removing everything from your safe deposit box and withdrawing funds from your joint checking account.

Check also with fraternal organizations, social organizations, etc. Think of every group with which he may have been a member, even if he was no longer actively involved.

Were there any installment loans at local stores? Check there for credit life insurance that might have been included with the loans. Some credit card companies provide insurance whenever tickets for airplanes and other mass transportation are charged on their card. If your husband's death was the result of this type of accident, notify your credit card company.

Unions and professional organizations

You may be entitled to benefits from your husband's union or professional organizations. Many of these organizations have insurance policies on their members, which may pay you benefits.

Writing a letter

In many cases, you might find it preferable to write, rather than call. If you find it too stressful, you may want to ask a friend to help draft it. A sample letter follows.

Mr. Jack Jones, Benefits Coordinator
Tremble Mining Union
Oshua, WV

Dear Mr. Jones:

I am sorry to report the recent death of my husband, Carl Smith. He was killed in a mine blast on December 4, 1993.

As his widow and the mother of his three dependent children (ages 2 - 13), I am requesting any benefits due to Carl's survivors. Enclosed is a certified copy of the death certificate. The following information may also be helpful.

Carl Smith Social Security Number: xxx-xx-xxxx
Carl Smith Union Number: xxx-xx
Joan Smith Social Security Number: xxx-xx-xxxx
Children's Social Security Numbers:
Jamie Smith xxx-xx-xxxx
Frank Smith xxx-xx-xxxx
Carl Smith, Jr. xxx-xx-xxxx

Thank you for your prompt attention to this matter. If you need additional information, I can be reached at (333) 111-1111.

Insurance companies

Phone each insurance company with which your husband had a policy. Request their beneficiary claim forms. If you prefer, call your local agent. He or she can provide the correct forms and assist you in completing them. When calling, you need to know:

1. Your husband's full name as registered on the policy.
2. The policy numbers.
3. Your husband's Social Security number.

If you aren't sure that you know all of the companies, or if you can't find the policies, don't give up. There might be life insurance, home mortgage insurance, accident insurance, workers' compensation, union insurance, bank credit card insurance, etc. It's worth exploring.

There is a free service that will search all policies that your husband may have had, and will send you the information. To get this service, send a self-addressed, stamped business size envelope along with a letter requesting information to:

Policy Search Service
American Council of Life Insurance
1001 Pennsylvania Avenue, NW
Washington, D.C. 20004

Insurance benefits

In our practice, we have found that many widows are reluctant to claim their life insurance benefits because they anticipate a tax hit. To the contrary, no income taxes are typically due when you receive life insurance death benefits. However, the death benefit is included in your husband's estate for estate tax purposes if he owned the life insurance. This does not affect you if you are a U.S. citizens.

Dealing with companies

Unfortunately, dealing with insurance companies is a universal problem with all the widows we have interviewed. It's a problem that they have asked us to address in this book.

Sandra received the following letter from an insurance company in response to her claim to collect her husband's insurance benefits. Her husband died within two years after taking out the policy. Therefore, the policy was still in the "contestable period." This is the two-year period during which an insurance company has the right to contest any claim if they determine that the insured lied on the application, committed suicide, or had undisclosed preexisting conditions.

> *Re: John Doe, Deceased.*
>
> *The Policy 5555555 was issued on April 26, 1992. Where life insurance policies in which the death of the insured falls within the first two years of coverage, it is our practice to investigate the possibility of a preexisting condition.*
>
> *We have requested medical records from several sources. We are still waiting to receive records from Dr. Jones. Once these records are received, we will review them to determine if a misrepresentation was made. When our investigation is complete, we will advise you of our findings.*

When she received the letter, Sandra was devastated. What a cold, cruel letter to write to a person grieving for her beloved husband. How dare they accuse him of "misrepresentation." Didn't they know that he was one of the most honest, decent men in the world?

When Sandra shared her letter with us, we wrote a long letter to the insurance company. Included in our letter was the following:

> *Our real complaint is with the paragraph which states, "Once these records are received we will . . ." You must understand the*

state-of-mind of not only Mrs. Doe, but any widow you are dealing with. She is going through tremendous stress and pain after nearly 40 years of marriage. She is trying to pick up the pieces of her shattered life. She is forced into the position of handling her own finances and dealing with people in governmental agencies (Social Security Administration, Veterans Administration, etc.) who are downright rude.

She misses her husband deeply. For you to tell her that you are going to determine if her late husband misrepresented something on his application is like driving another stake through her heart. Mrs. Doe said to me, "John would never misrepresent anything." She's right. He was a fine man and as honorable as they come. Of course, you don't know that, and thus you need to perform your investigation.

But the tone of your letter indicates that he is guilty of misrepresentation until you prove him innocent. Then, once you have completed your "investigation," you will advise her of your "findings." Sounds like a grand jury investigation or a special prosecutor investigation of Iran Contra.

A little compassion in the letter would have been nice: "We will certainly expedite the claim. Our sympathies are extended to you and your family." Just let them know you are not a cold, heartless insurance company that doesn't want to let go of your money.

We were pleased to receive the following reply:

Thank you for your comments regarding Mrs. Doe. Sometimes we tend to get so caught up in our claim review and payment proceeds that we unintentionally overlook the subtle words and actions we use to accomplish our goal.

We have begun a review of all of our claim correspondence to incorporate your suggestions. Our goal is to provide prompt and caring service to our customers, and your suggestions will assist us in the successful completing of that goal.

Once again, thank you for taking the time to provide us with your input. Your comments and suggestions are always welcome.

If you currently feel, or have felt, mistreated by a company, please let us know. It is our goal to make these firms aware that the manner in which they handle benefits and claims affects their customers and reflects on them.

Guidelines

✓ *Use a prepared script when calling for information on survivor benefits.*

✓ *Have necessary documents or information at your fingertips when calling.*

✓ *Expect some hassles and rudeness. This is not an easy task.*

✓ *Make a list of every employer, organization, agency, or insurance company which might provide benefits.*

✓ *Transfer IRAs and retirement funds into your name. You can wait to change the investment choices when you feel up to it.*

✓ *Try to make your phone calls in the mornings, preferably Tuesday through Thursday.*

✓ *Call someone in your support network whenever you feel overwhelmed.*

Part Eight

Setting Goals And

Feeling Good

Chapter 55

How Can I Build
Strength And Confidence?

One of our favorite sayings is, "How do you eat an elephant?" Answer: "One bite at a time." Taking things in small increments is the best way to rebuild your life. At first you may have to think and plan in terms of minutes, then hours. Soon you can take it one day at a time.

Don't begin to plan ahead until "today" is well under control. It may be just too overwhelming. Count each day survived as a successful day, one to be checked off. Build strength and confidence as you go. Pat yourself on the back for each new accomplishment. You don't have to be perfect; you just have to do it.

"We're like tea bags. We don't know our own strength until we get into hot water." (Bruce Laingen, Iranian hostage)

While boiling alive is never fun, it does give you the chance to test your strength. Now is the perfect time to discover your own unique qualities. Learn to appreciate and value yourself as "you," not someone's wife, mother, or child.

Discover yourself

Once you begin to heal, you can start to evaluate your interests and lifestyle, and begin clarifying your own values. During your marriage, you probably spent most of your energy molding yourself and your opinions to match those of your husband. Now is the time to discover **your own** feelings and choices. Now may be the time to diet, get a new hairstyle, perhaps change your furniture . . . make your new mark on the world. This growing and discovery process is probably one of the most beneficial events that will ever occur in your life.

The philosopher Nietzsche once said, "That which does not kill me makes me stronger." You are neither dead nor defeated!

> *I woke up this morning and realized that the past is over, and my whole life is ahead of me. Now I can do things my way! I decided to put in the pool I always wanted, and I called a contractor about finishing the remodeling.*

Shake off any feelings of being the victim of tragedy. As long as you think of yourself as a victim, you will be unable to get on with your life. Victims have no power or control. They're just buffeted and abused by circumstances. Realistically, you can't lose until you quit trying - which is exactly what victims do.

Attitudes

Ann Kaiser Stearns, in *Coming Back*, supplies a list of attitudes typical of survivors:

- *I will vividly examine the future.*
- *I will not be defeated.*
- *My God, I'm lucky.*
- *I will take advantage of the available opportunities.*
- *Nobody's perfect.*
- *There is still time for me.*
- *There must be some meaning to be found or seen in these events.*
- *I will not assume the victim posture.*
- *I can do it if I set my mind.*
- *I have to be willing to expand.*
- *I am consciously deciding to be in the company of good people.*
- *We will find a way to get what we want.*
- *I will accept life's challenge.*

You may identify with some of these more than others.

Choose one or two and stick them on your mirror or refrigerator as a daily reminder. Constantly encourage yourself.

Frieda was sharing her shift in identity with her support group. Previously, she had perceived herself as a hostess for her husband's business associates and a leader among the country club set. After her divorce, her life changed drastically.

Sure, I had to change my perception of myself. I may have lost a lot, but now I'm gaining a new sense of "me," and I like me.

A member of a divorce support group wondered about whether to change her name back to her maiden name.

I thought seriously about changing my name. I know some of you have, and it worked out well for you. But I've built a business and all my business contacts on my married name. It would really be hard to change all that. I thought and thought and thought. Finally, I decided that I had purchased that name fair and square through all those years of love and pain. I earned it. It's my name now, and I'm keeping it.

Forgive

Forgive others. Perhaps you or your husband were the victims of mental or physical violence. Forgiving will give you strength and remove one millstone from around your neck. Dropping grudges also helps you get on with your life.

There is a difference between forgiving and forgetting. We're not saying forget what happened. You learn by experience, but you can forgive. Like many Jews say about the Holocaust, "We may forgive, but we will never forget."

Failing to forgive puts the burden on **you**. It doesn't hurt the other person. Only you suffer. It takes energy to remain angry with someone. The question is, how long are you going to hold on to your anger? How can you put that energy to better use than by being angry with someone else?

Anger is a useless emotion after a short period of time. It accomplishes nothing, except to ruin **your** life. Give it up. Forgive. The past is past. Your future is in the here and now.

Family (ugh!)

Another tough discovery is realizing that, as hard as you are working to build your self-esteem and move forward rebuilding your life, your family may not be fully behind you. In fact, they may be undermining you every step of the way.

> The kids were finally all in college or on their own. I decided that it was time to do what I had always wanted to do. Seems like I had always done what everyone else wanted. I took early retirement from my job and went back to college. I had always wanted to be a teacher.
>
> Every time I was studying for exams, my ex-husband would call and start a fight. Although the kids weren't living at home, they still complained that I wasn't doing enough for them and had become selfish. On the surface, everyone acted like they were so proud of me and behind me all the way. But in the day to day reality, their actions constantly set me up for failure. I had to stay very focused on my goals to achieve them, and I resented the way I was treated. Graduation is next week, and I'm not even inviting my family.

Often your own family becomes your worst enemy, and we don't just mean your ex-spouse. Children, parents, close friends, the people you thought you could count on, often undermine your attempts to achieve new heights. They say they are behind you, but secretly they may want you to fail! Why? They aren't mean-spirited or consciously against you (most of the time), but your achievements can be a threat to them. They subconsciously need for you to fail in order for their status quo to be maintained. They may be afraid of how their lives will change, once you achieve your new goals. Unfortunately, this is one more burden you need to be prepared to shoulder.

This lack of support is a common denominator among

women growing through changes in their lives, regardless of the catalyst for change. Many people of all faiths have found great strength and comfort in the prayer used by Alcoholics Anonymous.

Serenity Prayer

God, grant me
The serenity to accept the things I cannot change,
The courage to change the things I can,
And the wisdom to know the difference.

The biggest problem for women is that they are used to external feedback (support or disapproval). That is why you expend so much energy trying to please others. Now it's time to shift that thought process and learn to please the person within . . . yourself. Develop an appreciation for your own ideas, accomplishments, and self respect.

Guidelines

✓ *Set goals! Begin to make choices that lift your spirits and improve your self-esteem.*

✓ *Surround yourself with encouraging quotes and supportive people.*

✓ *Forgive others and let go of the past.*

✓ *Don't give up if your family doesn't support you. It's important for you to reach your fullest potential.*

✓ *It's okay to be your own cheerleader.*

Chapter 56

How Do I Move Forward?

Sometimes life seems like an endless treadmill. When it gets going too fast and out of control, or when it becomes too depressing, we want to jump off. We're so afraid of change, or of not keeping up, that we struggle to just hang in there. Unconsciously we may be driving it faster and faster in our panic over falling behind and getting hurt.

Many women who find themselves suddenly single get on a depressive treadmill. Just as the treadmill is a continuous cycle, they find themselves in a cycle of depression. The cycle moves from feelings, to thoughts, to behavior, to low self-esteem, and back to negative feelings.

Feelings: Anxious, worried, overwhelmed.

Thoughts: Unclear, confused, out of focus.

Behavior: Procrastinate, run away from problems, inactive, ignore problems.

Action: I'm no good at this. I'm a failure. It's too much for me to handle.

Even when we dislike the way we face life, or the habits that we have, they are hard to break. Why? Because our human nature is such that we are more comfortable with the familiar, even if it makes us uncomfortable. Change is scary.

We have to be mighty uncomfortable before we realize that the risk of not changing is worse than the risk of trying something new. Plus, there is that hidden "fear of failure" we have to contend with whenever we consider new behavior.

We recently saw a quotation in some junk mail that struck home: "Worry is like a rocking chair! It keeps you busy but it doesn't get you anywhere." Being on the depressive treadmill is like living life in a rocking chair. You'll never get anywhere. So, what is the alternative?

The positive, optimistic treadmill is the opposite alternative. You can jump on board at any point. It, too, is a conveyor belt on an endless cycle. However, this cycle leads to positive self-esteem. It continuously reinforces itself. Let's look at the difference between the low self-esteem cycle described earlier in this chapter, and positive self-esteem.

	Low Self-Esteem	High Self-Esteem
Feelings	anxious, worried, overwhelmed	calm, optimistic, confident
Thoughts	unclear, confused, out of focus	specific, clear, well focused
Behavior	procrastinate, ignore problems, inactive	positive choices, take action, handle problems
Action	I'm no good at this. I'm a failure. It's too much for me to handle.	I can do this. I will do it. I did it. I am successful.

You may have to ease from one treadmill to the other, or you may take it as a "leap of faith." There are some steps you can take to get yourself into the positive cycle.

- Set reasonable, realistic, achievable goals.
- Break your tasks into small steps.
- Work on only one step at a time.
- Measure your progress, then reward yourself.
- Set realistic deadlines.
- Be accountable to someone (friend, support group).

- Be as gentle with yourself as you would with a toddler learning a new skill.

As Franklin Roosevelt said, "The only thing we have to fear, is fear itself."

Optimist International is an organization that encourages young people to excel and challenge themselves. At the end of every meeting, The Optimist Creed is recited. We think it will be meaningful for you as you work to move forward.

The Optimist Creed

Promise Yourself-

- To be so strong that nothing can disturb your peace of mind.

- To talk health, happiness and prosperity to every person you meet.

- To make all your friends feel that there is something in them.

- To look at the sunny side of everything and make your optimism come true.

- To think only of the best, to work only for the best and expect only the best.

- To be just as enthusiastic about the success of others as you are about your own.

- To forget the mistakes of the past and press on to the greater achievements of the future.

- To wear a cheerful countenance at all times and give every living creature you meet a smile.

- To give so much time to the improvement of yourself that you have no time to criticize others.

- To be too large for worry, too noble for anger, too strong for fear, and too happy to permit the presence of trouble.

Guidelines

✓ *Look at your thought patterns to determine if your self-esteem is low or high.*

✓ *Begin to replace negative thoughts and behaviors with positive ones.*

✓ *Set goals and take things one small step at a time.*

✓ *Reward yourself for each accomplishment. Take pride in the small achievements.*

✓ *Repeat the Optimist Creed daily until you can begin to assimilate positive thoughts and actions into your daily life.*

✓ *Focus on small steps toward a larger goal, to remove that goal's power to overwhelm and frighten you.*

Chapter 57

How Do I Stop Procrastinating?

You have gained a tremendous amount of information from this book. We have presented concepts and shown you how to determine your needs and achieve your goals.

Now, it's up to you. On the one hand, you can put this book away and say, "That sure was interesting." If you do that, you've accomplished nothing. We have all wasted our time.

On the other hand, you can take **action**. Hopefully, you completed the forms throughout the book and established your goals. Now it's time to move forward. Don't let procrastination destroy your efforts!

While writing this book, we continually thought about the best way to treat the problem of procrastination. We realize that procrastination is a debilitating condition that prevents good things from happening. We know that people fail financially due to procrastination. In fact, it's one of the primary causes!

Procrastination means putting off something that needs to be done now. If you need to clean your basement, but put it off, you are procrastinating. If you postpone calling someone you don't want to talk to, that is procrastination. If you let your CD roll over at the bank because you don't want to think about doing something else with the money, that is also procrastination.

We studied this problem for many years, looking for ways to solve it. We read books, talked with psychologists and psychiatrists, interviewed successful and not-so-successful people. We debated it endlessly ourselves. We want to be able to tell you just how to solve this problem.

No solution?

Unfortunately, we discovered that there is no ideal solution and no pat answer. Why? Because, in reality, procrastination itself is not the problem. It is evidence of something much deeper. Let's look at it a little further.

Procrastination is the result of a choice or series of choices. It produces the desired result, even though that result is usually negative.

> *Jody felt buried under her bills. She knew she had to do something. She looked through the classified ads for a second job, called for information, and prepared her resume. But she never got around to sending it out.*

What did Jody's procrastination accomplish? It kept her from making the extra money she needed. It allowed her to continue to have bad feelings, reinforcing her poor self-esteem. It prevented her from successfully straightening out her finances and breaking out of her "cage."

Because she remained burdened by the overhanging cloud of not doing what she "needed" to do, she continued to berate herself for not being successful. It kept her from breaking out of her rut and allowed her to continue to feel unworthy. Remember that depressive treadmill?

Self-destructive patterns

We know this is a tough concept to swallow, and may be difficult to believe. Jody certainly didn't want to believe that her behavior was self-destructive, and she didn't want to hear "it was your choice." Unfortunately, that was the truth.

So, back to the problem at hand. How do you stop

procrastinating? First, you decide that you **want** to feel good about yourself. Second, you decide you're **worth** it. Then, you decide that you will do **whatever** is necessary to feel a sense of accomplishment. Sure, this takes commitment on your part, but until you make the decision to succeed financially and feel good about yourself, you will continue to procrastinate.

Getting started

If you choose to follow the recommendations in this book, then you must choose to get rid of the behaviors that have been holding you back. Admittedly, that is easier said than done. There are several things you can do to get started.

Your payoff

First, think about why you procrastinate and what benefit you get from it. What is your payoff?

> When I put off doing things I know I should do, I feel really rotten. I continually think about what I have to do, and it ruins my day.

> I know I would feel better if I completed my tasks. I would be happier. I would be able to do the things I want to do. I would feel good about myself.

> Therefore, I guess the reason I procrastinate is that it allows me to continue to feel bad about myself. I can knock myself and tell myself how lazy I am for not doing what I need to do . . . just like Mom always did.

> I'm used to that. I've always had negative thoughts about myself. I don't think I'm pretty. I feel fat. I'm not as smart as other people. I could work harder. I could be more caring . . .

This woman is very honest with her feelings. She's really tough on herself, isn't she? Procrastination allows her to continue to have bad feelings about herself, something she's had for many years. That's the one thing she's really good at . . . knocking herself. Those bad thoughts allow her to remain where she feels most comfortable. After all, if she started feeling good about herself, she'd have to break out of her mold, and that really would feel uncomfortable.

Focus

Another problem is focusing on the unpleasant. You probably procrastinate because you want to avoid "unpleasant" tasks. Instead, focus on how good you will feel after you have accomplished those tasks. If you visualize feeling good after completing unpleasant tasks, then those tasks become less unpleasant.

Previously we said, "Focus on the goal, not the journey." That means focus on what you want to accomplish, and how good you'll feel after your achievements. Don't focus on the process of doing it.

Look at Olympic athletes. Do you think it's pleasant to get out there and train all day, every day? Of course not. However, successful athletes focus on the goal of winning, not the journey. For them, the pleasure of competition and victory outweigh any pain they suffer.

> *I have procrastinated all my life. I remember my mother yelling at me to clean up my room, and yelling at me to do my homework, and yelling at me to take a shower. It got to the point where I didn't do anything until she yelled.*
>
> *Looking back, I hated the yelling, but I got used to it. I guess you could say it became a comfortable routine.*
>
> *When I got older, I started reading some books on the subject and realized that procrastinating made me feel bad about myself. The more I thought about it, the more I knew that was true. I hated myself for putting things off. Sometimes it was embarrassing, especially when I ran into someone I had promised to call.*
>
> *So I decided that for the first time in my life, I was going to work on feeling good about myself. It wasn't easy, especially with my*

husband around. Mom didn't help either. That didn't stop me, though, because I was sick and tired of the way I felt.

Slowly, but surely, I started doing the things I really needed to do. I changed my focus to feeling good when I completed a task. And, you know what? I started feeling better about myself. I was proud of myself for what I was doing, and that kept me on track. It got to the point where I actually felt uncomfortable procrastinating. Now I feel so much better about myself!

Make a list

Make a list of things you are now putting off. If you really want to stop procrastinating, it's important to get all those tasks hanging over you out of the way. Indicate how you feel about not doing each task, and how you will feel once you accomplish it. Set a time limit for completion. Rank them, and begin with the most important first. As you accomplish each task, focus on how good you feel about yourself and the reasons you want to maintain those good feelings. Make copies of this form so you can use it over and over.

I am going to _____

Because I have not done it, I feel _____

_____

When I do it, I will feel _____

_____

I will accomplish this by _____

On a scale of 1 - 5 (1 being the highest), this rates a _____

My reward for accomplishing this task is _____

_____

Once you have completed your list, think about how you feel. Don't you feel relieved to get those things out of the way? Don't you feel less stress? Don't you feel better about yourself? Can you see how defeating procrastination really is? You really do feel better when you accomplish important tasks, and you feel miserable when you haven't. So remember how good it feels, and commit to retaining that great feeling!

The choice is yours! You must choose whether or not to break out of your old, comfortable habits in order to develop newer, better ones. You, and you alone, must choose whether your normal operating mode will be one of depression, procrastination and jealousy . . . . or one of honesty, happiness, success, and caring. It's up to you!

Guidelines

✓ *Head knowledge, without heart knowledge (putting it into action), is worthless!*

✓ *Only you can end the procrastination that destroys your self-esteem.*

✓ *The past is not an indicator of the future, if you choose to change.*

✓ *Set goals. List the things you need to accomplish. Prioritize them. Start* <u>*today*</u> *on the most important.*

✓ *Break tasks into small, achievable steps with absolute deadlines. Reward yourself as you accomplish each small step.*

✓ *Focus on how much better you feel about yourself after each accomplishment.*

Chapter 58

Who Is That Person In The Mirror?

Life is not a dead end street. It has a number of paths, all leading in different directions. The path you choose has everything to do with the kind of life you live today, and what you can look forward to in the future.

Remember the Yellow Brick Road from the *Wizard of Oz*? Dorothy, the Tin Man, the Scarecrow, and the Lion all set out on a path that would lead to fulfillment. Along the way, they discovered that everything they sought was already present inside them . . . just undiscovered. Their poor self-esteem was all that prevented them from accomplishing their goals.

The best paths begin with feeling good about yourself. It's very difficult to make choices when you feel bad about yourself and powerless to change things. So we have an exercise we'd like you to take. It involves saying some good things about yourself.

We know that can be difficult. You've been taught: "Don't brag on yourself. If you're good, you don't have to tell others. They will know. Don't show off or put yourself in the limelight."

That doesn't mean you can't tell **yourself** how good you are; that you can't tell yourself what you like about you. Everyone has good points. If you could see yourself as others see you, you would recognize the good in yourself. You may not feel it personally, but it is there.

For a few minutes, forget everything bad you've ever been taught about yourself. Forget the guilt trips and negative thoughts people have dumped on you. Instead, look at yourself as the good person you really are.

Take time to complete the following two pages. Be totally honest, and positive, about yourself. Don't worry, nobody will see it. If you would feel more comfortable, make copies of the pages before completing them.

My most attractive physical qualities are:

1. _____

2. _____

3. _____

My best personality features are:

1. _____

2. _____

3. _____

My best attributes, those that make me interesting and special, are:

1. _____

2. _____

3. _____

The characteristics of other women I find interesting are:

1. _____

2. _____

3. _____

Characteristics I want to personally develop are:

1. _____

2. _____

3. _____

4. _____

I will develop those qualities by doing the following:

1. _____

2. _____

3. _____

4. _____

The following people will encourage and support me as I grow: (Eg. church, club members, friends, co-workers)

1. _____

2. _____

3. _____

4. _____

Other places I can find help with my personal growth are: (Eg. support groups, magazines, school, library)

1. _____

2. _____

3. _____

4. _____

Change is so important to me because:

1. I'm worth whatever it takes to grow as a person.

2. _____

3. _____

4. _____

I will no longer:

1. _____

2. _____

3. _____

4. _____

Encouragement

In our interviews, many women told us that they have been encouraged by little one-liners. You, too, should diligently seek, clip, and post them. Use them as markers in this book. They will help you get through the bad days as well as the good. You need to make a point of searching for humor in the little events of life that will help lift your spirit. The following quotes were contributed by widows, divorcees, and clients who found them helpful.

I'm going to improve my circumstances. I'll do it today.

Life is 10% how you make it, and 90% how you take it.

Don't let your burdens paralyze your progress.

Though there are 365 days in the year, only three count. Two we can't do anything about - yesterday and tomorrow. Only today is "cash." Yesterday is a "canceled check" and tomorrow is just a "promissory note."

Happiness is internal, not external.

Happiness is a choice.

"Present" has two meanings: "gift" and "now." Each minute is a fresh gift.

We're seldom as fragile as we believe.

I can't fail unless I stop trying.

Be bold in what you stand for and careful what you fall for.

If you're going to laugh about something later, you might as well go ahead and laugh about it now.

Worry is like paying interest on a debt you may never owe.

Life is full of learning opportunities, not problems.

Where Do I Go From Here?

Congratulations! You have completed your journey with Ann and Steve. You have studied a wide range of subjects, including both emotional and financial issues.

On the cover of this book is a butterfly. We chose that symbol because, like most women, the butterfly isn't complete or free until it leaves its cocoon to fly on its own. Hopefully, you are ready to abandon your cocoon and fly.

However, there is still a lot of work to do. This book is designed to give you a broad overview and point you in the right direction. But a single book can't be all things to all people.

To help you move forward from here, Ann and Steve have developed a special audio course entitled, *"I Can. I Will! (Beyond the Book)."* With the excitement of their live seminars, they walk you step by step into the future you want for yourself. Six audio programs, plus a special workbook, guide you into achieving your hopes, dreams, and aspirations. Included as a special bonus is a free 20-minute consultation, in person or by phone, with either of the authors . . . the ultimate in personalized service!

This is an opportunity you don't want to miss. The order form is on the following page, with more descriptive information contained on page 356. Bring their unique style and empathy into your home, car, or office, and make your dreams a reality.

Whether or not you take advantage of this offer, Ann and Steve would love to hear from you. They can provide guidance and solutions to your specific financial problems. They also speak at seminars for companies, associations, public groups, and professional organizations. Don't hesitate to call them at (800) 777-0867 or write to them at: 2517 Moody Road, Suite 100, Warner Robins, GA 31088.

Order Form
(See page 356 for complete details)

<u>Investment</u>

____ *I Can. I Will! (Beyond the Book)*
6 audio tapes, workbook, and
20-minute consultation with authors - $89.95   _____
          plus
Choose **one** of the following free bonus tapes:
Special issues for widows   ____
Special issues for divorcees   ____
Special issues for marrieds & singles ____
Gifting to (grand)children   ____

____ *Keep Uncle Sam From Devouring*
Your Life Savings
by Stephen M. Rosenberg, CFP - $14.95   _____

____ Add my name to your mailing list for updates
and seminars in my area.   no charge

Shipping/Handling: Add $5.50 (tapes) $3.00 (book)   _____

                         TOTAL   _____

For **cash orders**, send check or money order with completed form to: Capital Publishing, 2221 Peachtree Road, Suite 103, Atlanta, GA 30309. For **credit card orders**, mail completed form to above address or call **1-800-864-2929**.

Name _____

Address _____

City, State, Zip _____

Phone (Day) _____ (Evening) _____

Please charge my (circle): MasterCard, Visa, American Express

Account Number _____ Exp. Date _____

I Can. I Will! (Beyond the Book)

This audio cassette course includes a workbook and six tapes:

1. Believe and Achieve. Take stock of yourself and your direction in life. Learn how to make decisions that others will accept and build your self-confidence and self-esteem.

2. Choose Not To Lose. Are you a potential victim? Learn how to make your own best choices, arm yourself against the unscrupulous, and avoid debt devastation.

3. Perception or Deception? Is your money really safest in the bank, or is that an illusion? Discover how to overcome the many threats to your financial security. Learn the secrets your banker and insurance company don't want you to know. Stop getting ripped-off by insurance salespeople. Use tax laws to your advantage.

4. Pickles, Not Nickels. Your nickel won't go far anymore! Learn the best ways to combat inflation, accumulate money, invest safely, and fool-proof ways to accumulate money for the future.

5. Accumulate At a Steady Rate. Don't wait to start investing. Learn how to reduce risk and increase returns to build security and wealth with little-known techniques, and simple methods to determine how much you must have to retire comfortably.

6. Destination, Not Procrastination. Discover your true financial worth. Shape your plans and make your dreams a reality. Learn techniques for getting what you want and effective ways to put your plans into action today!

Package includes a free bonus tape and a certificate good for a free 20-minute personal consultation with one of the authors.

Keep Uncle Sam From Devouring Your Life Savings

In his highly acclaimed book, Stephen M. Rosenberg, CFP guides you through the minefield of estate planning. Uniquely non-complicated, it has been lauded for its easy-to-understand language. The book is chock full of information difficult to obtain elsewhere: avoiding 16 problems that could sabotage all you've worked for; 9 little known hazards of joint tenancy; what attorneys don't want you to know about living trusts; 4 methods to keep from losing everything to a nursing home; little known ways to maximize gifts while reducing taxes; caring for minor and disabled children; how to reduce estate taxes, and much more.

"....can save you a lot of money," *Ken Dolan, Smart Money*. "...explains just what you need to know," *Washington Times*. "...written for the layperson." *Leonard Hansen, Mainly for Seniors*. "...easy-to-understand language," *St. Louis Post-Dispatch*.

Appendix A - Financial Inventory

Personal Data

1. Complete the following personal information.

Your Name _____

Your Social Security # _____ Date of Birth _____

Your Husband's Name _____

His Social Security # _____ Date of Birth _____

His Date of Death/Divorce _____ Date of Marriage _____

Children	Social Security No.	Date of Birth

Your Assets

2. Complete the following real estate information. List the type, the owner, the current value, the amount owed, and the equity.

Type	Owner	Value	Mortgage	Equity
Home				
TOTAL				

3. Complete the following information on ALL bank accounts. Include all types: checking, savings, money market, and certificates of deposit (CD). Indicate the ownership of the account: your husband alone; you alone; or joint. Use your latest statements to get the account balances. List each CD separately.

Bank	Type/Owner	Account No.	Current Balance
TOTAL			

If you have CDs, where are they kept? _____

Which bank has your safe deposit box? _____

Do you have access to the box? _____Yes _____No

If you have a personal banker, what is his or her name and phone number?

_____

_____

4. Complete the following on any investments you own. List them below
    indicating: name of stock, bond, or mutual fund; ownership (your hus-
    band alone, you alone, joint); approximate market value; and location of
    certificate. You may have certificates in a safe deposit box or they may
    be held by the fund or by your broker. Many people keep their invest-
    ments on deposit with their brokerage firm and only receive statements.

Name of Asset	Owner	Current Value	Location
TOTAL			

Do you have a financial advisor? _____ Yes _____ No

If "yes," what is his or name and phone number? _____

_____

_____

Your Debts

5. Complete the following, indicating the type of account, creditor (who you owe), name on the loan (yours, your husband's, or joint), and the amount owed. We have listed some possible creditors to help jog your memory. Don't forget to include recreational vehicles, vacation homes, and business investment loans.

Type	Lender	Borrower	Balance
Home			
Home Equity			
Sears			
J. C. Penney			
Dept. Store			
Dept. Store			
MasterCard			
MasterCard			
Visa			
Visa			
Discover			
Amer. Express			
Gas			
Automobile			
Friend			
Family			
TOTAL			

Be sure to check and see if credit life was taken on any of the loans.

Life Insurance

6. Indicate the name of the insurance company, the agent, the death benefit, and the beneficiary. Your policies will be in your safe deposit box or your home. If you have trouble locating policies, see Chapter 54 about replacing lost policies. The beneficiary can be found on the application, which is usually part of the policy.

Company	Agent	Death Benefit	Beneficiary

Retirement Plans

8. If you or your husband have retirement plans, list them here. Include the type of account (IRA, 401(k), 403(b), Deferred Compensation, Pension, Profit Sharing, etc.), the current value, and the trustee, custodian, or bank.

Type of Account	Current Value	Trustee/Custodian/Bank

Personal Financial Statement

YOUR ASSETS

Liquid Assets:

Checking Accounts _____
Savings Accounts _____
Certificates of Deposit _____
Money Market Accounts _____
Savings Bonds _____
Mutual Funds _____
Individual Stocks & Bonds _____
Insurance Cash Values _____
Annuities _____

Total Liquid Assets _____

Personal Assets

Home _____
Personal Property _____
Other _____

Total Personal Assets _____

Retirement Accounts

Employer Plans _____
IRA _____
Keogh/SEP _____

Total Retirement Accounts _____

Miscellaneous Assets

Business Interests _____
Money Owed You _____
Other _____

Total Miscellaneous Assets _____

YOUR TOTAL ASSETS _____

YOUR LIABILITIES

Mortgages

    Home   _____
    Other   _____

    Total Mortgages   _____

Credit Cards

    Department Store   _____
    Gasoline   _____
    Bank Cards   _____

    Total Credit Cards   _____

Personal Loans

    Education   _____
    Automobile   _____
    Finance Company   _____
    Money Owed Others   _____

    Total Personal Loans   _____

Miscellaneous Loans

    Life Insurance   _____
    Business   _____
    Other   _____

    Total Miscellaneous Loans _____

    YOUR TOTAL LIABILITIES   _____

YOUR NET WORTH

    Total Assets   _____

    Minus Total Liabilities   _____

    YOUR NET WORTH   _____

Personal Income Statement

Use this form to see where your money is going, or to make a budget for yourself. You should be able to obtain most of the data from your checkbook.

YOUR INCOME

Salary/Wages   _____

Self-Employment Earnings   _____

Interest/Dividends   _____

Rental Income   _____

Social Security   _____

Retirement Plans   _____

Other   _____

TOTAL INCOME   _____

YOUR EXPENSES

Food   _____

Rent/Mortgage   _____

Credit Card Payments   _____

Automobile   _____

Utilities   _____

Medical/Dental   _____

Vacations   _____

Gifts   _____

Education   _____

Savings/Retirement   _____

Investments   _____

Insurance   _____

Taxes   _____

Maintenance   _____

Contingency/Emergency Fund   _____

_____   _____

_____   _____

TOTAL EXPENSES   _____

NET INCOME (Income less Expenses)   _____

Appendix B - Child Support Enforcement Agencies

AMA

Support Enforcement
ley Street
gomery, AL 36130
242-9300

KA

Support Enforcement
Vest 7th Avenue Ste, 410
orage, AK 99501
276-3441

ONA

Support Enforcement
ox 40458 Site Code 966C
iix, AZ 85067
252-4045

ANSAS

Support Enforcement
ox 8133
Rock, AR 72203
682-8398

FORNIA

Support Program Branch
Street - MS 9-010
amento, CA 95814
654-1556

ORADO

Support Enforcement
Sherman St., 2nd Floor
er, CO 80203-1714
866-5965

NECTICUT

au of Child Support
Asylum Ave.
ord, CT 06105
566-3053

DELAWARE

Division of Child Support
PO Box 904
New Castle, DE 19720
(302) 577-4847

FLORIDA

Child Support Enforcement
1317 Winewood Blvd.
Tallahassee, FL 32309-0700
(904) 488-9900

GEORGIA

Ofc. of Child Spt. Recovery
PO Box 80000
Atlanta, GA 30357
(404) 894-5087

HAWAII

Child Support Enforcement
PO Box 1860
Honolulu, HI 96805-1860
(808) 587-3695

IDAHO

Bur. of Support Enforcement
450 West State St., 5th Floor
Boise, ID 83720
(208) 334-5710

ILLINOIS

Div. of Child Spt. Enforcement
201 S. Grand St. East
Springfield, IL 62794-9405
(217) 782-0420 ext. 8758

INDIANA

Child Support Division
402 W. Washington St.
Indianapolis, IN 46204
(317) 232-4894

IOWA

Dept. of Human Services
Hoover Building, 5th Floor
Des Moines, IA 50319
(515) 281-6511

KANSAS

Child Support Enforcement
300 SW Oakley PO Box 497
Topeka, KS 66606
(913) 296-3237

KENTUCKY

Div. of Child Spt. Enforcement
275 East Main St., 6th Floor E.
Frankfort, KY 40621
(502) 564-2285

LOUISIANA

Support Enforcement Services
PO Box 94065
Baton Rouge, LA 70804-4065
(504) 342-4780

MAINE

Div. Support Enforcement
State House, Station 11
Augusta, ME 04333
(207) 287-2886

MARYLAND

Child Spt. Enforcement Admin.
311 West Saratoga St., 308
Baltimore, MD 21201
(410) 333-0642

MASSACHUSETTS

Child Support Enforcement
141 Portland Street
Cambridge, MA 02139
(617) 621-4200

MICHIGAN

Office of Child Support
PO Box 30037
Lansing, MI 48909
(517) 373-7570

MINNESOTA

Office of Child Support
444 Lafayette Rd., 4th Floor
St. Paul, MN 55155-3846
(612) 297-1113

MISSISSIPPI

Child Support Enforcement
PO Box 352
Jackson, MS 39205
(601) 354-0341

MISSOURI

Child Support Enforcement
227 Metro P O Box 1527
Jefferson City, MO 65102
(314) 751-4301

MONTANA

Child Support Enforcement
PO Box 5955
Helena, MT 59604
(406) 444-4614

NEBRASKA

Child Support Enforcement
301 Centennial Mall South
Lincoln, NE 68509-5026
(402) 471-9160

NEVADA

Child Support Enforcement
2527 North Carson St.
Carson City, NV 89710
(702) 687-4744

NEW HAMPSHIRE

Child Support Enforcement
6 Hazen Dr.
Concord, NH 03301
(603) 271-4427

NEW JERSEY

Child Support & Paternity Unit
CN-716
Trenton, NJ 08625
(609) 588-2385

NEW MEXICO

Child Support Enforcement
PO Box 25109
Santa Fe, NM 87504
(505) 827-7200

NEW YORK

Child Support Enforcement
1 Commerce Plaza PO Box 14
Albany, NY 12260
(518) 474-9081

NORTH CAROLINA

Child Support Enforcement
100 East Six Forks Rd.
Raleigh, NC 27609-7724
(919) 571-4120, 4144

NORTH DAKOTA

Child Support Enforcement
1929 N. Washington St.
Bismarck, ND 58507-7190
(701) 224-3582

OHIO

Child Support Enforcement
30 East Broad St., 31st Floor
Columbus, OH 43266-0423
(614) 752-9749

OKLAHOMA

Child Support Enforcement
PO Box 53552
Oklahoma City, OK 73152
(405) 424-5871, Ext. 2874

OREGON

Support Enforcement Division
1495 Edgewater NW, Ste. 29
Salem, OR 97304
(503) 373-7300

PENNSYLVANIA

Child Support Enforcement
PO Box 8018
Harrisburg, PA 17105
(717) 787-3672

RHODE ISLAND

Bureau of Family Support
77 Dorrance St.
Providence, RI 02903
(401) 277-2847

SOUTH CAROLINA

Office of Child Support
PO Box 1469
Columbia, SC 29202-1469
(803) 737-5800, 5810

SOUTH DAKOTA

Child Support Enforcement
700 Governors Dr.
Pierre, SD 57501
(605) 773-3641

TENNESSEE

Child Support Services
Citizens Plaza Bldg
400 Deaderick St.
Nashville, TN 37219
(615) 741-1820

;

Support Enforcement
x 12017
 TX 78711-2017
463-2181

Support Services
orth 200 West
ke City, UT 84145-9943
257-9156 or
538-4400

ONT

Support Services
outh Main St.
bury, VT 05676
241-2910

NIA

Support Enforcement
Franklin Farms Dr.
-199
1ond, VA 23288
662-7671

HINGTON

of State Enforcement
ear St., SE
pia, WA 98504-9162
586-3520

T VIRGINIA

Advocate Bureau
Capitol Complex
ing 6
eston, WV 25305
558-3780

CONSIN

au of Child Support
3ox 7935
son, WI 53707-7935
267-0924

WYOMING

Child Support Enforcement
Hathaway Building
Cheyenne, WY 82002
(307) 777-6948

AMERICAN SAMOA

Office of the Attorney General
P O Box 7
Pago Pago, American Somoa
 96799
(684) 633-4163

DISTRICT OF COLUMBIA

Paternity and Child Support
425 I St. NW, 3rd Floor
Washington, D.C. 20001
(202) 724-8811

GUAM

Family Division
238 Archbishop F.C. Flores St.
Agana, Guam 96910
(671) 475-3660 - 3663

NORTHERN MARIANA IS.

Attorney General
Saipan, MP 96950
(670) 322-4311

PUERTO RICO

Child Support Enforcement
PO Box 3349
San Juan, PR 00902-3349
(809) 722-4731 or 725-2134

VIRGIN ISLANDS

Division of Paternity
and Child Support
48B-50C Kronprindsens Gade
GRS Complex, 2nd Floor
St. Thomas, Virgin Is. 00802
(809) 774-5666

Index